Waltham Forest L

D0335098

0 8 OCT 2012		
trans- B 5/16		

TIM HENMAN

ENGLAND'S FINEST

SIMON FELSTEIN

Published by John Blake Publishing Ltd,
3, Bramber Court, 2 Bramber Road,
London W14 9PB, England

www.blake.co.uk

First published in hardback in 2005

ISBN 1 84454 111 8

British Library Cataloguing-in-Publication Data:

A catalogue record for this book is available from the British Library.

Design by www.envydesign.co.uk

Printed in Great Britain by Creative Print & Design (Wales) Ltd, Ebbw Vale

1 3 5 7 9 10 8 6 4 2

Papers used by John Blake Publishing are natural, recyclable products
made from wood grown in sustainable forests. The manufacturing processes
conform to the environmental regulations of the country of origin.

Every attempt has been made to contact the relevant copyright-holders,
but some were unobtainable. We would be grateful if the appropriate
people could contact us.

For Albie

Contents

Beginning

Nineteen seventy-four. Harold Wilson becomes Prime Minister as Labour is elected to power in the UK. US President Richard Nixon resigns in the face of an impeachment threat over Watergate; Gerald Ford succeeds him. Policemen find a new use for their helmets after streakers become a standard fixture at sporting events in Britain. Inspector Clouseau returns to cinema screens in *The Return of the Pink Panther*. Lego is named toy of the year. Norman Stanley Fletcher is sentenced to five years in prison as cult comedy *Porridge* is born. Carl Douglas's 'Kung Fu Fighting' knocks the Osmonds' final number one, 'Love Me For a Reason', off the top of the UK singles chart. Brought to life and unleashed on the same chart are the Wombles of Wimbledon Common.

Nearby, at the All England Lawn Tennis Club, Jimmy Connors is crowned Wimbledon men's champion for the first time.

On 6 September that same year a hazel-eyed baby boy named Timothy Henry is born in Oxford, Oxfordshire to proud parents Jane and Tony Henman, a family steeped in tennis history.

The dynasty can be traced back to the start of the twentieth century, when Tim's great-grandmother, Ellen Stawell-Brown, wowed polite society with her eccentric overarm serve. One of the first to deploy this innovative weapon at Wimbledon, she used it to beat five-times champion Charlotte 'Chatty' Cooper. Press reports at the time, while complimenting her 'indomitable pluck', criticised her for putting too much exertion into her serve. 'Apparently, she used to throw the ball really high, spin round once and then hit it as it came down,' says Tim.

Ellen retired from tennis to become a Berkshire doctor's wife and produced three children, one of whom, Susan, is reckoned to have been the last woman to serve underarm at Wimbledon. 'As the story goes,' Tim says, 'my great-grandmother told my grandmother an overarm serve was a bit strenuous and told her to stick to serving underarm.'

Susan possessed a spectacular underarm serve, a wickedly spinning side-winder which slithered so low that it discomforted even those opponents who did manage to get it back. Sometimes it was delivered without having been practised in the knock-up, so opponents had little warning of what was about to come.

It was through tennis that Susan met and married Henry Billington, a Wiltshire farmer. This occupation did not stop Henry competing in post-war Davis Cup ties and eleven Wimbledon championships. He would rise at the crack of dawn to milk his cows, head off to a tournament and return home to do the milking again.

Billington was a player from the Fred Perry era, the 1930s, until the mid-1950s, reaching the third round of Wimbledon three times, in 1948, 1950 and 1951, as well as the quarter-finals of the French Open in 1939. The previous year he had given Donald Budge one of his toughest matches, when the American was en route to his first Grand Slam at SW19.

Henry and Susan were regulars in the mixed doubles on the lawns of the All England Club, and she even played there while pregnant with Tim's mother, Jane. 'My mother, while pregnant with me, was told by the doctor she wasn't to take on any smashes,' Jane explains. 'So, when playing once in a mixed doubles with her, my father played every smash himself. Months later she bumped into the man who had played against her. He said he would know how to beat her next time – by lobbing every shot at her. He was really shocked when my mother told him she had been pregnant at the time and that didn't apply any more.'

Jane played at Junior Wimbledon, along with her two brothers, Tim and Tony, who also entered the Wimbledon men's qualifying competition. She competed for both Berkshire and Oxfordshire at county level, as well as once playing against the last Brit to win Wimbledon – Virginia Wade.

After studying at the Katinka School of Dress Designing of London, Jane went on to design Great Britain's Winnie Shaw's silver-lined halter dress, which she wore at her final Wimbledon in 1977 in her second-round defeat to number-one seed Chris Evert. She has also built up her own sportswear collection, Jane Henman Designs, and has been a consultant for O. H. Hewitt, the Surrey-based sportswear manufacturer who is the official licensee of the Wimbledon clothing brand.

With such a background it was hardly surprising that Jane met her future husband at an inter-tennis-club cricket match. Tony Henman was an all-round sportsman who represented Oxfordshire at tennis, hockey, squash and cricket, and played football for Headington United in the days before the club became Oxford United. A lawyer by training, Tony also represented England's over-60 side at the hockey World Cup in Malaysia in 2002.

Tony and Jane produced three strapping boys, Michael, Richard and Tim. Richard, four years Tim's senior, is an abstract painter who was artist-in-residence at Radley College, while Michael, the eldest and five years older than Tim, followed in their father's footsteps and is now a partner in the law firm. But Tim always dreamed of one day making his point in a different sort of court. 'It was almost inevitable that one of us would go into tennis,' he said. 'But just because I had the background doesn't give me a God-given right to be a success. I've had to work at it like everyone else.'

The boys were brought up in Weston-on-the-Green, north of Oxford. With a population of some 500, the village has two pubs, a 500-year-old hotel, a small sub-post office and shop, and a duck pond.

The Henmans had a tennis court in their back garden, and Tim would play for hours against his two elder brothers. But he insists his parents never pushed him into playing more or spending hours practising, despite the family's well-established tennis roots.

'The most important factor from my background was that we had a tennis court at home, and I always had someone to practise with,' he said. 'But my parents would encourage me to play all sorts of sport. They just wanted me to do whatever made me happiest – which happened to be playing tennis. They had no ambition for me beyond that.

'But I think it was working so hard trying to beat my brothers that made me so competitive. It runs in the family because both my mother and father are very competitive when it comes to sport. We all want to win. Even then, I hated losing.

'There are times when losing really hurts. It's like a pain that won't go away. It's both a physical and mental thing and you don't forget it.

'You learn something from that, in particular that you don't want it to happen again if you can help it. And winning is so sweet that you just want more and more of it. Sometimes I just like to lie on my bed and enjoy that feeling for a while.'

Tim ascribes a large part of his mental toughness to the fact that he was always so determined to compete with his more mature brothers. 'We used to play sport all day and every day – football, rugby, cricket, hockey, squash – and for me to keep up with them was serious competition.'

But it was tennis he fell in love with.

He began playing, with the use of a shortened squash racket, before he had turned three, and was already trying to serve overarm and learning to volley with the help of his mother, who would hold him over the net. It was not long before he caught the bug. His playroom was stocked with tennis rackets his grandfather had used in Davis Cup ties for Britain. By the age of five he had already decided that tennis would become his life.

'I've made only one career decision in my life – and I was five at the time,' he explained, 'I decided I was going to be a tennis pro. It was a gradual thing. I didn't wake up one day and say, 'Tennis is going to be my profession', but I never changed my mind. I had no doubts or second thoughts about it. It's kind of scary but that was all there was to it. It was obviously a distant dream, but it was something I enjoyed so much and wanted so much.

'My parents realised early on that I had ability. I had good hand-eye co-ordination and they saw how keen I was. So they played an important part when I was very young. They just wanted me to be happy, and they didn't need to be Einstein to work out that I was at my happiest on the court.'

But what if Tim Henman the Great British tennis star never happened?

'I've never really had to make too many career decisions

because I have always been so focused on this one thing. My father and brother are lawyers and that has always interested me as a profession. They are always very interested in what I do and I am interested in what they do. We have discussed cases over dinner or whatever, so that is an avenue I have always thought I might go down.

'But I'm not sure that a desk job would really suit my character. People have said, probably quite rightly, that I am hyperactive. I would like to think that I would always have chosen sport. If I wasn't involved in sport in anyway I would probably be very unhappy.'

Golf has always been another passion of Tim's. His mother recalls: 'Tim once said he'd like to be a golfer if the tennis didn't gel. One golf pro who gave him a lesson went round shaking his head and saying Tim should take the game up for a living.'

One player whose exploits certainly captivated his wide-eyed attention, almost as much as any tennis player, was Nick Faldo.

'He adopted a stance that basically said he didn't give a moment's concern about how other people perceived him, be they opponents or the public at large,' said Tim. 'And he did whatever he believed to be right for his game; whether completely remodelling his swing or remaining oblivious to what was being said or written about him, and not letting it affect his focus on what he was trying to achieve. That is something I can relate to.' Instead, though, Tim chose tennis.

'Tennis is as great a way to earn a living as you can get. As a child, I wasn't particularly outstanding. I wasn't winning tournaments every weekend like some of the other kids – it didn't come easily to me. I had to fight all the way through. The result was that I was always trying to prove that I was good enough, that I belonged. That has always been an enormous motivation to me.

'When I played at my dad's club, I made-believe that I was playing one of the great champions and it was match point. I had to win. I used to think that I would like to follow in my grandfather's footsteps by playing at Wimbledon.'

That first impression was set in stone when his mother took him to Wimbledon to watch Bjorn Borg on Centre Court, his first Monday opener against El Shafei of Egypt, when Tim was just five. He fell in love with the beauty of the Swede's game, the atmosphere, the lush green of the turf, everything about it.

'I went to watch when I was six and I remember thinking, 'This is what I want, I want a piece of this. Now I pretty much play all my matches on Centre Court and it's amazing to reflect back and realise this it's me out there,' he professes. 'When I was growing up, Bjorn Borg was my role model. I saw him at the top of the game when I was very young and thought I would like to follow in his footsteps. When he retired, probably earlier than anyone would have expected, Stefan Edberg was somebody I looked up to too. I haven't modelled myself on him but I think it's been pretty easy to see as I've developed that it's been in a similar style of play, so I've been able to learn a great deal from him.'

Tim had told his mother of his ambitions very early on. 'It was good for him to have an aim and he told us at the age of seven that he wanted to win Wimbledon,' she remembers.

Jane would coach all three boys on the family court, but it was Tim who showed the most promise, even from an early age. His two brothers possessed neither Tim's aptitude nor inclination.

His mother recalled: 'As a child Tim always wanted to play tennis. I used to pick him up at school where his older brothers, Michael and Richard, would finish around forty-five minutes after him.

'He would insist on playing tennis while we waited for them.

7

So we'd go out on the school courts every day and hit balls while we waited for the others.

'Tim usually hit volleys, which most children don't like at such an early age. He'd always want to play tennis even when it was a glorious summer day and I'd ask him if he preferred doing something else. He was beating me by the time he was eleven.'

Tim attended Weston-on-the-Green Primary School from the age of five and then, between the ages of seven and eleven, the Dragon School in Oxford. As a pupil of this prestigious and very sporty fee-paying preparatory school, he was following in the footsteps of such notables as poet laureate John Betjeman, former Labour leader Hugh Gaitskill and historian Lady Antonia Fraser.

As a new boy at the Dragon School, Tim excelled in all sports, playing in the first teams for hockey, football, rugby and cricket, and went straight into the top tennis team on his first day. He was described by his tennis teacher as having a 'phenomenal talent from the day he was capable of picking up a racket'. Enid Volak, who taught Tim as a seven-year-old at the school, remembers him with equal fondness. 'Tim was very shy in class. But when it came to athletics and tennis he was out of this world. We knew we had a star on our hands.'

Tim was always small for his age, a factor that would count heavily against him as a teenage player. However, that did not stop him being made the school's captain of tennis in 1985, when he led their tennis squad to twenty-one wins out of twenty-seven. Tim is the only pupil to have won both the school's junior and senior tennis championships in the same year.

But he also won titles outside school. In 1983 he was a finalist in the first-ever short tennis tournament for nine-year-olds and won the Oxfordshire Closed Under-10 Singles. A year later he won the Oxfordshire Closed and Open Under-12 Singles, and by the end of the year he had played in his first Under-12 international match, for Great Britain against the Netherlands.

Tim had received his grounding in tennis as an eight-year-old, when he was taken to the David Lloyd Centre at Heston, near Heathrow. His coaching there had to fit in with his studies at school in Oxford, and, as his mother recalled, 'It was quite a nightmare. I would take him in the car after school, I'd have to eat in the car, he'd have an hour with his coach, and it would be back to Oxford late and exhausted. It was a full-time job. Worst of all was the endless washing. Your role as a tennis mum is as a support system.'

At the David Lloyd Centre, Tim was given personal lessons by Onny Parun, a former New Zealand Davis Cup player who reached the quarter-finals at Wimbledon in 1971 and 1972. 'He was a big influence early on, because that is an important age,' Tim said. 'It is when you begin to learn your trade – the techniques of different shots.'

'His best shot has always been his head,' said Parun, referring to Tim's fabled mental toughness. It was Parun who brought him to the attention of David Lloyd, a former British tennis player and brother of John Lloyd, who reached the doubles final at London's Queen's Club in 1977 before turning entrepreneur. 'He was setting up his own tennis scheme, and offered me the chance to take one of his scholarships,' Tim recalls. He was a natural candidate for the scholarship scheme, which offered the boys a normal education coupled with intensive after-school coaching.

Lloyd was first attracted to the young Henman when he witnessed first-hand just how determined he was to succeed. 'Of course racket skill is important, but most of all I look for the quality of never giving in,' Lloyd said. 'Tim really wanted success badly, even at that age. He had an arrogant streak. I remember he used to cry if he lost. The difference between Tim and many other hopefuls was he always believed he was going to win. He would never settle for second best. If he was playing his mother he would go out to beat her.'

Tim was auditioned for the scholarship along with a string of other nervous schoolboy hopefuls aged between ten and twelve. The selection process involved a basic physical challenge. 'We were dealing with an elite group of tennis-playing kids but first I made them run and run until they dropped,' recalled Lloyd. 'It was a simple test of character – if they dropped I kicked them out.'

But Tim did not drop; nor did another couple of lads, Marc Moreso and David Loosemore. The trio became the first beneficiaries of financier Jim Slater's private scheme, winning scholarships to board at Reed's School, in Cobham, Surrey, beginning at Easter 1986.

Tony Henman, however, needed to be convinced that his son could carve a niche in the hard, uncompromising world of professional tennis. 'My parents were somewhat cautious about me going away to school but I was adamant,' said Tim.

David Lloyd echoed the young player's sentiments: 'I told them I thought Tim had a great chance of being a very good player. And if he was going to be good, he couldn't go to university. In the end Tim convinced his father that he wanted to be a tennis player more than anything else, and his dad gave him one hundred per cent backing. 'To Tim's parents' credit,' said Lloyd, 'they accepted what so many others don't understand; that you can always go back to higher education at twenty-two or twenty-three but that that is far too late to start a serious tennis career.'

Tim has never forgotten the support of his close-knit family. 'My biggest blessing is that I had an ordinary upbringing with an ordinary family. That is something which has stood me in good stead for everything that has happened. I'm delighted to have given Mum and Dad something to be proud of. You see a lot of parents putting too much pressure on their kids, but I had none of that. My parents have always been incredibly supportive. I needed them to pay my way, to drive me all over the country. I'd like to think it's been worth it all.'

The Tim Henman adventure was about to begin.

2

The Slater Squad

Wimbledon, 1984. John Lloyd bows out of the competition at only the third round to Scott Davis of the United States, 4-6, 4-6, 6-7. Nine other British men were in the draw alongside Lloyd when the championships got underway; three of them reached the second round, but after that only Lloyd survived. Wimbledon fortnight was just approaching its second week and already the British interest had been terminated. It was yet another predictably woeful performance.

Every year at this stage there was a tendency to get rather black and moody about the exodus of Brits from Wimbledon. But the mourners failed to recognise that Britain was no longer a major tennis nation, and had not been for some time.

One man was about to change all that, though – Jim Slater, a one-time millionaire before the collapse of his securities company in 1974. Like millions of others, Slater had been sitting in front of his television, depressed by years of doom and gloom, watching the demise of British players once more that summer, but unlike others he decided to do something about it. 'I play tennis myself, not very well, but I'm a keen fan who always watched Wimbledon on television every year. I was just so fed up with the British guys never going beyond the last sixteen and reckoned it was because we didn't get to them early enough. I felt something ought to be done.'

Slater believed intensive training and competition at a young age, alongside a normal academic schooling, could produce a male tennis champion for Britain – the first since 1936 – and he felt he had the three essentials required to invigorate the sport: the private money, independent coaching and a school that offered the best education and sporting excellence.

Through the Slater Foundation, a charitable fund he had set up in 1970, he bankrolled former British Davis Cup player David Lloyd to talent-scout for boys as young as nine who could be moulded into potential champions, as tennis schools abroad were successfully doing.

'It's so competitive out there today that, if someone wants to be a player by 18, they haven't a chance, unless they are so talented as to be freakish,' Slater said. 'We wanted to catch them early and give them every possible advantage.'

'I spent around £300,000 on the squad over the decade. It might sound a lot but it was nothing compared with what the LTA [Lawn Tennis Association] were wasting at the time.'

'They didn't start training players until they were thirteen, so I had a chat with David Lloyd and set up the Slater Squad. I paid for three courts to be built at Reed's School in Cobham, Surrey, and for the boys' £8,000-a-year fees there and all the coaching.'

'David ran the squad and it soon proved successful with the likes of James Baily (winner of the Australian Junior Open in 1993) and Jamie Delgado coming through.'

So, while Slater underwrote the boys' boarding-school fees,

Lloyd oversaw the selection, coaching and training, and Slazenger, Ellesse and Diadora provided them with rackets, clothes and shoes.

'Jim came to me because the LTA turned his offer down,' explained Lloyd. Both men were frustrated by the failure of the official body to energise junior tennis. 'They gave us flak for trying to spot talent at ten. But I argued that we had to get in step with the world. You have only to look at the record books and see some of the names of the under-12 winners of the Orange Bowl [the most prestigious title in junior tennis] – names like Chris Evert, Jimmy Connors, John McEnroe and Brian Gottfried – to realise we had to act. We have to start preparing kids with the right mental aptitude to succeed.

'The choice of school was vital, and Reed's was excellent. We wanted a boarding school so the boys would be mixing with other kids, to make them more well-rounded as people. If they had just been isolated kids, it could have been boring as hell, but they integrated well, and we encouraged the boys to play other sports at school, with the exception of rugby. We wanted them to have some sanity, though not get battered and bruised, but behind the scenes they had to know they were trying to become professional tennis players.

'I don't think it is a fluke that the best player Britain has produced in years came out of a scheme such as ours. In getting boys at the age of twelve, we were going against the grain as far as the LTA were concerned. At the time, they insisted that this was too young but when we won all the under-14 titles in the country and Delgado went on to become the first British player to win the Orange Bowl event in Miami, they had to take notice.

'The scheme was a success – and it did work as a catalyst to the LTA. They are now taking boys aged ten and eleven. It is easier to mould them at a young age and instil them with the right ideas and attitudes.'

Jim Slater's foundation had first found fame in the world of chess. In 1970 Britain had no grandmasters. Slater subsidised the only existing British tournament and doubled the prize money to attract Robert Fischer of America and Russia's Boris Spassky, then world leaders, to play. He offered £5,000 to the first British grandmaster and £2,500 each to the following four. Britain came 26th in the Chess Olympics in 1970, but in 1984 it finished second and five years later had twenty grandmasters – more, per head of population, than any other country.

Slater describes his approach as that of 'a laser beam rather than a scatter gun. I am attracted to unusual, perhaps quirkish things, where a relatively small amount of money will have a relatively large effect. It created an interest and a competitive environment that became self-perpetuating.'

In the beginning the Slater Squad, known by their school as the 'Tennis Patch Kids', may have seemed little more than a rich man's folly, and even though it is yet to produce a British Grand Slam champion, it did create a people's champion, someone Britons could look up to, a player who competes at the very top of the game. Tim Henman's regular appearances on Centre Court as well as all the many other great tennis stages of the world not only justifies Slater's faith in his project but has also caused a huge surge of interest in British tennis. Nothing could make Slater more proud.

'Tim joined when he was eleven and although he developed much later on, it's amazing what he's doing now,' said Slater. 'It's great seeing him on Centre Court. The incredible atmosphere at Wimbledon when Tim's playing proves the point and makes it all seem worth it. In investment terms, it's a good dividend.'

The original intake was eight young players with stars in their eyes. Lloyd selected the nine-, ten- and eleven-year-olds he believed had the most natural talent, stamina, intelligence and, more importantly, the determination to succeed. They made up the Slater Squad, a living experiment in the kind of intensive training that British tennis had never undertaken.

But Henman is quick to point out that it did not involve twelve hours of tennis a day, floggings and cold showers. 'Until 3.30 in the afternoon, when lessons ended, I was just like everybody else,' he explained. 'There was nothing special about being a tennis player there. I was totally involved at school from eleven to seventeen. I certainly thrived in the environment we had. We were surrounded by very normal people at the school and when they went off in the afternoon to play their sports is when we became "abnormal" by playing tennis. It was very important for our grounding as people to be in such an environment. When you went back after practice at the club you simply joined the kids in normal activities. There was great competition there [within the Slater Squad], six to twelve kids of various ages and talents with a lot of healthy competition you need at that age.'

For Henman, tennis was a three-hour-a-day, after-school activity. They were bussed to another of Lloyd's clubs in Raynes Park, near Wimbledon, for two hours of tennis, and received individual coaching, followed by group gymnastics and lectures on the technicalities of the game.

'In the car with the kids I would play songs with subliminal messages such as "When the going gets tough, the tough get going"', Lloyd recalled. 'Young kids take that stuff in without beating them over the head with a brick.'

Five weeks of their six-week summer break were spent playing tournaments, and they were allowed home on Sundays and four full weeks a year.

Each boy was evaluated in detail for physical flaws, including kyphosis (rounded shoulders), lordosis (curvature of the lumbar spine) and discrepancy in leg length. Personal training plans were followed, to correct any problems, and the boys trained with weights of up to 50 per cent of their capacity. They were taught to control their physical responses, to produce adrenalin at specific times and to control their reaction to stress with visualisation, relaxation and breathing techniques. The constant pressure of work, both sporting and academic, was designed to prepare them for the intense situations they would encounter on court in the future.

'You grow up quickly and become very independent,' said Henman. 'You learn you don't always have your parents or coaches to help. Once you step out on the court you are on your own.'

From the outset, Henman was an A-student of the game, as Lloyd confirmed: 'The drive and determination of a true winner was with him even before we took him into the Slater development scheme at Reed's School. We had to be tough with the others because kids often don't want to do that extra bit of training, but Tim never put in a bad practice session. Never. He took it all so seriously; and he used to cry when things didn't go right. That wasn't a weakness. Simply, it showed that he cared.

'When I say he had a selfish streak in him, I mean it in the best possible sense. You need it if you are going to succeed in a game like tennis. He also had the ability to shut everything out and want it badly. I think Tim would have made it wherever he was – he is so self-motivated. When he was twelve, I told him: "There's only one person in the world who can make you world champion and that's you. I can give you a chance but it's down to you."'

One of Tim's coaches, Steve Matthews recollects: 'We were looking for a combination of everything, natural ability and just desire. Tim had that little sparkle we were looking for. His work rate was phenomenal.'

But, although talented, Tim was not considered the best of the bunch. French Open champion Sue Barker, who sometimes drove him and his tennis colleagues around, certainly did not see an embryonic champion in the youngster. 'I've got to say no, there was nothing particularly special in his game in those days,' she explains. 'Tim certainly wasn't the most natural player, but he was such a hard worker. At that stage you're looking for someone with a bit more obvious talent and there was a very talented left-hander in the Slater squads around then but he didn't have the discipline that Tim had.

'That's why Tim has got better as he has got older, the typical British player in fact. Virginia Wade was much better when she got older, Roger Taylor was and so was Ann Jones. I was the exception to that rule. I was one of those who sprang up and whose career, if not burned out, at least fizzled out.

'Tim has grown into his career. He is so studious and so particular about everything.

'I've known Tim so long and through those years in the Slater Squad with David Lloyd when I used to give him lifts home in the minibus. I was a real Auntie Sue to the kids and I would always be stopping and getting them a Coca-Cola and a Mars bar on the way home.'

In fact not even his fellow Slater boys would have picked Tim out as the star of the litter.

'Up until fourteen I would beat him,' said Adrian Blackman, the former under-12 and under-14 British number one. 'At fourteen he didn't stand out.'

'If you'd asked me who was going to make it when we were fourteen or fifteen I doubt I would have said Tim,' concludes Gary Le Pla, two years below Henman.

That honour was reserved for Marc Moreso, the shining star of that first intake. He was the gifted one. Lloyd said of him: 'He had more talent in his little finger than any British player I have ever seen. He used to bounce balls around his head; he could sit at the piano and play a tune he'd never seen before. A real talent. But also my biggest disappointment I have of the Slater Scheme. I couldn't channel that talent.'

Moreso, who once coached the Princess of Wales at the Chelsea Harbour Club, would, over a five-year period, beat Henman every time the two Slater boys played.

'Marc had the most ability on the court,' Henman said. 'But I don't think he had it between the ears. I was the most determined.' He was not wrong there. For the Tim Henman story is not the story of an enormous talent, but rather the application of enormous effort to make the very most of what natural ability he had. It is sheer determination and single-minded focus that has taken him to success.

Moreso recalls one moment which suggested early on that Henman might be the one. 'I remember one time at tennis practice the coach asked, "What's your goal?" We all said I want to be number one in the world, or top five, apart from Tim, who said I want to be top fifty. He was so damned sensible. It showed he was taking the tennis thing seriously, and he was making realistic goals.

'Tim was the nearest thing to a professional aged twelve that I have ever met. At school he was not the most technically gifted player, but he was by far the most hard-working. He always had to win. He lived for sport. If it wasn't tennis he would be playing football or golf.'

Jamie Delgado, two years younger than Henman and the only other member of that squad still plying his trade in tennis, having once played for Great Britain in the Davis Cup, said:

'Tim is a talented player who has worked hard and taken all his chances, while maybe I haven't. The actual differences between us are quite small but very large when it comes to rewards. Tim and I were level pegging as kids but there were lots of guys level with him in those days and he has outstripped us all. Tim has kept learning and never makes the same mistake twice. He's bright like that, very smart. He deserves everything he gets because he has worked so hard for it.'

Henman has his own take on what makes him so driven to succeed where so many other British players have failed. 'You have to understand that I'm two very different people. When I'm away from the court I'm very relaxed and easy-going, quite calm – but that's because I've released a lot of my energy playing. On court I'm a very different person. I'm not this nice guy that everyone imagines me to be. It's perfectly true that I have a lot of self-belief and I'm a little arrogant but if you're going to make it in sport then I think you need to have that.

'When I'm playing I'm cold and ruthless. As far as I'm concerned it's kill or be killed. It's in complete contradiction to my image. Tennis is a battle between two people, there's nothing friendly about it at all.

'It's very in-your-face – which is what I love about it. One of you goes on to play the next round and the other goes home and doesn't come back. It doesn't get any harder than that.

'I understand why people wonder whether I'll be just another British player who fails to fulfil his potential. I saw it happen to a number of players while I was growing up and that made me all the more determined to push myself even harder so that I didn't go the same way.

'I don't want to be just another promising player who didn't make the grade. I've got a lot of ambition to do well.'

Yet his love for the sport was not just limited to his endeavours on the court. Even classmates at his boarding school at Reed's, originally set up to educate orphan children, tell of his passion for tennis and unswerving single-mindedness to succeed. One former schoolmate said: 'He was always sports-mad, and at any opportunity would have sports trivia quiz sessions with anybody who would want to. It's quite well known that his nickname at school was Sport Billy. He was good at tennis obviously, but also hockey and cricket. He could have gone a long way in hockey but tennis was always what he wanted to do.

'He knew everything there was to know about Wimbledon. Former champions? He knew them all. He even knew the ones that everybody else had forgotten about. He could rattle them off, and nobody knew if he was right or wrong, because we didn't have a clue about any of the people he was mentioning.

'When you went around to his house, sport was always a big part of the conversation. But his folks never seemed to push any of the boys into sport at all. They were all just genuinely interested in all kinds of sports.

'He did look really young when he was at school, and kept to his close circle of friends. He was never in any trouble – none more than any other student – and, as I say, sport took up a lot of his time.

'There was the odd time when we were around sixteen or so, and we wanted to go to the pub near school. We were all underage, but we could just get away with it. And we used to try and avoid Tim – not because we didn't want him around: it was that he looked so young that it would have made us all get caught.'

Another school friend, who still keeps in contact with Henman, said: 'It is a credit to him that he has done so well for himself in his chosen career. He worked extremely hard at it, and the benefits are paying off, as everyone can see.

'There were always flashes of absolute brilliance. He never had the quickest serve, but there were times when you played him and he returned a shot in a way that you would never have even thought of. The placement of it, and the timing – the intelligence it took for a shot like that – you were just left shaking your head, saying: "Too good."

'And looking back, when you take into account what he could pull off on the court, and his attitude at the time, it's no surprise he has gone so far.

'When the rest of his mates were getting into girls, smoking or whatever, Tim stayed focused on his tennis. I'm sure everyone you meet will tell you that he was the most single-minded person you could ever meet when it came to what he wanted to do in his sport.

'But off the court he is a normal down-to-earth bloke. He has this public perception of being a boring guy, but he's not. I think it's because he focuses on his tennis rather than making an image for himself that makes people think he's dull. He's not a plucky loser like Eddie the Eagle, or a wacky waste of talent like Gazza. He's a tennis player, but that's not enough for some people.'

But, weeks into his new life, Henman suffered an injury to his arm which almost put paid to his tennis aspirations before he had even got going. He was suffering from a painful bone disease called osteochondritis diseccans, which affects the joints and is common among young farm workers who bale too much hay before their muscles are strong enough to take the strain.

'It was one of those overuse injuries when my bones were still relatively soft,' Henman recalls. 'I played so much that I pulled a piece from my elbow.'

He had to stop playing altogether for six months, and it was two years before he played another tournament. The problem did ease but it left Henman with a bent arm. Luckily a straight arm is not a prerequisite for hitting a serve.

'It had to repair itself, but I never once thought about chucking it all in. I think I knew then that I was going to have many years ahead of me and that eleven or twelve is probably not the most important stage of your career. I think in the end it instilled a lot of mental strength in me to believe, "OK, this is the way it is, but I'm going to come back and I'll be better for it."'

Yet, had Lloyd not kept faith with him, that would have been it. Fortunately he recognised the career-threatening problem immediately. Lloyd suspected that Henman was suffering from the same bone condition that almost forced his own brother, John, who went on to become British number one, to call time on his fledgling career. Expert medical opinion was needed urgently.

'Luckily I had an uncle,' said Lloyd, 'Alan Murley, who was not only a doctor but a top-rate sportsman. He had played tennis for Essex and cricket for Essex juniors and came up with the right diagnosis.

'Everyone but me and Tim wanted him to give up. But I felt he could do it and go on to become one of the world's fifty best players.

'It is a very rare condition in the elbow which affects the normal formation of the bones. There is too much pressure on a young joint which is still growing and if you don't treat it right away then your arm never straightens again. John's arm never completely straightens to this day and Tim is the same. If we hadn't got him treated it would have been a serious problem.

'The key thing is to spot it early. We were fortunate John had been through the same thing and so we knew what we were dealing with straight away.

'It was a tough time for Tim and would have finished a lot of kids. But we didn't kick him out just because he couldn't hit a ball for a year. Instead, we used to take him to the club so that he could work at strengthening other areas of his body and it meant he could still train with the other lads while he was on the mend. He used to watch his mates, like Jamie Delgado, practising while he had to stay off court. You can imagine how much that hurt him.

'He used to cry a lot. But that was natural. People tried to tell me that tears are a sign of weakness but I disagree. They were tears of fury and frustration more than anything else, not fear. It was because all the other kids were able to play tennis, not the sort of crying you get from a whinger.

'He was fortunate in that Jim Slater agreed to go on paying for Tim's education while he recovered.

'At twelve-years-old a lot of children would have been destroyed by the experience but Tim was mentally strong and didn't get bored during his year out because he was with his friends. Eventually Tim got back on court and in retrospect I think the experience hardened him up. That is why Tim is so mentally strong; it's rubbish for critics to say that he bottles matches.'

'It took him two years to recover and he amazed us with his levels of conviction,' says Mareso. 'Most young lads would have given up – but not Tim. I remember him looking me in the eye and saying that he would be British number one.'

Yet, amazingly, one teacher failed to recognise Henman's never-say-die spirit. 'It's rather embarrassing,' admits Mike Hewlett, who taught him at Reed's. When Henman topped the academic marks of the twenty-two pupils in form 3C, his teacher was moved to comment in his written report on the boy: 'Tim seems a well balanced, friendly individual, but what I have not really seen evidence of is the killer instinct which I expected of the tennis scholar!'

Who ever said teacher knows best?

Henman gained ten GCSEs, though he openly admits to failing Chemistry. 'I passed the others with a few As, a few Bs and a few Cs. It was nothing dazzling by any means, but I got by.'

Academic prowess was obviously not uppermost in his mind, though he did start A-levels, until he realised it was having a detrimental effect on his tennis and chucked it all in.

'I remember Tim telling us just before one half-term he couldn't keep up with his A-levels because Europeans and Americans were getting ahead with their tennis,' said his mother, Jane. 'He was just sixteen when he made that decision. So many people asked what he would have to fall back on, which was a rather negative attitude. You can take A-levels any time. Tennis has a limited span.'

One school friend remembers: 'When he left it was fairly sudden. He obviously would have been thinking about it for a while, but I remember him coming up to me before assembly and telling me he was off to pursue his tennis career – just like that.'

Tim left school towards the end of 1990 to go full-time on the tennis circuit. 'It was obviously a big decision at the time,' he says gravely. 'But the experience you gain from playing professionally from that age is invaluable. I don't think anyone has successfully combined education and tennis. It's a risk I had to take.'

But Henman's coaches had little faith that he could make it as a singles player. Even David Lloyd admitted that he considered him too small, though he was hoping to emulate his brothers, who are both over six feet tall. 'At fifteen I was tiny,' Henman said. 'I've always been pretty skinny, at sixteen I was five foot six. In juniors height has a massive impact on results. I was then probably number ten for my age in the UK. When you look at our tennis standards, that's pretty awful.'

Lloyd felt Henman would be better suited making a living as a doubles player. Perhaps he was right. After all, the majority of Henman's major title wins during his period in the Slater scheme had come in doubles tournaments. Between 1985 and 1990 he had won five doubles events (Bristol Open Under-12 1985, Gloucestershire Open Under-12 1986, Under-14 British Hard Court Doubles 1988, Under-14 doubles at Solihull and Sheen 1988), compared with two singles crowns (Bristol Open Under-12 1985 and Under-16 Reebok Junior Grand Prix at Gunnersbury 1988).

Henman disagreed, though. With the help of Bill Knight, a former Davis Cup player who had just been appointed manager of men's national training at the LTA, he returned to the LTA coaching structure and competed on the world junior tennis circuit, travelling the globe. It was all a big adventure.

When he was seventeen he toured for eight weeks in South America with a coach and five other young players, competing in Venezuela, Peru, Bolivia, Colombia and Ecuador. 'In Bolivia we stayed in a place where you got a bucket from reception, took it upstairs, and that's what you washed with.'

In Venezuela he and his tennis mates stayed on the twenty-eighth floor of a hotel. 'We started getting toilet rolls and throwing them out of the window at people,' he recalls. 'We got pretty accurate at it. We were going to the supermarket and buying twelve-packs of toilet roll. Then we saw people with walkie-talkies looking up in our direction; after that the phone started ringing in our room. We panicked a bit and thought, OK, we'll put the latch on the door and pretend we're asleep. There was a knock at the door and we thought, we won't answer that. Eventually we were hiding in the cupboard.

'Finally, the manager and a policeman cut through the chain with wire-cutters. The manager said, "Have you been throwing things off your balcony?" We took one look at each other and said, "Yep." They were actually pretty good about it and they said, "Don't do that again." We said, "Never again."'

In 1991 Henman endured a disappointing first full year on the junior singles circuit. In the opening tournament of the year, on the grass courts of the New South Wales Championships in Sydney, he defeated Andrew Turner of New Zealand 6-1, 6-3 in the first round, but was eliminated in the last thirty-two by 11th seed Corrado Borroni 5-7, 1-6. This was followed by a first-round exit at the hands of Michael Hill, predominantly a doubles player, at the Australian Open Junior Championships. Henman threw away a one-set lead before being dismissed by the Australian 7-5, 3-6, 5-7.

He fared only slightly better at the National Junior Championships in Nottingham in August, reaching the third round before being defeated 6-1, 6-2 by Lincolnshire's Andrew Richardson.

The diminutive Henman appeared to be having better success in the doubles game. He reached the quarter-finals with Richardson at the New South Wales Championships that year, and won the under-18 Midland Bank British Junior Championships doubles crown with Jamie Delgado, an ally from the Slater days.

Perhaps David Lloyd had been right after all.

But 1992 was to prove otherwise. In February, at the LTA Junior Indoor Circuit Masters at Nottingham, the unseeded Henman won his four-man group and beat Jamie Delgado in straight sets to reach the final, before losing to top seed Mark Schofield from Darwen.

Things got worse before they got better. Henman went out in the first round at the Junior French Open to Germany's Bjorn

Jacob 6-7, 6-1, 9-7, and did the same at Junior Wimbledon. He remembers that match well: 'In my only Wimbledon as a junior, I lost 6-2, 6-1 to a Mexican clay-courter called Enrique Abaroa, who has hardly set the world on fire since. I played a great game to break service and go two-one up, then I lost eight games in a row. It's fair to say there weren't too many people who held much hope for me.'

Many would have taken the hint after that and set about getting a job, or at the least some A-levels. But Henman kept believing, and in his final junior tournament he got his reward.

In August at the National Junior Championships, on the eve of his eighteenth birthday, he reached the semi-finals without dropping a single set, conceding just nine games in three matches.

In the semi-final, which would be contested in the best of five sets, he met Mark Schofield. After spending the opening set trying to get his first serve in working order, Henman, who was not even seeded, put paid to the top seed, winning 2-6, 6-3, 7-6, 6-2.

The final was a similar scenario. Henman required a set to get his serve going, but after that he dispatched his opponent, Cheshire's Nick Baglin, 3-6, 7-5, 6-4, 6-4. The *Sunday Times* wrote: 'It was a fairly contested affair won by Tim Henman, who went out in the third round last year, but he has grown up a bit since then. He has grown a few inches, given up school and pinned his hopes on a career as a tennis professional.'

It was the ideal way to celebrate turning eighteen. Having finally made an impact as a junior, the next step for Henman was the dog-eat-dog world of senior satellite tennis, the one beneath the top level, and the ultimate goal, the Association of Tennis Professionals Tour.

3

Early Days

Twelve months is a long time when you are eighteen. By July 1993, in the space of a year, Henman had grown six inches to six foot one and added two stone to his slender nine-stone build. The extra height and strength had allowed him to develop an intelligent and varied all-court game, as he acknowledged: 'As a junior I had pretty good technique. Now I've got the strength and reach, and on the serve that has helped tremendously.'

With his body maturing, it seemed that now was the right time to make his first foray into the world of Association Tennis Professional (ATP) tennis. He had started 1993 774th in the world and playing on the satellite circuit, the one beneath the ATP circuit, where the world of five-star hotels and pampered luxury is replaced by terrible courts, dodgy hotel rooms and poor food.

Come July, though, and sitting just outside the top 600, Henman was making his first appearance in an ATP Challenger event, as a wild card in Bristol. A bumper crowd turned out in the sunshine for the opening day of the £35,000 tournament, and Henman rose to the occasion in front of his home crowd, easily claiming his first success at Challenger level 6-0, 6-3 against Colombia's Miguel Tobon, world-ranked 257. He followed that up by defeating experienced Frenchman Eric Winogradsky 7-6, 6-3 in round two, to set up an intriguing contest against Britain's current tennis darling Chris Bailey in the quarter-finals.

Just over a week earlier the British number three, ranked 240, had won the adulation of screaming schoolgirls and a proliferation of sponsorship deals when he took world number six Goran Ivanisevic to five sets in the second round of Wimbledon. Bailey may have lost 7-5, 6-7, 7-6, 4-6, 7-9 in a thrilling Centre Court battle with the Croatian, but, in the process, he became a national hero, such was the calibre of British tennis stars at the time.

Most of the hardy spectators, particularly the teenage girls, had come to Bristol to worship their new idol, and he didn't disappoint, sweeping Henman aside in just forty-nine minutes, giving the teenager little room for manoeuvre throughout in a 6-2, 6-1 win.

November saw the next opportunity for Henman to shine, on a national scale at least, with the start of the Volkswagen National Championships in Telford, where he was seeded 8th. Having propelled more than 200 places in the world rankings to 415th, since his debut Challenger event he had bypassed Paul Hand and Nick Adams to face a quarter-final bout with British number one Jeremy Bates, who had won 36 of his 42 singles in this event, on his way to four titles.

The pair had practised frequently together in recent months and Henman had made a favourable impression on the number-one seed. 'He's improved a lot over the last year,' Bates said of his opponent, thirteen years his junior. 'Everybody likes him and we are all hoping that he climbs up the rankings.'

Bates had looked as solid as a rock during the first two rounds, conceding only five games. But he was to be severely tested by Henman before eventually scraping through a pulsating last-eight match – thanks, in part, to thirteen aces – 7-5, 7-6. Henman's game showed a refreshing flexibility, as did his footwork, while further reinforcing Bates's view of him. In all his years, Bates said, he had never been given such a tough match by a British teenager. 'He put me under a lot of pressure, and, more importantly, took advantage when he did. If I hadn't served as well as I did, we might still be out there. Tim shows all the signs of having what it takes to be a good player. I think he is a very good prospect.'

After the nationals in Telford, Henman continued his steady climb up the rankings by winning a satellite event in Israel. He carried that rich vein of form over into the 1994 campaign, winning eighteen singles in a row at the four-leg Indian Satellite circuit, falling only two wins short of a clean sweep at Chandrigar. He also came through a stronger field to win the British Satellite Masters at Croydon, which moved his ranking up to 222nd in the world.

Henman had excited even the most cynical observers with his stylish performances, and was rewarded for his fine run of form with a first-ever place in Tony Pickard's Great Britain Davis Cup squad, alongside Bates, Mark Petchey and Danny Sapsford, to play Portugal in the Euro-African Zone Group One tie in Oporto in March. 'I've been working hard and things have been going well, but I didn't think this would happen so quickly,' he said, after hearing of his Davis Cup call-up.

He impressed greatly in practice in Oporto, with Pickard considering him 'the one bright light in the British game', while one of his Davis Cup teammates remarked that 'he already attacks the ball so much harder than anyone else of his age group'. He may have made an impression on his colleagues, but he failed to feature, as Great Britain was defeated 4-1.

Nevertheless, his exploits with the Davis Cup squad, as well as on the satellite scene, provided him with the confidence, and the ranking, to try his luck on the greatest stage of them all – the ATP.

Henman trekked to the Far East with Bates – who was soon to become the first Briton to claim a grand prix title for seventeen years, in Seoul – to take in his first major ATP Tour event. 'It was grand to travel with Jeremy,' recalls Henman. 'He was a great help and, seeing he seems to be playing better and better, it was a real bonus to be able to practise with him.'

Proof came in the Japan Open in April, Henman's first qualification on the senior tour. The £720,000 event in Tokyo featured an all-star line-up that included Pete Sampras, Boris Becker, Michael Chang and Ivan Lendl. Showing few signs of nerves, Henman marked his ATP Tour debut by defeating the American Kelly Jones, a former world number-one doubles player, 6-2, 6-3.

'By the time I'd broken him for the second time, I thought he was becoming quite brittle,' said Henman. 'In the second I was happy just to keep my nose in front once I'd got ahead.

'Playing here has been a very exciting and new experience. Instead of having British juniors on the practice courts next to you there's Pete Sampras and that gives you a real lift. This is where you want to be and where you want to stay.'

Little did Henman know that, far from practising alongside Sampras, he would very shortly earn a tilt at the world number one in the third round in Tokyo. He secured that dream match after a great comeback against Australia's Darren Cahill, a semi-finalist at the US Open in 1988, coming back from losing the first set 6-2, to win the second set on a tie-break 7-5 and then romp away with the decider 6-1.

Sampras was on a seventeen-match winning streak and had won all but two of the seven tournaments he had entered so far in 1994, including the Australian Open. For his debut week in a top-level tennis event, the qualifier could not have asked for more of a challenge than a match against the most formidable player in the game.

Unsurprisingly, their third-round contest followed the form book, with the top seed and defending champion Sampras dominating 6-1, 6-2 in less than an hour. Sampras was awesome, losing only three points out of twenty-one on serve, with 61 per cent of his first serve going in. Nonetheless, he gave Henman an encouraging assessment after their match: 'He's not a bad player. He hits well and has a good forehand. But he needs to develop a big weapon. At age nineteen, he's still got a lot of time.' In his own youth Sampras had been a prodigy, winning in 1990 his first Grand Slam (US Open) at the same age that the Briton was now.

Henman had been blooded in high style in his first ATP Tour event. 'I really enjoyed it out there, it was good fun,' he said. 'That is what you play tennis for – meeting the top players on the show courts. I got three games off him, so I don't look on it as disgracing myself. It was a little daunting, but a very good experience for me, especially with the sort of year that he has had. I think you can learn a lot of things from players like him. I think the thing that struck me most about him was his serve. It is unbelievable and sometimes it was just not physically possible to get to it. That's something I have got to work on.'

Henman's first venture on the ATP Tour yielded almost £10,000, easily his biggest pay cheque yet, and lifted him to 184th in the world rankings.

A failed attempt to qualify for the Hong Kong Open followed, and so Henman ended his Asian adventure with a brace of hard-court ATP Challenger events. Unseeded in Nagoya, Japan, he upset 8th seed Eyal Ran of Israel, before losing in round two to Japan's Gouichi Motomura, and in Manila, in the Philippines, he reached his first professional final, losing to 5th seed Michael Tebbutt of Australia 2-6, 2-6.

A return to the more familiar surroundings of Europe failed to inspire Henman to qualify for his first Grand Slam at the French Open, where he lost in the first qualifying round in straight sets to Wayne Arthurs of Australia. As result, along with compatriots Chris Bailey and Mark Petchey, he headed for a Challenger on the grass courts of Annenheim, Austria, in search of further ranking points.

Bailey was the only one of the trio to emerge successful from the first round, with Henman losing in straight sets 6-3, 6-2 to Canada's Sebastien Lareau.

Good news for Henman, now placed 161st, followed a week later, when he was given the chance to take on the world's top stars after receiving a wild-card entry to his first major tournament on home soil, the pre-Wimbledon Stella Artois Championships at Queen's Club. The draw was headed by the world's top three players, Pete Sampras, Michael Stich and Stefan Edberg, while Boris Becker and Goran Ivanisevic were also included in the line-up.

Henman booked his date with one of the big boys, after defeating qualifier Peter Lundgren of Sweden in round one 7-5, 7-6. In round two he faced 5th seed and Australian Open finalist Todd Martin. Henman underlined his potential with a battling display against the American, before losing to the eventual winner that year 6-4, 6-4.

'I thought I played very well,' concluded Henman, who

walked away with a cheque for £3,000. 'I need more matches against players of his calibre because you learn a tremendous amount playing people in the top ten.'

Martin uttered a few compliments during the match and more after it. He forecast a successful future for the nineteen-year-old and suggested he would not need wild cards for much longer. 'He's going to be a very good player in the future. He has a ton of shots and, for his thinness, a great amount of power which will be accentuated once he fills out and grows into his height. Great Britain may not win the Davis Cup next year but you have some talented players who often don't get the credit they deserve.'

For now, though, Henman was more than grateful for his wild-card invitations, and received two more. The first was to play at the Manchester Open, where he lost in the first round in three sets to America's Alex O'Brien; the second was to participate in his first Grand Slam on the hallowed turf of Wimbledon.

The previous June, after losing in the Wimbledon qualifiers, Henman was playing in an unglamorous satellite event in Spain and his world ranking was near 800 – almost off the graph. Now he was sitting inside the top 200, and set to emulate his heroes in treading the grass at the greatest Grand Slam of them all, at SW19. But being in awe of the place was not an option; he had a job to do there.

'No, of course I'm not daunted about Wimbledon,' he said. 'It's what every British player particularly works towards. I like grass. I played a lot of junior tennis on grass and it's something I feel very much at home on. Wimbledon is the most prestigious tournament in the world and I am very much looking forward to it.'

As Wimbledon drew closer, tongues were already wagging

as to which British hope had the best chance of progressing there, and Henman's name had been floating around more than most.

Mick Dickson of the *Daily Mail* wrote: 'Tim Henman is a genuine international prospect who, at nineteen, is older than he looks. Henman has risen more than 200 places in the world rankings since the start of the year and almost 500 spots in the last twelve months. Much of the improvement has been the result of sheer hard grind on the satellite circuit. He has the talent to make it big if he can handle the inevitable hype.'

The Independent's Owen Slot described him as 'a skinny, serious 19-year-old from Oxfordshire notable for the elegance of his groundstrokes and a ranking that has shot up 650 places – into the mid-100s – in 14 months. To him will national expectation turn.'

William Kings noted in the *Evening Standard*, in his piece headed 'Henman is a diamond in pack of wild cards', that 'At just nineteen years of age Tim Henman is regarded as the best thing since sliced bread. Well, maybe not quite that but, in tennis terms, perhaps the best thing that's happened to Britain since Jeremy Bates burst on the professional scene in 1982. The personable young man from Oxfordshire is certainly being groomed as the natural successor to Bates. And the consensus on the circuit is that, with the right handling, this tall, slim, unassuming young man is really going places.'

Unfortunately Henman's pre-Wimbledon exposure lasted far longer than his run at the actual tournament. After winning the first set of his first-round tie with Germany's David Prinosil, he succumbed tamely and lost in four sets 6-4, 3-6, 2-6, 2-6. A return to another 1twelve months of obscure Challenger events and relative anonymity beckoned.

But the British number three wasted no time getting back into the swing of things after his Wimbledon disappointment, making the quarter-finals of the Bristol Challenger and the last four at the Winnetka Challenger in Illinois. During this period he was also called upon to make up the first Davis Cup squad selected by new coach Bill Knight, which included Bates, Petchey and Bailey, for the crucial Euro-African Zone Group One relegation play-off with Romania.

Henman made his Davis Cup debut alongside Bates in the doubles, beating Dinu Pescariu and George Cosac 6-2, 6-7, 5-7, 6-2, 6-1, which delighted the crowd at Didsbury, Manchester, but ultimately proved insufficient to stop Great Britain losing the tie 3-2 and tumbling out of Group One.

In September, and now 146th in the world, Henman returned to the Far East to play a series of hard-court Challenger events, starting in Seoul, where unexpectedly he lost in the second round to Korea's Kim Nam-Hoon, who was ranked outside the top 700.

Henman's second tournament took him to Singapore. Little did he know what a lasting impression this place would leave on him. He had made good progress at the Singapore Challenger, beating two players ranked in the top 200 in order to progress to the quarter-finals and a meeting with compatriot Chris Wilkinson.

It was in this match that disaster struck. Henman was trailing the British number four 7-5, 5-4, when he slipped and tumbled to the ground, clutching his left ankle, after pushing off in an attempt to attack the net. Unable to stand, he was forced to retire hurt with an apparent ankle strain. 'I just pushed off on the leg and there was this big crunch,' he recalls.

He headed straight home to Britain for treatment. 'It was a twelve-hour flight. I was told I'd just strained my ankle but I said to the physio, "I don't think that's quite right" because I heard this big snap as I did it. It felt as though someone had hit me on the ankle with a mallet.'

On his arrival back in England it became apparent that he had in fact broken his ankle in three places. 'I tried not to think about it too much but if you've broken something you tend to worry about your career prospects.'

Henman was forced to miss the National Championships in Telford, and went under the knife. The injury's legacy was three pins, each about two inches long, which permanently hold his repaired bone in place and will be clanking around inside his ankle for the rest of his days. 'From a tennis point of view I don't think it was the best thing to happen, but I felt a little bit stronger mentally coming through something like that.'

He recuperated at the National Sports Centre at Lilleshall, alongside more seriously injured footballers such as England international and Liverpool defender Mark Wright and Scottish international striker Kevin Gallacher, who was plying his trade with Blackburn Rovers. It was three months before he could train again, and five months before he could play.

A softer soul may have called it quits, but not Henman. He fought back to fitness and returned the following February to play in the carpeted Wolfsbury Challenger in Germany. There he made a winning return, coming back from a set down, to beat 268th-ranked Fernon Wibier of the Netherlands 2-6, 7-6, 6-3, but subsequently lost in round two in straight sets to world number 141 Sandor Noszaly of Hungary.

However, it was not until May that his recovery was judged to be complete. Before then he had failed to record back-to-back wins in any of the Challengers in which he had participated, in addition to flying to Paris in an abortive attempt to qualify for the French Open. His ranking had slipped to the outskirts of the top 300, plummeting from 146 to 272.

'At least the ankle was fine,' he said, 'and that was the important thing.'

His fortunes were about to take a huge upturn, with the opening of the grass-court season. He started by flying to Austria in an attempt to qualify for the main draw at Annenheim's grass-court Challenger. 'That was the big turning point,' he believes. Not only was he successful in his aim but he went on to reach the semi-finals.

At Queen's a week later he justified his wild card into the Stella Artois event by beating 16th seed Martin Sinner and then, at Nottingham, 2nd seed Jonas Bjorkman on his way to a quarter-final place, his first on the ATP Tour. It was an encouraging three weeks, which sent his ranking up to 219th in the world. He had also collected more prize money in those three tournaments than he had from all the other tournaments he had played so far in 1995.

His progress since his recovery from that career-threatening injury had certainly impressed Britain's latest Davis Cup captain, David Lloyd. 'What I like is his attitude,' said Lloyd. 'He's selfish, which is important as you must be single-minded to achieve in tennis.'

Henman himself admitted: 'I would say now I'm definitely back to where I was, if not improved. The last three weeks have been very encouraging and I feel very happy about the direction in which I am moving.'

A fitter, stronger and more confident Henman was further lifted, less than a week later, by scoring his first singles win at Wimbledon. The recipient of a wild card, he recorded his first victory at SW19 by beating Paul Wekesa, at 107 the highest-ranked player in Kenya's history. A familiar foe, Wekesa trained regularly at Queen's and the two had practised together there a month earlier.

The only time Wekesa, seven years Henman's senior, looked in contention in the match was towards the conclusion of the opening set, when Henman was broken after throwing away a set point at 5-4.

Other British players may have suffered a drop in confidence but Henman battled through the disappointment to win the subsequent tie-break 7-3. Wekesa appeared overwhelmed. Henman dropped a mere five points in the second set, rocketing through it 6-0. He then established an early lead in the third, with some accurate passing shots allowing him to break serve. After that it was just a case of how long the Kenyan could hold out. Henman took the first of the two match points he set, at 5-4, sealing the victory with an ace, which was received with a tremendous ovation by the home crowd.

Afterwards, far from being jubilant at winning for the first time at the Wimbledon Singles Championship, he claimed it was more 'a relief'. But in truth it was a notable victory for Henman, made even more so by the fact it had earned him a tilt at the reigning Wimbledon champion, one Pete Sampras, in the second round. Yet, rather than being unnerved by the prospect of a second encounter with Sampras, after being allowed a mere three games in Tokyo the previous year, he was relishing it. 'I was trying to concentrate on my match [with Wekesa] and not think about the consequences,' he said.

'I look at it as a great honour for me to be playing the defending champion and a chance to beat him. Pete Sampras hasn't lost here for two years and I believe he is the best player on grass in the world. It's what you put in all the effort for and all the pressure is on him. You cannot go on court thinking you're going to lose before you start.

'It's a different surface [to Japan], so the points are going to be played in a different way. In that match, I was serving and standing back quite a lot of the time. On grass I will be coming forward a lot more.'

The American was not playing as well as he had been at the time of their first head-to-head. He had yet to win a Grand Slam in 1995 and had been pushed off his number-one perch by Andre Agassi. Relieved to get his quest for a Wimbledon hat-trick underway after needing four sets to win through in round one, Sampras guarded against over-confidence. 'There is no reason why Henman shouldn't think he can beat me,' he said. 'It's grass, and anything can happen.'

But predictably it didn't, as Henman found the defending champion too formidable an obstacle to advance any further. Sampras lost only three points on serve in the 6-2 first set and two points in the 6-3 second.

Henman, however, inspired by the fanatical support that had gathered at Court One, battled the American evenly in the third set. He broke for the first and only time in the opening game of the third, hitting a running cross-court forehand that sent Sampras diving in vain on to the grass. The American was forced into saving two more break points at 5-5, as the set headed to a tie-break. The two were even at 3-3 in the shoot-out but Sampras's experience aided him as he won the next four points, to send Henman tumbling out.

The young Brit had certainly won the crowd's approval, as well as the American's respect. Sampras, who went on to win his third Wimbledon title in a row that year, said: 'He's got a pretty good all-round game and a pretty good head on his shoulders. He does everything pretty well and has got the tools of the trade, but I think he needs a weapon.'

Indeed, Henman's main problem was that he lacked a big serve and was trying to go for rather more than was perhaps wise. He made twelve costly double faults, despite showing himself to be a highly skilled net player, producing fifteen winning volleys.

The beaten Briton was aware of his limitations and was determined to improve the situation. 'I definitely need to become stronger,' he said. 'But this was a great experience and something I can go away and learn from.'

Unfortunately, hours later, it was not the Sampras match that would thrust Henman's name into the newspapers the following morning. A day that began with the excitement of playing the defending champion on Court One ended in ignominy in a doubles match with Jeremy Bates shortly before twilight on Court 14.

The British pair were leading in their first-round doubles match against Henrik Holm of Sweden and Jeff Tarango of the United States 7-6, 2-6, 6-3, when the fourth set was in the midst of being decided by a tie-break. After Henman missed a net cord, which had handed his opponents a 2-1 lead in the shoot-out, he lost his cool and lashed out with his racket at the offending ball, attempting to ferociously volley it towards the far end of the court. But it was a dismal effort.

The ball hit Caroline Hall, a ballgirl crossing the court to retrieve another, at close range on the side of the head, right behind her left ear. The shocked sixteen-year-old, who had only been on court as a relief for another girl during her break, instantly fell to the ground before getting up and fleeing back to her position in tears, still rubbing the ear and crying. She was eventually helped to the side of the court, where she was treated with ice before being taken home and later seen by a doctor.

Henman was devastated. The Australian umpire, Wayne McKewen, summoned the tournament referee, Britain's Alan Mills, who officially defaulted the pair, to a chorus of boos from the 1,800 fans around the court.

It was the first time in the Open era that anyone had been disqualified from the Championships, and only the third time in any Grand Slam event. Germany's Carsten Arriens had been kicked out of the French Open that same year for throwing a racket that struck a line judge in the leg, while, unsurprisingly, John McEnroe was defaulted from the Australian Open in 1980 for verbally abusing officials.

'The whole thing was so unexpected that everyone was totally shocked by it – me, the umpire, Alan Mills the referee,' Henman recalls. 'It was obviously an incident I didn't mean to happen but I had to take responsibility for it and deal with it. I think most people who know me felt it was out of character.'

A statement from the referee's office said: 'the rules precisely state that a player must be in control of his actions on court, and in such cases there is no choice but to default automatically on the basis of unsportsmanlike conduct.'

The incident also roused the wrath of Henman's opponent, Jeff Tarango, who had once dropped his shorts in a match with Michael Chang. He thundered: 'If I had hit the girl in such an incident I would have been thrown out of tennis. With the speed of the ball, it could have killed the girl.'

Tarango, however, went on to infamy of his own later in the Championships, when he called an umpire 'the most corrupt official in the game' and stormed off court. After the match his French wife ambushed the umpire and slapped him.

Henman, clearly emotional and close to tears, later held a press conference. Shaken and contrite, he said: 'I was not very happy at losing the point and very angry. I went to hit the ball at the other end of the court, to be honest, I was hitting the ball hard. Just as I was throwing up the ball to hit it, the ballgirl ran in front of the net. It's a complete accident, but I'm responsible for my actions. If I had missed the ballgirl, if she had not been there, I don't think I would have got a code violation. There was no one in line with the ball before I was about to hit it. As I hit it, she ran straight out in front of me so I'm the responsible party. As soon as I had hit the ball and I had hit her, I had a pretty fair idea that I may be defaulted.'

All England Club chairman John Curry sat next to Henman during the news conference and confirmed the disqualification. 'It was obviously an accident but the rules are very clear. If you hit an official, accidentally or otherwise, it is disqualification,' he said.

It was arguably the most embarrassing moment of Henman's career. 'That was one of the toughest situations I've ever had to deal with, but whether it's tennis or anything else, if there's an issue I like to tackle it straight away. I remember coming in the next day and it was as if I'd murdered someone, I felt awful. But it wasn't because of people's reactions: between that Wednesday and the end of the tournament I must have had between 500 and 750 letters from the public, and not one of them was negative.

'Every one of them said, "I think it was an awful decision, I don't think you should have been disqualified," or words to that effect. So obviously that was a big morale-booster. The reason I felt so bad on the Thursday was the coverage in the newspapers. There were big headlines saying that I had hit the ball so hard I could have killed the ballgirl. When there are stories like that all over the newspapers there are times when you think, I don't really need this. But come the Thursday afternoon it was all sorted out.'

Henman returned to Wimbledon the next day to present Hall with a large bouquet of yellow and white flowers. He hung his head in shame when he met his victim, who had suffered swelling and bruising behind her ear, and told her: 'I can't say how sorry I am. I hope these flowers will make up for it in some way.' They posed for pictures together on a practice court and Henman put his arm round her and kissed her several times for the benefit of photographers.

'By Friday everyone was saying I was the nicest guy. It is amazing how the situation evolved. Looking back on it, I don't think the media could have a better opportunity to be as negative about me. And in the end I think I dealt with it, and maybe I came out of it a better person.'

Henman was later fined £1,300 by Wimbledon referee Mills for smashing a ball at a ballgirl, and a further £650 for being defaulted as a result. The total fine was deducted from his prize money and forwarded to the Grand Slam Development Fund.

Caroline Hall was not allowed to talk to reporters under rules governing the conduct of ballboys and ballgirls. However, in a statement issued by the All England Club press officers she said: 'It was a bit of a shock and my head is still quite sore. I know it was a complete accident and I was just very unlucky, as was Tim. Tim has said sorry, but I had already forgiven him because I know he didn't mean the ball to hit me – there are no hard feelings. I'm really sorry that the game had to end that way, especially since the Brits were winning. They didn't even think about the match; in fact Jeremy was the first person to rush over and check that I was OK, and he really comforted me. They were more worried about me than the score.'

It was the only black mark for Henman on what had been a highly productive grass-court season, which also included, post-Wimbledon, appearances at the Manchester Challenger and a semi-final berth at the Newcastle Challenger. But, having made a public apology, and being the professional he now was, Henman rapidly put his misdemeanour behind him. The only way to make people forget about it was to progress in his tennis career.

Now sitting at 150th in the world, he headed to the United

States and the heat of Indianapolis at the RCA Championships, and pulled off what he described as 'my best win of the year' by upsetting 16th seed Cedric Pioline of France, a US Open finalist in 1993, in straight sets, to reach a second-round spot.

He followed that up by getting through four rounds of qualifying, without dropping a set, to gain entry to his first-ever foreign Grand Slam championship, at the US Open. There he beat fellow qualifier Juan Albert Viloca of Spain 6-3, 4-6, 6-3, 6-2, but failed in his attempt to become the first Briton to advance to the third round of the men's singles since Andrew Castle in 1987, losing in four sets to 75th-ranked American Jared Palmer.

But it was his globe-trotting marathon from early October, a hectic programme that was to take him from Kuala Lumpur to Beijing, Seoul, Telford, Beijing again and then Andorra, that began to get him on the map for the right reasons. Three titles were his reward.

In Seoul he produced a series of superb displays to win his first Challenger tournament, dropping just one set, and then doubled his Challenger trophy tally with a win at Reunion Island a month later.

Henman also halted Jeremy Bates's phenomenal run of three consecutive wins in Britain's Guardian Direct Championships by eliminating him in the semi-finals, at the expense of just three games. In the final he beat that famous all-Canadian Yorkshireman and clear favourite Greg Rusedski, after coming back from losing the first set, to become the youngest-ever winner of the national title.

His tennis performances in the second half of the year had been highly profitable, and were exemplified by his end-of-year rise in the rankings into the top 100, at 95.

'Knackered but happy,' was Henman's own résumé of his

effort and accomplishment over the past six months. 'The top 100 is a barrier which people judge you by, but now I've broken it I won't be resting on my laurels. This is just the beginning.'

Breaching the top 100 had looked an impossible dream twelve months before, when he was hobbling around on crutches while recovering from a long-term injury and, as a result, slid down the rankings. Now suddenly he found himself a truly rare British sporting commodity: a young tennis player with fantastic hand-eye co-ordination who was being widely tipped to break into the higher echelons of the world game.

His game, especially his serve, forehand and footwork, had come on leaps and bounds, contributing to his winning fifty of his last sixty-six single matches of the year – even though he had yet to develop a really big shot. 'I'm not doing anything particularly different but I am now picking the right shot to play at the right moment. And I do have a lot of confidence. I'm looking forward to 1996,' he remarked.

After breaking the top-100 barrier, he now faced the prospect of competing at a far higher level, for he would now be playing regularly on the full tour, rather than in Challengers, and this meant direct entry into many more ATP Tour and Grand Slam events.

Nineteen ninety-six was going to be a big year for Tim Henman.

4

Breakthrough

Revitalised after a short break, and injury-free, Henman began the new season, his first on the full tour, in just as impressive form as he had finished the last.

After qualifying for his first Sydney Outdoor Grand Prix, he played a wonderfully intelligent match to unexpectedly snuff out the power-packed challenge of Australia's Mark Philippoussis, ranked more than fifty places higher, in straight sets, to go as far as round two.

He continued to upset players ranked significantly higher than himself, when he made his Australian Open debut, taking another big leap forward in his burgeoning tennis career when he out-hit world number 26, the Czech Petr Korda, in four sets. Korda commented: 'He went for everything and everything turned to gold. He's got great potential and if he can play consistently at this level he can easily reach the top twenty. But, up to now, he has got hot and then cold.'

Unfortunately, Henman's form happened to follow the

Czech's words. In round two he showed up cold, failing dismally in his attempt to follow one convincing win with another. Up against Sweden's number 34, Jonas Bjorkman, he bowed out in straight sets, in a one-sided encounter. He managed to win just six games off the Swede, as his serve failed to get going.

'I was beaten by somebody who was doing everything better on the day,' Henman admitted. 'He served better and he returned better. Everything I tried to do, it seemed he had a better answer. I think I now have to improve my consistency against top-ranked players. I know I can play one good match, but after playing one I need to play a second. At least I've recognised the problem.'

Despite a disappointing ending to his trip Down Under, Henman did receive a boost, by way of news that he had risen to his all-time highest ranking of 86, as players receive bonus points for beating higher-ranked players. Even so, inconsistency continued to follow him wherever he went.

From Australia he departed for Shanghai, where he was seeded 2nd in a weak entry. He reached his first ATP Tour semi-final, but lost to 130th-ranked Andrei Olhovskiy of Russia.

Returning to Europe, Henman took in two events in France, coming close to the best win of his career against world number 12 Sergi Bruguera of Spain, a former French Open champion, before going down 6-1, 3-6, 6-4 at the Marseilles Open and, lamentably, a week later at Cherbourg, being knocked out in round one in straight sets by world number 123 Omar Camporese.

Indoor ATP Tour events, unseeded, in Rotterdam and Copenhagen, brought two more last-four finishes, and included the scalps of world number 22, the Dutchman Jan Siemerink, and world number one, Pete Sampras (who withdrew through injury), in the Netherlands, and 8th seed Marc-Kevin Goellner in Denmark. Such results saw Henman hit 58 in the rankings, and it was only just March.

At the end of that month he flew to Key Biscayne, Florida, to play in the Lipton Championships. Taking his Masters bow, he dropped just three games against American Steve Campbell, ranked 138th, but was once again foiled in three sets by Bruguera, in round two.

Henman also produced another repeat in that match with the Spaniard. In an episode reminiscent of his last trip to Wimbledon, he let his feelings get the better of him. During the opening game he whacked a ball at the umpire's chair, which earned him a warning, and then, with Bruguera leading 5-3, 30-0, he fired a ball down the court in frustration, for which a point was deducted from his score.

Henman may have been progressing up the ladder quite rapidly since his injury, but if he was truly going to get to the top and make a name for himself for the right reasons, he had to learn to curb his impulses.

Disappointing performances followed in the first rounds in New Delhi, where he suffered one of the most crushing defeats of his professional career, losing 6-1, 1-6, 6-0 to world number 100 Frederik Fetterlein, and in Tokyo where he was also defeated. To make matters worse, he had picked up a virus in the Far East, initially feared to be glandular fever, which left him bedridden for five weeks and so deprived him of match practice ahead of his debut on the clay courts of Roland Garros.

He was 'ring rusty' when he did take to the court in Paris for his first-round match against Belgium's Kris Goossens, forty-eight places his inferior, and was defeated in straight sets 4-6, 4-6, 5-7. He never looked at ease on the clay surface, of which he had limited experience – a pattern that was to continue for years to come. On this occasion, as well as failing to serve well enough to make an impression, he had no answer to the Belgian's forehand.

Then came another huge blow for Henman, who had slipped to 61st, at the start of his favoured grass-court season. He was eliminated at only the second phase at Queen's to Russian doubles specialist Andrei Olhovskiy, a player ranked forty-nine places below him.

But Henman's unpredictable form took a turn for the better at the Nottingham Open, where his tennis senses appeared revitalised. He gave an assured performance in his first-round match against 3rd-seeded American MaliVai Washington, to take his first top-twenty scalp 6-3, 7-5 in just seventy-five minutes.

Delighted though he was, Henman managed to keep his success in perspective. 'Now I have to set my sights on beating players of his standard more often, and I know that to do that it is going to take a lot of hard work, though it was MaliVai's first match on the grass so that was to my advantage.'

In round two he came from behind to beat Michael Joyce of the United States 6-7, 7-5, 6-2, before being unlucky to be edged out in a tight three-set match with 5th seed Jan Siemerink, in his first major grass-court quarter-final. For Siemerink it restored some Dutch pride, after the national football team had been humbled 4-1 by England at Euro '96 a few days earlier.

With Wimbledon just around the corner Henman was in buoyant mood. Coincidentally, he was in a car travelling to Wimbledon when he heard he had been drawn to play Russia's Yevgeny Kafelnikov, the 5th seed, in the first round. He could hardly have faced a tougher opponent, and a comment in *The Times* the next day said it all. 'Tim Henman hits a wall first time out: Kafelnikov.'

He had no chance. Kafelnikov had arrived on the back of becoming the new French Open champion and was a quarter-finalist at SW19 the previous year – something Henman could only dream of emulating at that point in his career, or so it seemed. 'You've got to look at it as a good opportunity,' he said, but even he must have had severe doubts about how much he believed what he was saying.

But there would be one positive aspect to having such a high-risk first-round opponent. He would fulfil a lifelong dream of experiencing the splendour of Wimbledon's Centre Court. Ever since, at the age of five in 1980, he had seen his first Centre Court match – Bjorn Borg's first Monday opener and three-setter against Egypt's El Shafei – this is where he had yearned to perform and now, to his elation, he had been handed that chance.

He was greeted on that most famous of tennis venues with rapturous applause from the home faithful, who, in hope rather than expectation, prayed for their man to cause an upset. 'I'll never forget that feeling of walking out on to Centre Court that year in front of your own fans and they're cheering and waving flags,' he recalled. 'It was so special and made me feel so proud – the hairs were standing up on the back of my neck and it brought a bit of a lump to the throat.'

Whereas so often in the past his compatriots have found the pressure of a success-starved crowd too much to shoulder, this young player appeared to thrive on the traditional highs and lows of the British response. 'They were phenomenal,' Henman remembers. 'They hung on in there and stayed behind me, throughout. Until you have played in front of a Centre Court crowd you cannot understand what it is like. I didn't know how I would feel when I got out there because this was my first match on Centre Court, but I felt good in the knock-up and I think that showed in the first two games.'

Henman burst out of the blocks and took supreme control of the match, winning the first set on a tie-break and then breaking the Russian early in the second to take a two-set lead. He was displaying a full range of strokes and a maturity beyond his tender twenty-one years. Kafelnikov never looked at home on the lush grass, especially after he aggravated a knee injury, which required him to wear a knee support from midway through the first set.

There were moments when it seemed Henman might have wrapped it up in straight sets, but Kafelnikov survived three break points at 3-3 in the third set and then proceeded to make life most uncomfortable for his opponent. Besides, winning in straight sets is just not the British way of doing things. That's far too boring.

Having forfeited his two-set lead, Henman now appeared to be on the verge of adding his name to that long list of great British 'nearly' men when he stood at two match points down at 5-3 in the final set. Oh, how we love a good British loser!

But his response to adversity was to produce two successive aces, worthy of Boris Becker in his prime, to gain deuce and take the game. 'They were very timely, but really I felt I had nothing to lose at that point. My only thought was that I wanted to make him serve out for the match.' In that aim he succeeded, but amazingly the blond Russian was found wanting. He double-faulted, presenting Henman with a couple of break points, and the Briton devoured the first with a confident forehand down the line.

More drama was to come, when Henman began to suffer pain from cramp. He valiantly fought on, saving a break point in the eleventh game with a winning serve, and reached match point in the next game by simply outrallying his opponent. It was crunch time, the biggest moment in his career. The crowd were on the edge of their seats. Henman lured Kafelnikov into the net. The Russian responded with a backhand. But it was weak and failed to reach the other side of the net.

After three and a half gruelling hours of rollercoaster tennis,

Henman had scored the biggest upset of the Championships, and in that split second it took for Kafelnikov's backhand to hit the net Henmania had been spawned. Truly breathtaking, and certainly a far cry from the previous year's Wimbledon exploits. The crowd packing Centre Court rose to give their new hero a standing ovation. His mother, Jane, turned to friends and remarked: 'I am exhausted, but I feel terrific.' His father, Tony, remained the only person seated in the entire arena. It really was a great reward for all the early tutoring they had given their son. Like Dad, Henman resisted the temptation to overdo the celebrations.

He recalls: 'When I was two sets up I knew I could win but, a break down in the fifth set, I was saying: "Shit, it doesn't seem that long ago that I was in complete control of this match." This was a turning-point for me, not just in the match, but in my career.

'I remember thinking that I'd watched a number of British tennis players making names for themselves at Wimbledon by playing really well, but the sad fact was that they lost in those matches. I decided I didn't want to be put in the same bracket.'

At the press conference after the match he said: 'To beat a player like Kafelnikov is the top moment in my career, and my aim is now to do this kind of thing more often. Mentally I am twelve months more experienced. I have had my highs and lows but I have learnt from them.'

Kafelnikov offered no excuses: 'I'm sure Tim will be much more confident after today's match, because he lost the match once,' he said. 'He has got a pretty solid game. It is good enough that he can win a couple more matches. I don't know about him and the seeded players, but of the others, he is the most dangerous.'

Henman was beginning to command respect on a global scale,

and when he lost just sixteen games to fellow Britons Danny Sapsford and Luke Milligan in the next two rounds, the weight of expectation exploded.

Before the tournament had got underway, Henman had lived anonymously and travelled by bus and Tube quite unrecognised. Now suddenly he was a sensation, fans were queuing all night for tickets to his matches, girls screamed and Britain fell in love with him. It really was the start of Henmania.

'My life changed in a couple of days,' he recalls. 'I was on the front pages of all the newspapers, photographers camped outside my house. It was like becoming a pop star. It didn't upset me but it showed how long everyone had been waiting and wanting there to be a British tennis star, someone of our own to cheer on.'

Even Henman's next opponent, Magnus Gustafsson, a baseliner from Sweden ranked 37, had joined in the euphoria. 'He reminds me a little of Sampras, the way he plays,' he said. 'I've seen him many times before, and I am very impressed with his game. He's a man for the future, that's for sure. He has nice strokes, they are taken from a coaching manual – and as a person he is a great guy.'

But Henman refused to get carried away by the hype: 'Obviously when I'm arriving and leaving the courts there is a lot more attention than I'm used to, and that I would expect. But that's probably part of the package. I don't like it, I don't dislike it. That's the way it is. If people are going to put expectations on my shoulders or put extra pressure on me, that's up to them. If people want to take a photo when I arrive or when I leave, that's their choice. I'm very much trying to concentrate on what I'm doing. I think probably with each match I've become a little more confident with the way I am playing. But I suppose it's a new experience, the fourth round of a Grand Slam tournament, and it's something I'm really enjoying. I'm delighted it's happened at Wimbledon, because there's no bigger tournament, and being in front of the British public is extra special.'

The revelation of British tennis continued his fine work against Gustafsson. From start to finish, in a match continually interrupted by rain, Henman was going for winners: big shots on big points in the foremost match he had yet played. He started beautifully, winning his first service game to love and racing to a 3-0 lead after exposing his opponent's frailty at the net; volleying seemed a complete mystery to the Swede.

Three times in the match Gustafsson broke Henman's service, yet this failed to dent his confidence and concentration. Each time, almost immediately, the Briton broke back. Serving for the match at 6-5 in the third set, he momentarily faltered, but he remained composed, and disposed of Gustafsson with a crisp forehand volley at the net. It was the first time since 1973, when the honour went to Roger Taylor, that a British man had reached the quarter-finals at Wimbledon.

But Henman had not just kept his nerve to reach that milestone; he had also retained his modesty: 'Obviously, I'm very pleased to be in the quarter-finals, but I have to keep looking forward,' he said. 'I'm pleased with what I've achieved, but there's still more tennis to be played. The sense of history has not sunk in yet, but the crowd support was great. I hope I can live up to their expectations. They definitely lifted me. Sometimes it can make life more difficult for my opponents when it seems like they're probably playing against 15,001 people.'

The flags of St George, temporarily lowered after England's Euro '96 defeat at Wembley against Germany a few days earlier, were hoisted proudly over the All England Club, and the confidence of the Euro '96 anthem, 'Three Lions', that football was coming home turned into claims that it could be tennis that was coming home that summer. Unlikely perhaps, but not outrageously so. After all, the only seed left standing in Henman's path to the final was his quarter-final opponent, 13th seed Todd Martin of the USA.

Sadly, the mounting enthusiasm of the Henmania phenomenon sweeping the country was not mirrored at this, the most important British tennis match in years. Instead of being greeted by 13,000 flag-waving fans, Henman walked on to the court at 11a.m. to find half the seats empty. His loyal army of fans were unable to see the match, after it was postponed as a result of nearly four hours of torrential rain the previous day. The match was put back twenty-four hours to official ladies' semi-final day, and this therefore meant all Centre Court tickets had been sold months earlier, so none would be available on the gate for Henman's fans.

Not even the Royal Box could be filled in time for his match, which started early to help ease the congestion caused by numerous rain delays throughout the tournament. The Duchess of Kent and Prince and Princess Michael eventually appeared just before the end of the second set.

Henman produced some moments of sparkling tennis, notably with his searing forehand, but Martin's powerful game, which included a ferocious return of service far stronger than anything Henman had encountered throughout the fortnight, frequently tested the Briton on his own serve and more than once led him to make the mistake of trying to lob the six foot six American.

Henman had his chances to win the first set, including two break points and three set points, none of which he could capitalise on. The most controversial of them all came at 5-4 on

Henman's first set point. Martin's serve was initially called out by the line judge, but it was overruled by the umpire, to send the game into deuce.

The opening set eventually came down to a tie-break. Errors by Henman gave the American a 4-1 lead, before he pulled it back to 5-5. But Martin replied with an ace to earn his first set point, and with Henman struggling with the incessant swirling wind he double-faulted on his serve to concede the opening set.

There was nothing between the two as they battled through the second set, even though Henman looked dangerously vulnerable. At 4-3 to Martin, rain halted play for half an hour, but on the duo's return a second tie-break of the day was eventually played out.

Martin blew Henman away in the shoot-out, racing to a 6-1 lead. And despite Henman's denying the American on his first set point, he was helpless to deny him a second time as Martin aced his way to a two-set lead.

Three more times they were driven off court in the third, and for the first time in the match, sandwiched between the first and second interruption, someone dropped their service.

Predictably, it was Henman, and with Martin now leading 4-2 and two sets up, the end looked nigh.

It was simply a match too far for Henman, outfoxed by a rival who always had an edge in power and accuracy. He had certainly not embarrassed himself, and the crowd acknowledged this as he exited to a standing ovation.

Martin was generous about the prospects of his young British opponent. 'There should be a lot of optimism surrounding Tim because he's going to be a great player,' Martin said. 'I can't say enough good things about him. To deal with everything he has had to for the last week, after his win over Kafelnikov, I think it's a remarkable effort to have kept his mind on the game. This won't be his last quarter-final at Wimbledon – one day Tim might even win it.'

Henman may have lost, but there was still plenty to be optimistic about. 'Overall I can reflect on the greatest tournament of my career so far,' he said. 'Coming through against Kafelnikov was the highlight and I just hope there will be more and better Wimbledons for me in the future. I was disappointed with my match today but know I lost to a better player on the day. I've shown that I can compete with some of the very top players, and now I think it's my job, my aim, to go and join them. I have got the credentials to do just that. This is a big breakthrough. A step in the right direction. I'd like to think I can win Wimbledon one day.'

He had entered Wimbledon labelled merely as the first guy to be disqualified at SW19, but left it as the pride of British tennis. The country adored him. Mothers and daughters loved him for his clean-cut features and great physique, fathers liked his good manners and ambition, and even sons admitted to admiring his pluck.

Henman admitted: 'My fan mail has gone from around a hundred letters to thousands, including proposals of marriage. I don't go looking for the fame and adulation. I know things are expected of me, but I don't concentrate on things like that or allow them to faze me. All I know is that I am on a high.'

His income had also started to accelerate, with bigger prize money and potential sponsorship offers rolling in. But Henman would have shunned it all if it meant improving his ranking. 'Since reaching the Wimbledon quarter-finals there have been a lot of interest and sponsorship proposals. But it is tennis that motivates me, not money. I've no idea what the deals involve.'

His performances had almost halved his world ranking, from 62 to 39. This time the previous year he was ranked a lowly 276th as he fought his way back from that severe ankle injury. Now, in addition to his rise up the rankings, he was on the verge of claiming a place in the Grand Slam Cup tournament, a controversial event with £1 million for the winner. It had commenced in 1990 amid acrimony between the International Tennis Federation and the then Association of Tennis Professionals. Only the sixteen players that perform best in the year's Grand Slam tournaments are invited to Munich's Olympic Arena to take part. Henman was currently joint 17th in the standings with Sweden's Thomas Enqvist.

If he was going to make it to Munich he had to prove that his Wimbledon accomplishment was not a one-off.

His first opportunity to prove so was on his Olympics debut in Atlanta. But after a tense and error-strewn 7-6, 6-3 win against Japan's 85th-ranked Shuzo Matsuoka in the searing 38∞C heat at Stone Mountain, he failed to overcome doubles specialist Todd Woodbridge, ranked 43rd, in the second round. The nerve of the Australian proved a little too strong for Henman, as he beat him in two tie-breaks.

It was another in a long line of knocks to Great Britain's medal hopes, which eventually yielded a solitary gold, thanks to rowers Steve Redgrave and Matthew Pinsent in the coxless pairs. But Henman had not given up hope of a medal yet, and just a day after bowing out of the singles he teamed up with Neil Broad to launch an assault on the men's doubles.

Born in South Africa, Broad had acquired British nationality in 1990 with the optimistic hope of representing Britain in the Davis Cup at a time when his own country was still barred from the Olympic arena because of apartheid. He and Henman went to Atlanta with a single Davis Cup match behind them as a pair. They had lost that match in Slovakia to Jan Kroslak and Karol Kucera, but revenge was sweet as they beat the same duo to progress to the second round at the Olympics.

Henman had never really considered himself a doubles player, but he had such talent that he and Broad managed to stun second favourites Grant Connell and Daniel Nestor from Canada and Czech Republic 5th seeds Jiri Novak and Daniel Vacek in the last sixteen and the quarter-finals respectively, to find themselves just one win away from a medal.

That one win would have to come against defending champions Germany in the semi-final. Boris Becker and Michael Stich may have been responsible for striking gold in Barcelona in 1992, but they had been replaced by Marc-Kevin Goellner and David Prinosil, who refused to give up the title lightly.

The German pair won the first set 6-4 and early in the second set threatened the Brits with two break points on Broad's serve. Had the British pair lost that game they would have been looking down the barrel of defeat. But the burly Broad fought his way out of trouble and the pair then broke the Germans, for the first time, in the subsequent game. From almost being 2-0 down they were now 2-0 up. The British team levelled after an hour, but neither side gave an inch through the drawn-out final set. There were no breaks until the seventeenth game, when Broad made two timely interceptions at the net.

But in the next game his nerves appeared to turn to jelly, when serving for an Olympic medal. His over-hit volley brought the score to 30-30 and it required Henman's calming influence to get them back on course. Broad responded with two aces to give Great Britain its first Olympic tennis medal since the sport had been readmitted to the Games eight years earlier, amid scenes of wild excitement. Ironic really, considering that tennis was discontinued as an Olympic event after 1924 because the British were winning too many of the titles: fourteen out of the thirty-three on offer. How times had changed.

Silver couldn't be converted to gold in the final, however, as

Henman and Broad were predictably beaten by number-one seeds, the world-famous Australian pairing 'the Woodies'. Todd Woodbridge, Henman's Olympic singles conqueror, and Mark Woodforde won handsomely in straight sets in little more than a hundred minutes as the four-times Wimbledon and reigning US Open champions continued their dominance of doubles worldwide.

Even so, it was a proud moment for the British pair as they stood on the podium to receive their silver medals. Henman said: 'I'm still well pleased with what we achieved. We went out today believing we could win gold but a silver medal will set off just as many celebrations back home and I look at it as just one more major step in gaining experience in my career. Just being at the Olympics is special and being part of the opening ceremony was a tremendous experience. We've really enjoyed ourselves, I don't think we came into the tournament with great expectations but we've had a good week and hopefully this is another step forward for British tennis.'

It may have been a welcome boost to claim an Olympic medal, but it meant nothing in terms of ranking points. Henman still had a lot to do to prove he could be force on the ATP circuit all year round and not just during two weeks in June. The perfect opportunity to substantiate that would come in less than a month's time at the US Open, where qualifying was no longer part of his schedule.

Henman was due to open against the Swede Mats Wilander, a former world number one, and was likely to meet his Wimbledon conqueror and number 12 seed Todd Martin in round three, should both progress that far. It was certainly a tough prospect but these two were precisely the calibre of opponent Henman needed to beat if he was to break into the top twenty.

But then, on the eve of the tournament, Wilander was forced

to withdraw because of a strained groin, a major boost for Henman, who would now face Roberto Jabali, a lucky loser from the qualifying competition. The Brazilian was to be Henman's third opponent, after a display of player power, not seen at a Grand Slam since the 1973 Wimbledon strike, had forced the US Tennis Association (USTA) into agreeing to 'remake' the men's singles draw.

Several players had complained that the USTA had disregarded, for no good reason, the ATP computer rankings in framing their seeds and had only then announced them after the draw in order to fill the slots in such a way as to favour the home players.

Henman had initially been paired with Andrei Olhovskiy of Russia before the revised draw paired him with Wilander, who was then replaced by Jabali because of injury.

The Briton produced a workmanlike performance against the Brazilian to seal a straightforward 6-2, 6-3, 6-4 win. He then strode confidently into the third round, the first Brit to do so since Andrew Castle in 1987, in straight sets with a devastating combination of severe serving and superior volleying, at the expense of world number 159 Doug Flach, who had beaten his US compatriot Andre Agassi in the first round of Wimbledon that year.

Henman's 1996 achievements had already earned him £184,000 and he was now in touching distance of a place in December's Grand Slam Cup, which carries a guaranteed prize of £66,000 even if you go home without a win.

It was unlikely but if he required extra incentive this would come from his being on a collision course to face his Wimbledon dream-destroyer Todd Martin, with a chance to seek vengeance on the American's home patch. Four-times US Open champion John McEnroe warned his fellow countryman he was in for a testing time with Henman: 'He's the most talented British player I've seen – no, the best I've ever seen. Period. When he gets a little bit stronger – watch out!'

Even before the match got underway, Henman held the upper hand as Martin was playing through the discomfort of an injury which spasmed the length of his playing arm and was a legacy of his first-round encounter with Younes El Aynaoui.

Americans may not have known who Henman was before this match, but they certainly would afterwards. At 2-2 he broke Martin three times in a row to capture the first set and lead by a break in the second. He suffered a blip at 2-0, playing three uncertain games to trail 2-3 and was then forced into saving two break points in the sixth game and a further two at 4-5, to deny Martin the set and cause a tie-break. Henman responded well and played a controlled shoot-out, winning 7-4 to double his one-set lead.

Another early service break in the third saw Henman lead 3-0, and though he double-faulted to drop his serve at 4-2, his resolve never flickered. Leading 5-4 on Martin's service, he hit an extraordinary blind backhand smash that left his rival gaping, and after the American double-faulted to give Henman his first match point, he sealed it with a crisp forehand to exact revenge and win through to the last sixteen.

The comprehensive reversal by Henman, in his first experience on Flushing Meadow's Centre Court, carried an authority that reduced the noisy, chauvinist crowd to near silence.

After the Briton walked off court McEnroe rushed to congratulate him. 'The British should be pretty pumped up. This guy has great potential,' he said. David Miller of *The Times* agreed, writing: 'There is every reason to believe that Henman can become the most accomplished British men's player since the era of Perry, Austin and Hughes before the war.'

Afterwards Martin sportingly refused to hide behind any excuse. 'The elbow felt fine,' he said. 'I just think I caught Tim on one of his best nights. The reason for the drop in the level of my play was because of the way Tim played. He lost focus a little bit, missed a few first serves when he needed them, but that was matched by his ability to rise to the occasion – the sign of a very good player. I think he has tremendous potential.'

Henman had become the first Briton since John Lloyd in 1984 to make the last sixteen in the US Open, and he admitted: 'Wimbledon was the highlight of my career – but this is definitely alongside it. I didn't make any unforced errors and I took my chances. It's just very special.'

Now, if Henman was to emulate his Wimbledon achievement two months ago and reach another Grand Slam quarter-final, he would have to bring to an end the glittering career of one of his heroes. Swede Stefan Edberg, a champion at Flushing Meadow in 1991 and 1992, was playing in his fifty-fourth and last Grand Slam before retiring. In the past Henman had practised with him in London, learned from him and been inspired by him, as well as modelling much of his play on him.

The prospect was well within the compass of Britain's accelerating meteor and he promised his admiration for the ice-cool Swede would not deter him. 'If there's one player who I've learned most from it would be him, in his style of play and the way he handles himself. He's definitely been an inspiration, but I won't be worried about ending his Grand Slam career, I'll just be concentrating on my game.'

Henman endured a nervous start against the Swede, who broke him in the third game and at 3-1 had a further two break points. But Henman had begun to develop a habit of getting his serve in on the big points and held on to narrow the gap to 3-2.

Edberg served for the set at 5-4, but he played a poor game and Henman made the most of his first break point to level and send the set into a tie-break.

Masterful in the shoot-out, Henman took a 3-0 lead, with two points against service, then ran round his backhand to hit a glorious forehand drive to Edberg's backhand corner and reach set point at 6-2 with the same shot. Edberg never recovered from losing the first points of the tie-break and immediately put a backhand wide to go a set down.

The second set began with a flurry of break points – fourteen in the first five games, eight to Henman, six to Edberg – but neither player could convert. The set continued to go with serve, until another tie-break was forced to settle the set. This time Edberg took the spoils 7-2, Henman losing his first set of the competition. That, he says, was the turning point. 'I think in the second he had the majority of the chances, but then if I had taken one of the break points in the first game of it maybe the momentum would have really swung my way.'

After that Edberg took over. Both players held their serve at the start of the third set but Edberg looked to be holding his resolve better and Henman was forced to save a break point at 2-2, but could not repeat the trick at 4-4, when he over-hit a backhand volley at the net to give Edberg a service break. The Swede was again serving for the set at 5-4, just like in set one, but this time he made no mistake and produced an impressive service game to take the set.

It got worse for Henman in the following set as he dropped his serve – to a double fault – in the opening game. Edberg held serve comfortably to go 2-0 up, but Henman refused to fold. He broke back for 2-2 with some inspired groundstrokes, but was then dealt another blow after holding serve to lead 3-2. Discomfort from a groin injury had been mounting in his left leg for a couple of days, and he was forced to call for court-side physiotherapy at the change of ends.

On resumption it was evident that Henman looked vulnerable. He held serve just once more, and effectively conceded defeat in the ninth game, losing his service to love with three unforced errors, to trail 5-4.

Edberg was able to clinch victory in style the very next game. Henman missed an attempted cross-court winner – 15-0 – hit his return long – 30-0 – hit another weak shot into the net – 40-0 – and Edberg, with three match points, fired down an ace to settle it.

The former world number one punched the air in triumph, a gesture met with a roar of acclaim from the crowd. He had managed to sustain his swansong and gain a place against Goran Ivanisevic in the quarter-finals.

Henman refused to blame his defeat on his fitness troubles: 'I'm disappointed, I had my chances in the second set, but the whole thing has been a great experience for me. I would have liked to be the guy who ended Stefan's Grand Slam career, but I can reflect on a good tournament and another positive step forward. Stefan's obviously at the end of his and hopefully I'm at the beginning of mine. I learned a great deal from playing someone like Stefan, such a great player.'

His injury sustained at Flushing Meadow, which he admitted receiving painkillers for during his run to the last sixteen, forced him, on doctor's orders, out of action for three weeks. 'I've been having treatment twice a day since I returned from the US Open – icing, ultra-sound and stretching,' he said. 'The doctor has told me I must relax for a while. It's been a huge summer and I've basically played solidly for fourteen weeks. The injury is just a case of wear and tear after a long season, and the rest should have done it some good. I don't know how much good because for the last week I have not been doing anything, just visiting family and friends.'

Henman's US Open exit also dealt him a second blow with the news that despite moving up to 33rd in the world rankings, he had finished 20th in the qualifying order for the Compaq Grand Slam Cup. It would now require four withdrawals for him to get a shot at the first prize of £1 million.

Nevertheless, on his return from injury at the end of September, the goal of finishing the season inside the top twenty was still attainable. His first two tournaments after coming back both yielded last-four finishes, at Lyons and Ostrava, where he beat world number seven Wayne Ferreira from South Africa in the last eight, to push his ranking up to 25. But in his final three tournaments of the season he suffered successive first-round defeats to Edberg in Stuttgart, 24th-ranked Carlos Moya at Paris and Byron Black, the world number 49, in Moscow's Kremlin Cup.

Rather than end the season in spectacular fashion in Germany, it looked like Henman would be ending it at 29th in the world and in the less glamorous surroundings of Telford in the Guardian Direct Championships.

After once again defeating Greg Rusedski for the second year in succession to claim the national throne, he had planned to rest after winning £265,407 worth of prize money that season. However, following his promotion to second reserve for the Grand Slam Cup, which would earn him £30,000 for doing nothing, following the withdrawals of Thomas Muster and Stefan Edberg (who rightly chose tradition and the Davis Cup in Malmo over mere money for his final match before retirement), Henman was informed on the eve of the tournament that he would in fact be opening the richest tournament in the world against home favourite Michael Stich. The late withdrawals of

American trio Pete Sampras, Michael Chang and Todd Martin saw him upgraded to an active participant in this knockout affair.

Henman had never played Stich before and the big-serving, six foot four German was particularly menacing on indoor courts, having won this tournament in 1992 and made the final again in 1993. But that didn't deter him. He may have been looking drained a few weeks earlier after a hard year on the road, but after a short rest with not a racket in sight, he seemed refreshed in his play against Stich and finished the contest off in just sixty-two minutes.

Outplaying the German number two, thirteen places his superior, Henman appeared to have recaptured much of the sparkle and quality he had shown at Wimbledon and the US Open, especially on his backhand, which he regularly scudded past Stich. He broke the former Wimbledon champion's serve twice in the first set and once in the second to seal a quarter-final place 6-3, 6-3 and a cheque of at least £150,000.

Henman was clear, though, that money was not his motive. 'Don't get me wrong, I prefer to have the money than not have it, but it's not the reason why I play the game. I've always said it's more my hobby than my occupation. It's nice to play in a tournament like this where there are obviously huge amounts of money at stake. I was very pleased with my performance and I feel great.'

His star was certainly shining bright, and this was brought home when he and coach David Felgate dined out in Munich's best Italian restaurant to celebrate his first-round win. The meal ended, Henman went to pay the bill, only to find that Andre Agassi, who had been sitting at a nearby table, had already taken care of it. That was confirmation, if ever he needed any, that he had made his mark on the ATP circuit and gained the respect he craved from his peers.

Henman was certainly not short of confidence as he went into his last-eight tie with MaiVai Washington, a Wimbledon finalist that year, having already beaten him in straight sets in the ATP Tour event at Nottingham in June. It took Henman a while to settle to his task against Washington, as a first-set tie-break loomed. But he looked likely to win the tie-break, having dropped only five points in six service games in the opening set, and he did eventually prevail 7-3 after forty minutes of play. His service was a revelation throughout the match: he consistently served at more than 130mph and hit a total of twenty aces.

With the first set in the bag, Henman was in complete control. Looking sharper and leaner, he was pushing Washington into more and more errors as his shots became wilder. Henman's returns were blistering, and when he needed to get involved in a rally, his forehand found the lines with impressive regularity. Only when he served for the match at 5-1 in the second set did he make a couple of rare mistakes to give Washington his first break points of the day.

'At 30-love I thought let's try and make life easy, but I missed an easy volley and he went on to break me,' Henman recollected.

However, he did not waste his chance second time round, reaching 40-15 and then forcing yet another error from Washington to win the contest 7-6, 6-3 after seventy-five minutes.

The twenty-two-year-old Briton was now assured of more than £260,000 from this tournament alone, doubling his prize money for the entire year, and he still had a chance of winning the £1million first prize. To get close to that vast sum, however, he would have to beat three-times Wimbledon champion Boris Becker in a best-of-five semi-final, with the odds and a capacity crowd stacked against him. It would be arguably the toughest test of his short career so far.

'It has to be up there with one of my best matches indoors or outdoors,' he said. 'I'm aware of the money. Make no bones about it, but I'm pleased with the way I've blocked it out of my mind. I'm happy to be playing in an event where there are huge amounts to be won but I'm focused on winning matches, not the money. But, to go through and play Boris Becker over five sets in his home town, you don't get much better than that. Well, perhaps if it was on Centre Court at Wimbledon – but that's probably his home too.'

Most people would have forgiven Henman for showing signs of stage fright in front of an 11,000-strong German contingent, with one Union Jack bearing the legend 'Go Tim Go' the exception, but for a set and a half he valiantly matched Becker serve for serve, blow for blow. 'He had me at full stretch,' conceded Becker.

Henman was at ease from the moment he fired in a 118mph delivery in his opening service game, which he won to love. He was immaculate and unchallenged on serve in the first set, and briefly threatened Becker in the fourth game, earning the set's solitary break point, only to be foiled by a high-kicking second serve.

But, when it came to the key points in the first-set tie-break, Henman did not have the power, experience or luck to counter a player who had won six Grand Slam titles. Becker gained a mini-break at the start when he smashed a forehand into the net cord, which fortuitously plopped over and Henman could not recover, going down 7-2.

An absent-minded service game from Henman, at the start of the second set, saw Becker take a 2-0 lead, but a wonderful lob helped secure an immediate break-back and a couple of searing returns even earned Henman a break point for a 4-2 lead. But, frustratingly, he wasted the opportunity with a dismal return of service, which he ballooned wide.

Henman appeared to lose his way after that, as Becker began crowding him at the net like a bully and broke to love for a 5-3 lead, effectively sealing the set and the match. Disheartened and demoralised, Henman lost much of his consistency in the third set as Becker came at him ever more relentlessly. The Briton had his service broken twice early on, and a tame double fault was his final signal of surrender as Becker wrapped up the proceedings in an hour and fifty minutes, 7-6, 6-3, 6-1.

Nevertheless, the German was impressed with his opponent. 'He's only been on the circuit two years and he's already come a long way. Who knows how far he can get? One day Tim may win Wimbledon. He has a great first serve, he's got good hands and he comes up with some surprising shots sometimes. All in all, he's a player with a good future.'

Becker was not the only one Henman had impressed with his performances in Germany. His first-round opponent, Michael Stich, said of him: 'Tim is very good. He didn't make many mistakes against me and gave me a real hard time. He can certainly get to the top. But there are no guarantees. He is very talented. It now depends on how he reacts to the various pressures.'

It had been quite a year. Back in January Henman was ranked 95th in the world. Now he sat at number 29 after a season in which he made headlines by travelling 65,000 miles while playing seventy single matches and 176 sets of competitive tennis, winning 933 games and losing 813. His exploits had seen him become the first proper tennis star Britain had produced in decades and helped catapult him into the ranks of the seriously well-paid sporting celebrities, earning over £1 million from his on-court earnings and sponsorships.

5

Ups and Downs

Henman was now a household name, to the amazement of the man himself. 'It has been unbelievable,' he said. 'I suppose it emphasises how much the public are crying out for a British tennis star. I mean, I've had a good year, but not when you compare it to the top guys. Suddenly, I'm being asked to do all sorts of off-court things. In Moscow, while I was playing out there recently, Tina Turner was in concert. Her manager happens to be English, and he sent a message asking if I would like to come and see the concert and meet her afterwards. Imagine that? I would have gone up to her in complete awe, and she would probably have turned round and said: "Who the fuck are you?"'

He recalls the first time he realised he had become famous. He had been back in the country just a couple of days after his US Open exploits, and was stuck in traffic. 'There were two guys in an estate in the lane beside me and I could tell they recognised me because they both had a wide-eyed look on their faces. I drove past them but, a few seconds later, came to a halt, and their car sidled up next to me again. This time the driver was staring at me, and the passenger was leaning right over the steering wheel to have a look.

'There was this brand-new, shiny Audi in front of them, and I could only watch as the guys, still staring at me, went straight into the back of it. I drove off feeling a little guilty, and looking at the mess behind me in my mirror.'

Now that is fame.

But Henman was the first to admit he had won nothing yet. 'I've got so much more to achieve,' he said. 'Being 25th in the world, and reaching a Wimbledon quarter-final, is not what I want to be remembered for. I don't want 1996 to be known as Tim Henman's year.

'What is exciting for me is that I can clearly identify areas where I know I can improve. I don't expect to be playing my best tennis for another three or four years, and it may well be that, so far, I've only scratched the surface. Next year will be tougher because all the top players know my game now, but I have proved to myself I can definitely play with the best of them.'

For his part Henman knew exactly what he would need to do in order to climb the rankings further. Recalling his Grand Slam Cup match with Becker, he said: 'There's a lot to be gained from a week like this. Boris definitely takes some beating, but it's a consistency thing. When I'm playing my best tennis, I'm able to stay with someone of his calibre, but it is his consistency – he's able to keep playing like that for four or five sets. At the moment, I probably couldn't do that.'

His first objective for the new season was to transform his six semi-final appearances into places in the finals of ATP events. And he did not have to wait long to achieve it. Despite being unseeded in his first tournament of 1997 at the Qatar Mobil Open in Doha, he dropped just one set in four matches to make his first ATP Tour final. However, he could not quite manage one better and win the event, succumbing 7-5, 6-7, 6-2 to Jim Courier, the American with four Grand Slam singles titles to his name.

'A lot of people will see it as the breaking of a jinx,' Henman said. 'Certainly I have learnt from the past and reaching my first final was the reward for that. My ambition at the start of this year was to reach a tour final and I was delighted to have done that so quickly in the New Year.'

After losing to Courier he dashed to the airport to catch a series of flights to Abu Dhabi, Bangkok and Sydney spanning fourteen hours. He had to overcome jetlag and fatigue to compete in the Sydney International Open that day, but within five days he was in his second-ever ATP final.

His route to the final had been tough and he demonstrated remarkable powers of recovery to oversee wins against the likes of double French Open champion Sergi Bruguera and world number three and top seed Goran Ivanisevic, his most prized scalp. But Henman had little time to digest his momentous 4-6, 7-6, 6-1 win over the Croat, before facing the unseeded Spaniard Carlos Moya in the final the very next day.

Henman started nervously against the world number 28, and he was fortunate not to lose his serve in the opening game, though he was broken in his next service game, to fall 2-1 behind, as Moya scored freely off his powerful forehand.

But, storming back, Henman immediately took Moya's next two service games to seal the opening set 6-3 in just thirty-three minutes. He opened up in the second with a combination of fluent movement, some great angles and outstanding tactical awareness. Moya's forehand had become erratic and Henman took full advantage with deep approaches which allowed him to get to the net and put constant pressure on his opponent.

Moya was allowed just one service hold in the entire second set and was eventually swept aside 6-1, which brought Henman his first ATP title of his four-year career as well as making him the first British player to lift the Sydney men's singles title since 1902.

'It's great to come away with the title. This is definitely extra special,' said Henman after his fifty-two-minute triumph. 'It's the sort of start to the year I couldn't have dreamed of. I'm happy with the way I'm playing and hopefully I'll manage to continue that form. It's a great feeling. I said at the beginning of the year that I wanted to make finals, and win a major tournament. I made a final in the first week, I won in the second week. I made a New Year resolution to win a tournament in 1997 – but once you achieve targets, you go back to the drawing board and set your sights even higher. I like to set myself targets and now I want to break into the top ten and do well in the Grand Slams.'

Henman was zooming up the charts faster than the pop sensation of the day, the Spice Girls, sitting proudly at number fourteen, only the fourth Briton in the twenty-three-year history of the men's rankings to appear in the top twenty, while forcing his way into the Grand Slam title reckoning.

Ex-Wimbledon champion Pat Cash certainly thought Henman was the man to end Great Britain's Grand Slam drought. 'I'm sure Tim will win a Grand Slam event in the next couple of years – perhaps Wimbledon. He's calm, he's got a good sense of humour and he doesn't let things worry him. I reckon he's capable of a top-five spot in the world rankings too.'

Further good fortune shone on Henman when local favourite Mark Philippoussis, the big Australian prodigy with possibly the most formidable service in world tennis, was obliged to withdraw two days before their scheduled first-round encounter at the Australian Open because of an arm injury. He had been responsible for Pete Sampras's exit from the same tournament the previous season.

Philippoussis's replacement was a lucky loser in qualifying: Andre Pavel of Romania, ranked 135th in the world.

Henman went into the tournament with more singles victories – nine in ten matches – and more prize money – £60,000 – than any other player in the world so far that year.

He did not have to exert himself too greatly in the 38∞C heat, which caused his feet to stick to the surface, against Pavel and dismissed the Romanian, a thick-legged player who appeared heavy-footed around the court, in straight sets 7-5, 6-4, 6-2.

Henman was developing a vocal band of supporters Down Under, similar to cricket's 'Barmy Army', and he used that to his advantage against second-round opponent Guillaume Raoux, ranked 82nd. Despite two stoppages for rain, the Briton kept his cool and concentration to chop down the Frenchman 6-3, 6-3, 6-4, hitting eleven aces and dropping only seveteen points on his serve.

The win set up an enthralling showdown against Michael Chang, runner-up the year before. The previous week Henman had beaten the world number three, Ivanisevic, and now he was setting his sights on the number two. A win over Chang would virtually guarantee him a place in the top ten, with all the bonus points that a win over a higher-ranked player brings with it.

Henman got off to a good start, serving out to love, to lift the expectations of the holidaying Brits and expats, wearing England football shirts and carrying the Union Flag, who had descended on Melbourne Park. But Chang was not to be distracted from the task at hand. 'The crowd did not bother me,' he said. 'It makes exciting tennis. The atmosphere was great and it was a lot of fun to play out there.'

He proved his point, justifying his number-two world status by continually returning the best Henman could muster. Chang was wearing the Briton down by making him play extra shots and running down volleys capable of beating other players. Henman began to lose power and rhythm in his serve and Chang cashed in, running away with the next six games to humiliate him in the opening set 6-1 in just twenty-four minutes.

Henman showed signs of a recovery in the second set, breaking for 3-1, and then held serve for a deceptively comfortable 4-1 lead as he started to make it torture for the little Chinese American. But again Henman's service let him down when he double-faulted to drop it, although he did manage to break back immediately to lead 5-3 and serve for the set. However, his normally reliable serve deserted him again as he was broken to love with four unforced errors, and soon Chang was level at 5-5. Henman's forehand was beginning to break down under the pressure of the occasion, and so it proved in the tie-break. Chang raced to a 5-1 lead, profiting from some errors, though many were largely forced, and was soon leading by two sets.

In the third set Chang broke in the eighth game, the fifth time in the contest, once more to love as Henman double-faulted. Serving for the match at 5-3, Chang earned two match points but needed just one of them as the match finally drifted beyond Henman's reach.

The Barmy Army, who had exhausted their vocal cords with their less-than-musical renditions, among them the national anthem, adapted to include Henman's name, gave their hero an emotional send-off, despite the fact Chang had demonstrated that the difference between rankings of 2nd and 14th can be significant.

Statistics can be overused in tennis, but the fact that his first-service rate was only 45 per cent, and in the first set fell to 27 per cent, which is barely one valid serve in every four points, demonstrated that Henman had simply not been good enough, or sufficiently experienced, to deal with Chang.

'It was a bad day at the office, simple as that,' he admitted afterwards. 'I'm just sorry I couldn't give the Barmy Army more to cheer about. They are always a great help, but I just couldn't get going. I served badly and made life difficult for myself and easy for him.

'Michael is the quickest player on tour, but I didn't take my chances and that adds to the frustration. I have always focused on the positive and I will forget about the performance and think about the start to the year I have had. It won't take me long to see I am moving in the right direction. I can learn from this match and will get over the disappointment quickly.'

Even though he had reached the third round of the Australian Open for the first time, it did little for his ranking, which dropped two places to number 16. Yet Henman could be proud of what he had achieved in the southern hemisphere after sealing his first ATP title.

A third ATP final of the season followed in mid-February at the European Community Championship in Antwerp, where he also received his first seeding in a mainstream ATP Tour event: 8th. No British player since the open era began in 1968 had reached three big tournament finals in the space of a mere eight weeks. Henman conceded just one set in four matches en route to the final, but failed to take a single set off 23rd-ranked Marc Rosset of Switzerland, as his serve misfired once more, resulting in his leaving Belgium with a silver tray instead of the gold-studded racket that such greats as Ivan Lendl, John McEnroe and Pete Sampras had lifted in the past.

More concerning for Henmaniacs, however, was the fact that

Henman had been sporting an ice pack on an inflamed right elbow after victory in the last eight at Antwerp against Spaniard Francisco Clavet, even though it was being played down as a precautionary measure. However, after a second-round exit in Milan his right elbow problems resurfaced and doctors advised him to pull out of the Champions Cup at Indian Wells, California.

During this period he was offered some light relief when his fellow ATP professionals voted him Most Improved Player for 1996, ahead of Spain's Felix Mantilla and the American Alex O'Brien, at tennis's answer to the Oscars, the annual ATP awards ceremony, at the Jackie Gleason Theatre, Miami Beach. Pete Sampras, Andre Agassi, Boris Becker and John McEnroe had been similarly honoured in the past, so he was in good company. 'Winning this is definitely something I'm pleased with,' Henman said. 'It means recognition amongst my peers, so I've obviously made an impression. It's the first time a British player has won such an award. I'm hoping it's the first of many, for me and for British tennis.'

Henman made his first outing as the ATP's Most Improved Player at the Lipton Championships in Key Biscayne. It was also his first match since the end of February, after three weeks out with a swollen elbow. Yet, despite his being seeded 14th and receiving a bye to the second round, all this tournament proved was that his elbow problems were still nowhere near cured.

Against twenty-year-old qualifier Julian Alonso, Henman managed to take the first set on a tie-break, but began to show signs of the injury in the second set and as a result his serve suffered. The Spaniard, ranked 228 and in his first ATP hard-court tournament, began to take control, outplaying Henman in the next two sets, and eventually caused the upset of the round 6-7, 6-2, 6-3.

'It probably wasn't the smartest thing to play today, but it seemed OK in practice. It's disappointing and things aren't improving,' Henman confessed after the match. He was suffering from a sharp pain which travelled down the nerve in his arm when he hit the ball poorly. He had been troubled by the elbow periodically since taking a tumble as an eleven-year-old, which had stopped him playing for eighteen months and threatened his future in tennis before it had started.

'It's not tennis elbow,' he said. 'It's loose body that's floating around in there. It dates back to a problem I had when I was eleven. For some reason it often flares up and gets irritated. Rest seems to be the only cure. I don't really feel it's possible to go after my serve like I want. When I mis-hit a ball I can really feel it.'

Having struggled with the injury for the past few weeks, Henman decided to fly home after his second-round defeat in Florida and underwent arthroscopic surgery. Ten small pieces of bone were removed from his right elbow, which needed complete rest, meaning all training was restricted to leg work and he could not even drive a car.

'I was pleased with how the operation went and I am looking forward to competing again soon,' he said. 'It was a frustrating few weeks for me. Obviously having an operation does interrupt things, but it's definitely improving, so hopefully I'll be able to get back on the court. It's just a question of waiting and seeing really. I'll just have to see how my elbow reacts when I start practising again and I'll take it from there.'

Henman had to wait six weeks before resuming practice, but at least he had been somewhat lucky with the timing of the operation in that the majority of the points he had to defend that year in order to maintain his ranking were to come later on, during the summer.

He returned to action at the Masters in Rome in mid-May, on a clay surface, which he was still relatively unfamiliar with.

He had missed that part of the season with a virus the previous year, and in 1995 he was more concerned with improving his game on hard courts. As a natural serve-and-volleyer, he found the slow brick surface did not suit his game, and he had barely played since late February. With the French Grand Slam just two weeks away, he had little time to adapt to clay, but he was staying upbeat and just relishing the prospect of returning to tournament play. 'The rehabilitation has been very good. I've been playing for just over two weeks and now it's one hundred per cent. I started off slowly, and was playing probably a little bit cautiously. But once you break down those psychological barriers it's been one hundred per cent full out.'

Seeded 14, he found the going tough in his first match after elbow surgery, only his second on clay in two years, and he progressed to round two only because his opponent, Spain's Roberto Carretero, retired with a thigh injury with the score standing at 4-6, 7-5, 2-0 in the Briton's favour.

However, Henman's return to competitive tennis was short-lived, as he succumbed to Davide Scala, an Italian qualifier ranked 210th in the world. After leading 6-1, 1-0, 40-15 with a break, he managed to lose the last two sets 3-6, 4-6, to make an early exit from Italy.

Struggling with the after-effects of elbow surgery, the clay surface and just about any opponent, Henman headed to Austria as 4th seed at the Raiffeisen Grand Prix, but crashed out 6-4, 6-2 in the first round to Sjeng Schalken of the Netherlands, ranked 81st.

Henman was virtually an apprentice on the comparatively slow clay courts of Europe and this had been underlined by his early elimination in both tournaments to journeymen players, in the build-up to the main clay event in Paris. He was struggling for any sort of form but, amusingly, still found himself seeded 14th for the French Open, his first seeding in a Grand Slam championship. His reward for being the first British man to be seeded at the French Open in fifteen years, since Buster Mottram, came with a draw against Olivier Delaitre, one of the home nation's wild cards.

Sitting on the borderline of the seeds and with Wimbledon fast approaching, Henman desperately needed to find form and points, but his chances of progressing far were slim. In fact on the Wednesday before the start of the French tournament he was on the verge of withdrawing altogether. The enhanced pliancy in his elbow meant it was still readjusting and so was still causing him a great deal of discomfort. Fortunately a new course of anti-inflammatory pills and treatment with a new machine using electrodes, belonging to ATP Tour physios, had wiped out the swelling and transformed his state of mind.

'There is no doubt it has affected me in matches and in practice,' Henman said of his elbow trouble, 'as much mentally as anything. I was getting a bit depressed, but over the last couple of days it has been one hundred per cent, it has been quite a relief.'

But any hope that his form on court would be transformed proved to be unfounded, and his misery hit a new low courtesy of a controversial decision that ultimately dumped him out of the French Open, once more at the first hurdle.

Delaitre had taken the first set 6-2, but after an early service break in the second, Henman's serve began to fizz, causing the Frenchman's previously tight-knit to unravel, and the Briton surged into a two-set-to-one lead. But, at 1-1 in the fourth set, Henman's frustration boiled over after he was deprived of a vital point.

An angry exchange with the umpire followed after he refused

to overrule a double fault which gave Delaitre a crucial break point, even though Henman's claim looked justified. That game lasted twenty-six minutes – equal to the time of the second set – and contained thirteen deuces before Delaitre finally achieved the break of serve. Henman reacted by throwing a racket to the floor and offering further words to the umpire.

Delaitre, a complex man who is happy to admit he spends long sessions on a psychiatrist's couch, admitted later: 'It was the game of the match. If I'd lost it I think I would have lost the match. But I knew if I could break him, then physically I was stronger, because Tim had lost two or three months after his elbow operation.'

Henman took just one more game in the set, as the signs of weariness became etched into his face. He had only once played five sets, at Wimbledon the previous year, but, despite his having the pluck to slug out the final set, it was his opponent who prevailed. Roared home by the partisan Court Two crowd, Delaitre took the set 6-4 to claim the spoils, after a contest lasting three hours and thirty-five minutes.

Although disappointed with his early exit, Henman said: 'My preparation probably hasn't been ideal and I haven't had the best of results in the last four weeks. I think if I had been able to hold on to my serve I would have been able to maintain that momentum. Once he was able to break, that's when he sort of got a second wind. I didn't play quite as well as before and he improved.'

At least the start of the grass season would provide a welcome respite, after his barren experiences in the slippery dust bowls of Europe, and release him to play his serve-and-volley game.

But the real worry was whether Henman had enough time to mount any sort of challenge at Wimbledon, less than a month away, and emulate his run to the previous year's quarter-finals, after only recently coming back from elbow surgery. Henman had claimed it had not given him any problems at the French Open and refused to blame his recent injury for his first-round defeat. Yet he was still worried he could suffer a reaction later, as had been the case after Rome.

Henmania had gripped the country again with the start of Wimbledon fast approaching, and Henman was painfully aware that the nation was desperate for him to become England's first Wimbledon men's singles champion since the late Fred Perry in 1937. He said: 'It's inevitable that people's expectations will be high – quite rightly in light of the results I have had since Wimbledon last year. But the most important thing is my performance on the court. It may seem selfish, but I have never played to a crowd, I simply play for myself. I can't deny there is pressure to do well at Wimbledon, but the pressure I'm under is more self-inflicted.'

Grass-court preparations commenced, as always, at Queen's Club for the Stella Artois Championships, where tournament officials put on extra security to deal with the ever-growing young girl fan base that flocked to Kensington to catch a glimpse of Henman. 'We haven't seen anything like this since the arrival of Andre Agassi,' said a spokesman. If Henman was to stand any chance of getting to the latter stages at Wimbledon a productive run at Queen's was vital, in order to advance his desire for a seeded berth at SW19.

He remained vulnerable because of a lack of match practice since injury, and his world ranking had suffered accordingly: he had dropped out of the top twenty, to 22nd, for the first time since he won his first ATP tournament, in Sydney in January.

Having received a bye in the first round, on the basis of his 4th seeding, Henman started in the second round against compatriot and close pal Andrew Richardson, ranked 253.

Unsettled by nerves and struggling to master blustery conditions, Henman allowed the six foot seven Lincolnshire giant to strike a psychological blow by winning the first set, before rallying to lose just five more games and win the next two sets. It was his first victory for more than a hundred days. But it did little to improve his performances.

Henman was still struggling in round two against Germany's world number 105, Jens Knippschild, a player treading grass for the first time in six years, who broke a million schoolgirl hearts by taking their hero out in straight sets.

With Wimbledon now just two weeks away and the nation's hopes resting on his slim, youthful shoulders, Henman continued to insist that his lacklustre form was nothing to fret about. 'I'm not worried – after all, I always lose here after only one win,' Henman joked. (He had yet to record back-to-back victories at Queen's.) 'I would like to have won the match but there's no reason to hit the panic button. I do need more matches but there's still no reason why I can't have a good run at Wimbledon.'

Providentially, despite Henman's four months of scratching for form after elbow surgery and being outside the top 16, the Championships' seeding committee handed him one of the prestigious spots among the 128 starters, with a seeding of 14, after six players had withdrawn. 'This is the second time I have been seeded in a Grand Slam,' he said. 'Obviously I am pleased, but all that matters is that I won't play Pete Sampras in the first round. Beyond that, there is no guarantee of anything.'

He also commented on his unconvincing recent form: 'It's probably fair to say that I haven't wasted my best tennis before Wimbledon, although I felt things were starting to happen. I wasn't playing great tennis this time last year.' A look back at the formbooks for this time the previous year confirmed his findings. He had won only one game in two months at the same point the year before, and it was not until the last warm-up competition before Wimbledon that he began to show form. That tournament was the Nottingham Open, where he had reached the quarter-finals. After another disappointing showing at Queen's, Henman accepted a wild-card invitation with a 4th seeding at Nottingham, in his quest for further match practice to sharpen his game and rebuild his dented confidence.

And once again it proved just the tonic. Displaying renewed confidence and quality, he achieved three consecutive victories to go one step further than the previous year and make the last four in the Nottingham Open before losing in three gruelling sets to Karol Kucera of the Czech Republic.

'My preparation for Wimbledon is spot on,' he beamed. 'I'm pretty sure I'll deal with the attention, just like last year. I would have preferred to have won it, but the most important thing is that I've got in some matches. My game has improved in the last week and I'm serving much better. I feel positive.'

Next stop Wimbledon.

It was time, and that meant all British eyes were on Tim. Expectation would dog his every step. His many new-found sponsors would expect promotion, journalists would expect snappy quotes, fans would expect autographs and everyone would expect victory.

'I don't know about that but I'm certainly going to be giving it my best shot,' Henman said modestly. 'I definitely believe I have the ability to win Wimbledon and I certainly have the desire and determination. You also need a little luck with the draw and to hit your very best form at the right time. Last time I was the underdog and no one expected too much from me. This time they'll be expecting me to do better and anything less will be a let down. I'll just go out and give everything. But I'd like all the fans to know that when they're cheering me on, it really does make a difference.'

Any doubts that Henman's achievements the previous year were a fluke were instantly dispelled as he ran into the kind of form that had propelled him into the nation's hearts and the higher echelons of men's tennis. With the help of his ever-expanding fan base, he blitzed his way to the third round without dropping a set, after crushing wins over Canada's Daniel Nestor, ranked 105th, and world number 94 Jerome Golmard of France.

'I am having treatment on my elbow but there are no problems with it,' he remarked. 'There is definitely a buzz about Wimbledon with all this British success but I don't find coping with the pressure too much of a problem. I'm happy the way I have been playing and I feel very confident.'

For the first time since 1909 two consecutive days were lost at the Championships to the bad weather and so the committee gave the go-ahead for a second 'People's Sunday', an arrangement inaugurated to much acclaim in 1991, when the first week had also been a washout.

A carnival of British patriotism greeted Henman on Centre Court for his third-round match on People's Sunday, against Dutchman Paul Haarhuis, one of the journeymen of the European tennis circuit. A sea of red, white and blue encircled the court as hordes of flag-waving supporters provided an electric atmosphere, bellowing soccer chants and performing Mexican waves throughout the match.

'They were like a Wembley crowd,' Henman gasped. 'At times I thought the roof was about to come off. So many "oohs" and "aahs" can be a bit distracting, but when they called my name it gave me an amazing buzz. From the word go, I did not hear a ball. The crowd set the tone for the whole match and I could never, ever have better support. They had an effect on the match, without a doubt.'

Given the tension, both men settled remarkably well, but it was Henman who struck first, going 5-3 ahead with a searing forehand return. The noise was almost unbearable. To his immense credit Haarhuis held his nerve and broke back immediately, as Henman managed to blow three set points, two of them through double faults, and so the set headed into a tie-break.

In the first two rounds of Wimbledon that year Henman had won opening-set tie-breaks, but this time he squandered a 6-3 lead, with the final set point disappearing with yet another double fault, as the Dutchman sneaked it 9-7.

Henman could easily have fretted over losing the tie-break, but instead his game improved radically, especially his service, which began to reach speeds of 130mph. He was seizing on every error made by his opponent, who was beginning to look frail and worried. The next two sets passed Haarhuis by, 6-3, 6-2, as he failed to re-establish his hold on the match. A leisurely stroll into the second looked on the cards for Henman – but we should have known better.

Without notice, two poor backhand volleys in a loose service game at 1-1 in the fourth set gave Haarhuis the sniff of an opening and suddenly the fans were faced with a fifth-set decider.

Now the drama really started to unfold.

We knew about Henman's nerve and strength of mind from past experiences, but never had it been so dramatically illustrated as in this final set. Haarhuis was now playing the more measured, solid tennis. Henman spurned several break opportunities before being broken himself for 3-4 when he smashed a mis-hit by the Dutchman wildly into the net.

At 4-5 Haarhuis was serving for the match, but the crowd

would have none of it. They chanted, they shouted Henman's name, though at times some could barely watch, peering through fingers or over programmes.

It was Henman's ultimate test. He raced to a 0-30 lead, but Haarhuis won the next three points and suddenly he was on match point. With the pressure piled so heavily on the Dutchman's head that it almost drilled him into the turf, he double-faulted to bring the game to deuce.

The atmosphere was at boiling point. Haarhuis double-faulted again, giving Henman a sudden chance to break back, and on the very next point Haarhuis netted a volley to send the massed ranks into delirium.

It went with serve much of the time after that, with groundsmen being forced on at every changeover to tread down the badly scuffed surface. The fact that Henman was making such hard work of it only added to the spine-tingling tension. He failed to put away a match point at 12-11, dumping a return into the net, but then, at 13-12, Haarhuis finally buckled.

The Dutchman made a volleying error and then failed to deal with two simple returns, to give Henman three match points. This time, presented with the kill, he took it, finally finishing Haarhuis off with a sensational forehand down the line that sparked off an explosion of relief and joy from the stands. It was grass-court tennis at its best, all four hours of it, especially the final set, which lasted ninety-four minutes.

Afterwards a dejected Haarhuis complimented the crowd: 'I always thought Wimbledon was a bit stuffy but this was different. The English have always given their soccer teams support, but never before like this in tennis.'

'I'm still in a bit of a shock over the crowd,' Henman added. 'I wished I could have taken them home with me. I've seen pictures in the papers and they looked incredible showing their support.'

The match had attracted Wimbledon's third-largest television audience of all time, behind the two Bjorn Borg v John McEnroe finals of 1980 and 1981, peaking at 12.8 million.

Henman's reward for partaking in the tie of the tournament was a plump fourth-round clash against another Dutchman. However, this one was regarded as far superior to Haarhuis, as he was the reigning Wimbledon champion, Richard Krajicek.

Despite being the title holder, Krajicek had yet to play on a show court that year. This had obviously rankled with him, and he gave notice that British hearts would be broken as a consequence. 'I'm going to pounce early and shut up Tim and his fans,' he proclaimed.

Talking the talk is one thing, but walking the walk is a completely different concept.

It was almost 6.30 on a damp but sunlit Tuesday evening before the two gladiators set foot on court, as rain delays had eaten into the afternoon's proceedings. The Henmaniacs were back in full force, and Centre Court was awash with emotion, with Union Jacks flying high and chants of 'Henman, Henman' pouring out from the stands.

Krajicek was taller, bigger, older, higher-ranked at number five, higher-seeded at 4th and, as defending champion, the favourite; but Henman started the better. In the eighth game the Briton had four break points to steal the lead, but so dangerous is Krajicek that his serve had been broken only three times in his previous ten matches, and he managed to foil Henman on each occasion.

The challenger then missed three set points in the resultant shoot-out at 4-2 and 6-4, before finally clinching it 9-7 with a firm, precise and unreachable forehand volley. The crowd went ever so slightly potty.

The second set followed a similar pattern to the first, only

Krajicek was squeezing on the pressure more now and had opportunities to break in the sixth and tenth games. But Henman showed strength of character to fend him off, forcing the match into a second tie-break. As in the first set, Henman contrived a set point, but Krajicek produced two stunning forehands and an ace to turn the tables and draw back level.

In the depths of despair after going to a set-all, Henman suddenly found the Dutchman producing the kind of shot-making that great champions can fall back on. With the match starting to turn his way, Krajicek broke to go 3-2 up and then, with the contest looking under his control, asked the umpire about whether he could go off because of bad light.

No sooner had the Dutchman been refused than Henman, with the crowd acting as his fuel, proved just how tough he was by stepping up another gear to play some of the best tennis he has ever produced at Wimbledon. Brilliantly, he broke back for 3-3, prompting another appeal from the defending champion. This was again rebuffed and, in the tie-break that followed, Henman's nerve held the stronger, allowing him to reclaim his one-set lead. The pair finally came off court in failing light at 8.39 after two hours and sixteen minutes of pulsating action.

Henman was relaxed, in his totally unselfconscious way. 'I'm not really the sort of person who is a bundle of nerves and I was happy to get some food and have a good night's sleep. I felt ready to go the next morning. I just wanted to continue with the thoughts that I had, to concentrate on my serve and not worry much about what he was doing.'

Loud cheers and a muffled chorus of 'Walking in a Henman wonderland' greeted Henman's re-emergence the next day and it was clear from the first ball that the overnight delay had not dimmed his competitive intensity. Krajicek appeared edgy and ill at ease; this time his shots lacked bite and control.

The Dutchman began with a double fault, and as early as the third game of the fourth set the determined running of Henman forced Krajicek into saving three break points, courtesy of two first-service winners and the aid of a close line call.

On his next service game, though, he would not be so fortunate. Henman rifled back four successive returns and Krajicek responded by making four catastrophic volleys, to lose his game to love, putting Henman one step closer to the next round. The Briton now had the crowd in the palm of his hand and did well to avert a scare in the very next game when Krajicek took a 30-40 lead with a signature backhand return down the line off his second serve. But Henman demonstrated just what made his future in the game look so promising, as he produced a big serve for deuce, then a fine service winner, and finally forced Krajicek into dumping a forehand into the net, to a Wembley-type roar from the stands.

Krajicek held to love on the next game, but Henman was now serving for the match. The champ was on the ropes. But could Henman land the knockout blow? Was he about to rise gloriously to the occasion or resort to a jelly-like existence?

On the first point Henman ran back and fired a devastating forehand pass on the turn. Fifteen-love.

Next, a service winner off his second serve, then another. Forty-love.

Match point. It was utterly silent. But when Henman landed his last precision volley down the line the 14,000-strong crowd rose to their feet in a frenzied delight.

Not only had he held serve, he did it to love and proved his chilling ability to rise majestically and play nerveless tennis on pressure points. Over two days he had bettered his opponent in every department, despite giving away so much in height, weight, experience and, to a lesser extent, power.

No Briton had put out the defending champion since Roger Taylor beat Rod Laver in the fourth round twenty-seven years earlier – yet another record broken by Tim Henman. 'This whole match for the sustained quality is some of the best I've ever played,' he said afterwards. 'To beat the defending champion you've got to be playing pretty well. I only had one break point against me today and came up with some big serves at the right time.'

He also commended the home crowds who had helped him reach new levels of performance. '"People's Sunday" set the standard and everyone that comes here will have seen that atmosphere and they're trying to repeat it. They are constantly behind me, constantly lifting me to new heights, and if there is ever a time when I'm struggling, they give me the confidence to battle on.'

The defeated champion agreed: 'The atmosphere was unbelievably loud, but what I really liked about the crowd is that once the point started you could hear a pin drop. I think they showed respect to the players. It was like playing against the whole of England.'

But just like the previous year, when it came to the quarter-finals and the chance for Henman to become Britain's first semi-finalist for years, the support faltered. Row upon row remained empty inside the stadium, as ordinary fans were again shut out, offered just 500 seats. The rest had already been purchased by rich ticket holders or businessmen who, rather than offer support to Britain's great hope, packed restaurants, the members' enclosures and hospitality tents where the free bubbly flowed like water.

Later the All England Club issued a statement expressing 'disappointment' at the number of empty seats on Court One. They cited the early 11a.m. start, implemented to catch up with play that had been delayed by the bad weather, and the fact that not everyone lived within easy reach of Wimbledon.

Henman was up against the unpredictable challenge of Michael Stich, the 1991 champion, who was to retire immediately after Wimbledon and whom Henman had defeated in their only other encounter at the Grand Slam Cup, at the end of the previous year.

Stich wanted to go out in a blaze of glory and Henman – in front of 11,400 spectators in a two-thirds full Court One – appeared to be doing all he could to help him as he double-faulted his way to disaster. It looked like he had reverted to his pre-Wimbledon form as he faltered on his serve and proved impotent in his all-court game.

Henman had already double-faulted twice when the eighth game came along, and he committed the same sin again for 0-30, 0-40 and 30-40, to drop his serve. Stich was now pumped up in his crusade and won the opening set 6-3.

But Henman's generosity did not end there. With Stich now firing in low returns and covering the net at all angles, the pressure led Henman into double-faulting again in the third game. More disaster followed with two more in the fifth game to give Stich another break and a 4-1 lead.

With just over an hour gone, Stich, ranked 88th, was already serving for a two-set lead and had three points for it. He needed just one. The German pumped his arms in eager celebration, in front of a subdued audience who knew the tide of the contest had turned his way.

Unusually, Henman, who had shown such icy composure against Krajicek, was now reduced to angry crashes of his racket against his bag at changeovers and shouting at himself. But none of it worked. At 3-3 in the third set he quickly fell behind again 0-40, and despite saving two break points he hit a third one long.

He was being outplayed, out-thought, and was never able to live with the kind of pressure that Stich piled on.

The dream that had gone on into Wimbledon's eleventh day was about to reach its last frame. At 5-3 Stich served out the third set to claim an unlikely semi-final berth.

Henman's great adventure had come to a pain-filled end after just eighty-eight minutes. He walked off embarrassed and with a tight-lipped look of anguish, his people slumped in their seats. Ten double faults in all, against one ace produced, was the simple reason why it was all over so quickly.

Heartbroken, the young Brit apologised to his legion of fans. 'It was probably my worse experience on a tennis court so far. To be in a quarter-final at Wimbledon and lose as easily as I did is very disappointing. It's difficult to understand how I can go from playing some of the best tennis of my career to some of the worst within twenty-four hours. I'm not going to make any excuses. I just played very poorly. My game, my attack is based on my serve, which just didn't work. When that happens other parts of your game fail and anything that could go wrong did go wrong. I'm sure the whole country is disappointed. All I can do is thank the people for their support and hope they've enjoyed what they've seen.'

Despite the disappointment and the manner of his defeat, Henman could walk out of the gates with his head held high. He was still only twenty-two, after all, and had a lot more to learn. He had also surpassed his 14th seeding and repeated his last-eight appearance of the previous season under far greater pressure. The fact that he was able to defend his ranking points from the year before meant he was likely to continue the rest of the year in or around the top twenty. He was now sitting at 18th in the world, but, following on from Wimbledon, suffered a hangover of epic proportions.

At the start of the North American hard-court season Henman failed to win a match in his first two tournaments. He suffered a mortifying 7-6, 4-6, 6-3 defeat in the first round of the Du Maurier Canadian Open in Montreal to home talent Sebastien LeBlanc, a wild-card entry ranked 885th in the world. Then, in the opening round of the Cincinnati Open, he was beaten by world number 21 Andrei Medvedev in straight sets. As a result, he dropped out of the top twenty and looked at risk of sliding still further.

'I couldn't put my finger on the problem,' he recalled. 'If I'd been practising poorly maybe I wouldn't have been so surprised. But I was hitting the ball great in Montreal in the days prior to that event so to play as poorly as I did was very frustrating. My game was at rock bottom.'

It was a month after Wimbledon before Henman finally won another match. This came at the Pilot Pen International at New Haven, Connecticut, Henman's last tournament in the build-up to the season's fourth Grand Slam at Flushing Meadow. Czech Daniel Vacek was the victim, as Henman came back from a set down and 0-40 on his serve to defeat the world number 67.

Henman's progress in New Haven, which was ended by Yevgeny Kafelnikov in the last eight, will never be recalled as a major triumph, but it was a milestone in a week that meant a great deal to him.

Nevertheless, it was not enough to earn him a seeded position at the US Open. And what made matters worse was that, as a non-seed, he was paired with Thomas Muster, the Austrian number five. It was going to be a tall order to repeat the previous year's last-sixteen finish, and it would need another example of Henman's big match temperament, demonstrated a year ago at Wimbledon against Kafelnikov and again this year against Krajicek, if he was to prevail.

Before the match Henman took considerable advice from Sweden's Stefan Edberg and put into practice the attacking philosophy which had enabled the Swede to defeat Muster in all ten of their matches.

Henman dominated throughout, smothering Muster's powerful baseline game with his own brand of serve-and-volley tennis. Suddenly he looked like he had finally picked up from where he had left off at Wimbledon, with a spectacular display of attacking tennis and follow-up play. His array of dropshots, lobs and acrobatic backhand volleys frustrated Muster in points where he believed he controlled, to such an extent that, at one stage, the Austrian ran round the net post and chased him off the court. 'It was just a bit of fun,' Henman said.

The Briton conceded only three points on his serve in the opening set and required just one break, in the second game, to win it 6-3. He moved two sets clear when he won the second set 7-3 on the tie-break, but after failing to convert either of his two break points in the second game of the third, he suffered a scare when his serve was broken in the very next game, allowing Muster to pull a set back.

However, the Austrian's exertions began to take an adverse effect on his left elbow, which generates much of his power, and he was rubbing the joint frequently from the third game of the fourth set.

Muster consequently lost his serve, allowing Henman to move 5-4 ahead. A magnificent drop shot gave him match point in the next game, and he clinched it with a lunging backhand cross-court winner to put an end to the 134-minute encounter.

Henman left the court quickly after his victory to get treatment for blisters on his feet, but commented: 'The result doesn't actually surprise me at all. The way I have been playing the last few weeks, I have felt very confident with my game. With his style of play, it works well to my game. I believed before the match I had the ideal game plan and I put it to work on the court. It was a good win.'

However, the cavalier who beat Muster on the Wednesday had gone AWOL by the time of his second-round match with Wayne Ferreira, replaced by a fumbling journeyman bearing a remarkable resemblance to the Henman who had lost to Michael Stich at Wimbledon.

And, just like at Wimbledon, after pulling off a big win over Krajicek, he came out looking totally flat in the next round. Even the 3-6, 2-6, 4-6 scoreline was identical.

Henman's succinct summation of his recent career said it all: 'When I'm good, I'm great – when I'm bad, I'm awful.'

Even Ferreira, who had worn heavy strapping on his ankle, admitted he expected more from Henman in their second-round clash. 'To beat Muster you must be playing well. I thought he would be playing really good tennis,' he said.

Henman knew he needed to find greater consistency to halt his alarming slide down the world rankings, which appeared to have originated after his elbow strife. He had been as high as 14th earlier in the year, but the fact he had failed to at least equal his last-sixteen finish of the previous year at the US Open meant he could drop even farther down the rankings, as his season looked like going into freefall and ending on a very bum note.

'I played a great match against Muster,' he said, 'but there have been too many highs and lows this year and we can't let it continue. I've got to be more resilient and find ways to dig myself out. I have moved my game in the right direction. It's things like this I must cut out. To beat Ferreira is not easy but it's a match I believe I should have won.'

With an unexpectedly empty four weeks ahead of him after his early US Open exit, and failure to make the Grand Slam Cup, which had now moved to the end of September, Henman took a wild card at the inaugural President's Cup tournament in the tennis outpost of Tashkent to play on the hard courts of

Uzbekistan, in a bid to swiftly banish the memory of his US Open misery.

After coming through a tough first-round match 6-4, 6-7, 7-6 against world number 233 Thierry Champion of France, Henman, the 2nd seed behind Kafelnikov, did not drop another set as he easily dispatched Russia's Alexander Volkov, the world number 151, American Vincent Spadea, ranked 114, and 6th seed and world number 55 Francisco Clavet of Spain, to make his fourth final of the year.

It was his first final since Antwerp in February, and if he was going to claim his second Tour title of the year he would have to exact revenge on the man responsible for beating him in that last final, the red-booted former Olympic champion Marc Rosset.

Henman began shakily losing his serve in the first game and nearly dropped it again in the third. He did recover, however, breaking back for 2-2 to send the set into a tie-break. Henman dominated the shoot-out, against one of the fastest servers in the world, claiming the last five points to win 7-2, before 5,000 spectators.

The second set proved a lot easier for Henman. He broke for 3-2 and then comfortably managed to serve out the match, delivering a total of seven aces, to become the first receiver of the President's Cup. 'I played good tennis from the beginning of the week,' he said after receiving the silver trophy from Uzbekistan president Islam Karimov. 'Once I got the momentum going I knocked him over. I was very aggressive and in a much better frame of mind than when I played him last time.'

After winning his first tournament in more than six months Henman still harboured hopes of climbing into the leading eight spots, which offer qualification for the ATP Tour World Championship finals in Hanover in November. It would require him to perform outstandingly well, considering he was still sitting at 20th in the listings, but there was no doubt this tournament win had set him off on the long European indoor season with his confidence restored. And so it proved.

Of the five indoor tournaments Henman participated in, he won ten matches, including two semi-finals, without being seeded in Basle and Vienna. He also achieved his quickest win in an ATP Tour event, beating Moroccan Hicham Arazi, the world number 39, 6-1, 6-0 in a mere thirty-nine minutes in the first round of the Paris Indoor Masters. But he failed to advance any further after this win and was beaten 6-3, 7-5 in the second round by the 10th-seeded Italian Open champion Alex Corretja of Spain, as some of his best tennis came to little because of early lapses and an inability to capture break points. Henman's outside chance of reaching the following month's ATP Tour World Championship in Hanover had been terminated.

He finished his ATP season with a ranking of 17th and a straight-sets quarter-final exit at the hands of top seed and world number 3 Pat Rafter, in the Stockholm Open, where he had matched his 8th seeding. It had certainly been a better end to the year than in 1996, when he lost in the first round of his last three ATP events, though that was of small consolation.

All Henman had left to look forward to in what was left of the 1997 season was Telford, where he was aiming to wrap up the British national title for a third successive year. But the only enemy he was likely to face at Telford was boredom, for with Rusedski away in Hanover he was way ahead of the rest of the contenders in the thirty-two-strong field. For that reason alone he had already decided that this would be his last campaign at the Guardian Direct Championships. 'I would like to win it three times in a row but after that I really cannot see what it will do for my career. I've always enjoyed it here, but a week's rest could be more beneficial. It would be better for a youngster to come through and enjoy the help offered by being the national champion. Hopefully, anyway, in future years I will be playing at Hanover.'

He launched his final campaign at the Guardian Direct event with a surprisingly hard-fought 6-4, 5-7, 6-1 victory over Nick Weal, and followed that with a thirty-nine-minute dismantlement of sixteen-year-old Scot Alan Mackin 6-0, 6-3, to reach the last eight and a match-up with Jamie Delgado.

Henman was well on course to finish a low-key week in Telford with a hat-trick of national titles. That was, until his phone rang at 11.30 on Thursday night, the day before his quarter-final match. In a very short time what should have been a comparatively quiet end to the week was about to develop into a frantic dash between Britain and Germany.

For Sergi Bruguera had been forced to withdraw from the ATP Tour World Championship suffering from a back injury after twice leaving the court for treatment during his 6-3, 6-1 defeat by Jonas Bjorkman the previous night. With standby reserve Thomas Muster having already filled in for hamstring victim Greg Rusedski, the call went out to Marcelo Rios (number 10), but he was back home in Santiago, Chile. Richard Krajicek (11) was injured, Alex Corretja (12) was ineligible under the ATP Tour's rules because he was playing doubles at an ATP Challenger event in Andorra. Petr Korda (13) was having a nose operation. Gustavo Kuerten (14) was in Brazil. Goran Ivanisevic (15) was injured. Felix Mantilla (16) was apparently not answering his phone. Time was running out. After the deadline of midnight (local time) passed, an SOS call went out to Henman.

With his coach, David Felgate, in Hanover for ATP board meetings, the Briton was easily contacted. 'I received a phone call at midnight on Thursday asking me to step in for Bruguera and to have the opportunity to participate in the World Championships was something I didn't want to miss.'

Henman would play a one-off round-robin match against Kafelnikov, but win or lose he could not qualify for the quarter-finals as Bruguera had already lost his previous two matches.

It was arranged that Henman would now open the day's National Championships programme against Delgado. After winning through 6-4, 6-2 in fifty-four minutes he was forced to skip the post-match press conference so that he could head by road to Birmingham Airport and take Flight 146 Alpha, a private jet, to Germany, at his own expense. He landed at Hanover airport an hour and a half later, at 16.30 local time, and by 7p.m, was on court playing Kafelnikov. Sixty-eight minutes later he had defeated the Russian, the eventual runner-up, in straight sets 6-4, 6-4, and then caught the last flight back to England.

For his night shift Henman raked in £62,500, as well as forty-five ranking points. 'I had mixed emotions about being there,' he said. 'I felt like I'd gate-crashed this party, that I didn't deserve to be in Hanover, but I had the opportunity and I took it. An atmosphere like that gives you a huge lift and makes you determined to qualify next time. It certainly wasn't a financial thing; I had already decided that if I received something I'd make a donation of a portion of the money to charity.'

The next day he completed an amazing and exhausting forty-eight hours by labouring to victory over Danny Sapsford in the nationals' last four, 4-6, 6-3, 6-3. 'I agree, it's not your average kind of day,' he said. 'I think I was mentally rather than physically tired after all that toing and froing.'

But by the time the final against Chris Wilkinson came around the following day, he was back to his best, to complete a straightforward 6-1, 6-4 dismissal of Great Britain's number four and a hat-trick of national titles.

Looking back on an erratic year interrupted by injury, Henman said: 'There are times when I play good tennis and it is up there with the best, but when I play poorly my standards drop too far. It is a case of me finding the middle ground. In future I will not be satisfied with the quarter-finals at Wimbledon. I set out with specific goals this year and if I look back there are a lot of positives. I can also look back and see how much better it could have been.'

Henman was already heading for multimillionaire status, having finished at number 16, one place higher than a certain David Beckham, in a list of British sport's twenty highest earners in 1997. The list, headed by Lennox Lewis, also included the sporting heavyweights Nick Faldo, Damon Hill, Stephen Hendry and Alan Shearer. With Henman now rubbing shoulders with the nation's finest, he had proved that Britain had finally found a player who could hold his head up high in world tennis.

6

Lucy

It was meant to be just another documentary, filming an insight into Tim Henman's career, but it was about to change his life forever. In December 1996 Henman had just finished his most successful season in tennis. He had made the quarter-finals of Wimbledon for the first time, the last sixteen at the US Open and qualified for the money-spinning Grand Slam Cup, where he reached the semi-final. For Henman it was already a year to cherish, but it was to get even better when a lady by the name of Lucy Heald walked into his life.

Lucy was an assistant producer on a documentary being made by her employers, Trans World International, the television arm of Henman's powerful sports agency, IMG. She produced tennis programmes for European channels and Sky TV.

It soon became clear for all to see that this was not going to be any ordinary documentary for either of them. 'During filming they would often chat together when the cameras were not rolling,' one of Lucy's friends recalled. 'There appeared to be an instant attraction between them.'

One year Henman's senior, Lucy was the daughter of a specialist cancer surgeon and had been brought up in Odiham, Hampshire, where, like Tim, she would practise her tennis skills on the court in the back garden of the family home. She shone academically, achieving ten GCSEs at the private Farnborough Hill School before gaining three A-levels and going on to earn a degree in social sciences from Durham University. Her former games mistress, Ann Berry, said: 'Lucy was one of those girls you know are going to make it in life, but never gushing or cocky. She has grace and composure.'

The couple's first date was at a Lawn Tennis Writers' Association dinner. 'He couldn't have chosen a more dramatic venue to introduce her,' recalled one guest. 'They looked totally smitten with each other. Tim was obviously in the limelight, but keen that Lucy met everyone.'

Henman spent Christmas that year with Lucy at her family's house but soon afterwards they were apart for more than a month as tennis dates took him across the world to the southern hemisphere. But he kept in regular contact with Lucy at the flat that she shared with a friend, which overlooks Wandsworth Common in south-west London.

Another friend said: 'Lucy's totally hooked on Tim. She has to work very hard at her job and obviously Tim has a lot of commitments with his tennis. But they spend every minute they can together.

'Lucy usually goes straight to his flat after work and leaves for work from there in the morning. On the days they have off together they go shopping and spend the evening at friends' houses or plush restaurants.

'She can't bear to think of having a night apart from him!'

The romance finally became public knowledge after Henman returned to Britain in late January and they were spotted going into his Chiswick home.

'When I first started going out with Lucy, I had fifteen photographers standing outside my house,' he recalls. 'That probably amounts to an intrusion of privacy. But the way I saw it, I had to go through it. It was something I couldn't change, and if I got too angry, let it affect me, well, it would also affect my game, and then everything would be lost.

'It is lovely that people are interested in what I do. When I go to a restaurant with Lucy, people come up and have a word, wish us well, and that is very flattering. She's a very relaxed sort of person and because she's involved in the business, she has a good understanding of my life.'

In fact Lucy's job allowed her to travel with Henman more than would otherwise be possible, as she was working at many of the tennis venues where he was playing.

'But the idea of giving up work to follow me around all the time isn't her at all,' he said. 'It would drive her mad, and if she were the tennis player I wouldn't do it for her. She's not too crazy about the whole image of being a tennis player's girlfriend. She has her own life. I like that. It's not all about me all the time.'

Lucy is a constant presence at Wimbledon, sitting in the same place in the players' box for each match. However, she refuses to speak publicly about her relationship with Henman, despite her media profession and generous offers to reveal all. Like him, she keeps a cool demeanour at Wimbledon, matching the self-contained style he displays on court by sitting quietly and clapping politely. On Centre Court, his frequent glances up to her are met mostly with her trademark inscrutable expression and donning of her sunglasses.

Her demure looks and unwillingness to squeak encouragement during matches won her the title 'Ice Maiden'. She is perhaps more reclusive than Henman and obviously perfect for him: very English, pretty in an unexciting way, stoical and easygoing.

'Lucy is just right for Tim,' one friend explained. 'She has a similar background and similar tastes. They have been going out together only since before Christmas, but they are inseparable. Lucy's family adore Tim and he is really close to them.'

The level of commitment they had to their relationship was demonstrated when, after just six months together, they bought a house in Barnes, south-west London, and moved in together.

'I can't say that it was a relationship waiting to happen,' Henman admitted to the *Sunday Mirror*. 'Given that tennis takes up so much time and is so consuming, it wasn't something that I was looking for. Nor was it something that I felt I needed, although it's lovely to be involved with someone.

'I don't feel that being with Lucy has been a distraction. I've discovered that having some stability in my life is not only a wonderful thing, but also that it has in turn helped with my tennis. I'm much more happy and content when I'm off the court, and thinking about other things apart from the next match, which is so important. Being with her makes me appreciate what I didn't have before.

'I'm very lucky because, on the one hand, she works in sport, so she understands the demands, the pressures and time away, but on the other she's not a tennis girl. She has no desire to hang around tournaments and be part of the circuit. That's not the sort of girl I want to be with.

'Lucy is my antidote to tennis, it's not something that we really talk about. When I get home from a tournament, or when I call her up when I'm on the road, the last thing I want to talk about is my forehand. I want to relax and chat about normal things. Going out to the pub or restaurant, doing things that everyone else does, really helps. I'm even getting a bit more domesticated.

'The thing I value most is having a normal boyfriend/girlfriend relationship and being like any other couple. I don't want to live in a tennis cocoon where it becomes my whole life. It's really important to be able to step away from that world, and Lucy enables me to do that.'

After Wimbledon, in July 1999 the couple took a private jet to Italy to spend a romantic ten-day break in a Tuscan villa – only the second time his demanding schedule had given them the chance to go on holiday together. While there the couple got engaged, but before publicly announcing the news they met up with Lucy's parents aboard a luxury yacht at Southampton so that Henman could ask her father for his daughter's hand in marriage. In a statement he said: 'We are delighted to confirm that Lucy and I got engaged while on holiday in Italy. We plan to get married later in the year during the very short tennis closed season. The service will be a private one with close family and friends.'

It is a measure of Henman's standing in Britain that news of his engagement to Lucy warranted front-page treatment. In previous years the fact that the leading British tennis player was going to marry would have prompted little more than a passing reference on the sport pages.

They married on 11 December 1999 at the little All Saints' Church in Odiham. Among the hundred or so guests at the ceremony were former British number one Jeremy Bates, as well as Andrew Richardson and Henman's coach, David Felgate, who were both best men. Among the other stars who attended the evening reception were Zoe Ball and her husband Norman Cook (Fatboy Slim), Sue Barker and Cliff Richard.

After the hour-long service, the couple emerged from the Norman church to applause from hundreds of well-wishers.

Henman described his wedding day as the happiest of his life. He told his official website (www.timhenman.org): 'It was a great day. It's something that I don't think you can really prepare for because it only happens once, but it definitely turned out to be a very special day. There were only a select few people that we wanted to share the day with, and I think that reflects my personality. I can understand that when I am on the court and I'm playing there's going to be a lot of attention which I can accept. However, on a very private occasion like my wedding day then we should be able to do just as we please and we did. It was a very private affair and that's very much the way we both wanted it to be.'

Within three years of their marriage the couple were expecting their first baby. 'It's fantastic news,' Henman said. 'It's a big responsibility, but one which both Lucy and I are really looking forward to.'

Rose Elizabeth was born on 19 October 2002 at 5.07a.m. at London's Queen Charlotte's and Chelsea Hospital, weighing eight pounds four ounces. Rosie had joined a tennis dynasty spanning four generations, and bookmakers William Hill were even offering odds of 250/1 that she would grow up to win the Wimbledon singles title.

Henman promised, however, that like his parents with him, he would not push his daughter into the sport. 'I'm not about to force a racket into Rosie's hand,' he said. 'But if she wants to play then I'll support her without question. But I'm happy she is not interested. Having a daughter is a pretty good way of working out that while you are going to go out on the court and try your best, at the end of the day it is just a game. Whether I have won, lost or drawn, all she wants is her food or her bottle.

'Having a family and a life away from the court is a good way of keeping things in balance. Whenever I get up in the morning or I get back in the evening, it's a great distraction to have. It's a good way, to a certain extent, of being able to switch off from what you have been doing throughout the day and from what you are focusing on.

'Having a daughter has had an impact on my game, because I'm a lot more relaxed about things. In the past I relied far too much on winning or losing, and put a lot of pressure on myself. When you have a daughter who is not the slightest bit interested in what you are doing, she doesn't care how you've done – she just wants your attention. I think that can help. But it doesn't distract me so much that I can't concentrate on what I am doing.'

Because of a shoulder injury, Henman was not playing, so he was able to be with his wife and daughter for the first four months of Rosie's life. Since then the very nature of his job has required him to spend a lot of time away from home for much of the year. But he got around that by taking them both on tour whenever Lucy could get time off work, and the trio were regularly spotted in players' restaurants around the world.

One journalist noted that they looked the picture of familial bliss, adding: 'It was really nice to see. Rosie seemed to have a strong personality of her own and really let her dad know what she wanted.'

But the family jaunts around the ATP were forced to come to an end at the close of 2004, when the couple became parents for the second time. Olivia was born on 15 December 2004 at 11.13a.m. at Queen Charlotte's and Chelsea Hospital, weighing eight pounds one ounce, joining the growing Henman family, which also includes Bonnie, their black Labrador, and Lucy's horse, Stella.

Again Henman was around for the first few months after the birth, because the baby was born smack in the middle of the off-season. 'I am absolutely delighted,' he said. 'This year has been fantastic for a number of reasons and to top off what I achieved on court with the birth of our second child is a real blessing. The last couple of years have been very special watching Rosie grow up and it's amazing to think she now has a little sister.'

7

Race for Number One

Rewind back precisely one year before Tim Henman popped into the world and another tennis superstar was born. Only this one was conceived on the other side of the Atlantic.

Greg Rusedski was born in Montreal on 6 September 1973 to Tom and Helen Rusedski. Greg's father came from Germany and was of Polish-Ukrainian descent, but his mother was British, born and raised in Dewsbury, West Yorkshire.

They were not rich by any means. Tom was a project development officer with Canadian Pacific Railroad and Helen worked in market research. They lived in a modest home, along with Bill, Greg's elder brother by three years, in Montreal's Pointe Claire district, where Greg's father was a member of the Clear Point Tennis Club. Watching his Dad play, Greg was hooked on the sport by the time he was six years-old.

The youngster had a natural affinity with a racket and ball and by the age of ten had started to enter tournaments. His parents supported him but struggled to find the cost of travelling, coaching and hotels, which involved their remortgaging their home and taking out substantial loans. He had sponsors, but they were in short supply, even after he became Canada's under-18 champion in 1991.

The recession of the late 1980s had hit the Canadian economy. In addition, Canadian sprinter Ben Johnson's failing of a drugs test at the 1988 Seoul Olympics, after winning gold and breaking the world 100-metre record, had burnt a number of companies and they were still afraid to trust individual sportsmen and women.

In 1991 Rusedski Jnr, still only seventeen, made his first appearance at Wimbledon and won the junior doubles with Moroccan Karim Alami, who has also since carved out a respectable tennis career, peaking at 25 in the ATP rankings in February 2000.

Rusedski also reached the semi-finals of the boys' singles at the All England Championships in 1991, a performance he repeated a few months later in the US Open. By his eighteenth birthday in September he had made the decision to turn professional, having already made his Challenger bow at Chicoutimi, Quebec in 1989 and scoring his first Challenger win in Singapore in 1990, where he reached the second round. By the time of his fifth Challenger, at the beginning of December 1991, he was already contesting his first final and pocketed a cool $2,120 despite losing in three sets to Germany's Bernd Karbacher. He finished 1991 at 603 on the computer rankings, but by the end of the next year he had rocketed to 158, thanks somewhat to his first Challenger title, in Newcastle in mid-July.

By 1993 Rusedski was a regular on the ATP Tour, and qualified for his Grand Slam debut at, of all places, Wimbledon, taking 2nd seed Stefan Edberg to three tie-breaks and four sets in the first round. He was rubbing shoulders with, and beating, the best of them.

His serve was clocked at 127mph (among the top ten fastest on the circuit) and he became the first Canadian since 1967 to win an ATP Tour title when he beat Javier Frana of Argentina, 3rd seed and world number 78, in three sets to win on the grass courts of Newport, Rhode Island.

By November, at the Tokyo Indoor Open, he was winning three-setters against world number 19 Wayne Ferreira, Richard Krajicek, ranked 10th, and world number seven Michael Chang on his way to a semi-final berth. A week later, at the indoor event in Beijing, he knocked out Sweden's Magnus Gustafsson, the 19th-ranked player, in three sets and world number 33 Brad Gilbert in the semi-finals.

It was in the Beijing players' lounge, after Rusedski had lost a three-set final against Chang, that the much-respected British tennis journalist Richard Evans met the Canadian and learned of a little item in his possession called a British passport, which he had held since birth as a result of his mother having been born in Yorkshire.

Evans wrote a couple of articles suggesting the Lawn Tennis Association should act on it, but they were reluctant to go chasing after him unless he made personal contact with them.

Britain was not exactly awash with tennis talent at this time. The country's highest-ranked player, Jeremy Bates, sat just inside the top 100, while Chris Wilkinson, Chris Bailey and Mark Petchey languished around the 150 mark. But here was a player capable of competing consistently with the best, and with a rare precious something that British tennis had lacked for many a year; he won. It was obvious, from the way he served and dominated the net with his long reach, that this powerful left-hander was tailor-made to win Wimbledon.

British tennis would certainly benefit, but so would Rusedski, who was well aware of the sure financial spin-offs to be enjoyed by a top player in a country which had a large tennis market and the world's biggest tournament yet was starved of international success.

The signs were all there. For a start, he had a long-standing English girlfriend called Lucy Connor, his future wife, with whom he had been smitten ever since he laid eyes on her when she was a ballgirl at a junior tournament in 1990. She lived in Putney, south London, and Rusedski was spending most of his spare time away from the tour there, as well as being a regular visitor to the LTA's practice courts in London. He had so far also deliberately avoided representing Canada in the Davis Cup, to keep his options open.

Despite an initial glut of newspaper hype surrounding Rusedski's apparent interest in becoming a British player, the situation simmered for over a year and by the end of 1994 was virtually forgotten.

But, after a year of agonising about where his future lay, which resulted in a disappointing season that saw his ranking drop from a peak position of 48 to 117 by the close of 1994, Rusedski finally took the first major step towards becoming a British player. This came in the form of repayment, around Christmas-time, of a voluntary $30,000 loan to Tennis Canada, the national federation, to wipe clean the slate of the modest financial backing it had given him as a promising youngster, thus ending the dealings between them.

In the spring of 1995, with Rusedski again one of the world's fastest-rising players, at 58 on the computer, as well as the biggest server in the game – he was measured in San Jose in February at 137mph – the LTA got the call British tennis had been waiting for. Rusedski officially confirmed to them his

In 1992, at the age of eighteen, Tim Henman won the British Junior Championships.
A year later, he turned professional.

Tim beat fellow Great Britain tennis star, Greg Rusedski, in the final of the Guardian Direct Nationals.

Above: Tim quickly developed a strong fan base as 'Henmania' swept Great Britain.

Below: Henman gives Wimbledon ball girl, Caroline Hall, a bunch of flowers and a kiss to apologise for hitting her with a ball during a mens doubles match with Jeremy Bates. He was disqualified from the doubles tournament as the ball had been struck in anger at an official.

Tim Henman and his
girlfriend Lucy Heald
during a walk along
the River Thames.

Above: As well as grand slam competitions, Tim has also taken part in many charity and exhibition events including the 'Ariel Champions of the Future' event at Regents Park Tennis Club with Nell McAndrew, Jonathon Ross, Penny Lancaster and Annabel Croft.

Below: Neil Broad and Tim Henman represented Great Britain in the mens doubles at the Atlanta Olympics in 1996. The pair were awarded silver medals after reaching the final.

In 1999, Tim and Lucy tied the knot in a very private ceremony. The happy couple now have two young daughters, Rosie and Olivia

Above left: Henman relaxes in the players lounge at the annual Stella Artois tournament.

Above right: Having beaten Andrei Pavel in a straight sets victory in the final of the BNP Paribas Masters Series, Tim poses with his trophy in 2003.

Below: Jane and Anthony Henman proudly watch their son play at Wimbledon with their daughter-in-law, Lucy.

A triumphant Tim Henman celebrates his impressive victory over Mark Philippoussis at Wimbledon in 2004.

intent to compete under the British banner. With the LTA's support a formal application was submitted to the International Tennis Federation (ITF), which on 22 May 1995 gave Rusedski the all-clear to represent Britain, on the basis that his mother was from Yorkshire, he had lived in Britain for three years and he held a British passport.

Rusedski would come straight in as Britain's top-ranked player and intended to fully integrate himself into British tennis by playing in the Davis Cup and the national championships. 'When I'm done with tennis, this is going to be my home until the day I die,' he proclaimed. 'In my heart, I feel British and my mother told me that I should go with what my heart says. I feel at home here.'

But not everyone was rejoicing at Rusedski's arrival. The first rumblings of discontent came from Mark Petchey, the twenty-four-year-old from Essex, who looked like he was about to be relegated to national number three by Rusedski and had lost his last eight Davis Cup singles matches. 'At the moment I'm having a problem dealing with it and I feel it's right I should stand up and be counted,' said Petchey, ranked 110 in the world. 'Over the last two years I have worked my butt off in the hope of establishing myself as British number one and, especially with Jeremy Bates's career coming towards its end, I thought it would happen.

'It's true that I have quite a lot to lose by this, both in financial and prestige terms, but I'm looking at it from a moral viewpoint more than anything else. The fact is that Greg is a product of the Canadian system, not ours, and has lived most of his life there.'

Incidentally, Rusedski's first ATP Tour appearance in British colours was against Petchey at the Stella Artois Championships, after a bout of tonsillitis ruled the former out of the French Open. And Petchey gave the new recruit a miserable debut, digging deep for a 6-4, 1-6, 6-3 victory that was undoubtedly the most satisfying win of his journeyman career. 'I certainly didn't need motivating for this one,' said Petchey. 'I had a point to prove. You can't stand up and say something and then fall flat on your face. He wanted to make a good impression and I was glad I didn't let him.'

However, Petchey was not the only one feeling bitter about Rusedski's admittance to British tennis. Chris Wilkinson, expected to be demoted to Britain's number four, followed Petchey in squawking his disapproval, but went further in actually quitting the country's Davis Cup squad in protest. 'Like other leading British players I have worked my butt off to represent my country and make a living from the game,' he angrily declared. 'Although we may not be world-beaters, there is still a lot of nationalistic pride in being the best in the country where you have been born and raised and in representing that country.

'I was British number one in 1993 and have fought back after a period of injury to a position where I could challenge to be number one again. I feel that this possibility has now been taken from me.

'Coming on the back of playing a South African [Neil Broad] in the Davis Cup team I feel there has been a cruel disregard for players like myself who have played for Britain at all levels. Now we will have a large chunk of our ambition and income taken away by overseas mercenaries.'

Henman, however, stood among those who welcomed the new arrival in the British ranks. At the time of Rusedski's entry into the British game, Henman had just returned to playing after breaking an ankle in a Challenger tournament in the Far East against Wilkinson, an injury which forced him out of the game for six months. Before that cruel blow halted his gallop, his ranking had rocketed from 434 in 1993 to 161 in 1994.

But with rehabilitation and recovery now firmly behind him, Henman was on his way back, already climbing to 231 in the world, after catching the eye with his performance on the previous year's satellite circuit, as well as by the way he had handled himself at Queen's, Wimbledon and in Britain's Davis Cup squad.

In a *Sunday Mirror* piece in 1997 Henman revealed his first thoughts on Rusedski's arrival: 'There was never a moment when Greg and I were formally introduced. We'd seen each other at various tournaments and said hello, but that was it. So from the moment the news came through that Greg was eligible for British citizenship and could play for our Davis Cup team, some people were convinced that there must be some animosity between us.

'They were sure I'd be jealous and would have my nose put out of joint because it might affect my position in the team and rankings. Some of the players were upset and said so. They thought that Greg getting a British passport when he'd been born and brought up in Canada was coming in through the back door. They were probably more worried about how his arrival might change things for them. But that didn't bother me – I've always felt that if you want to be the best then you have to be prepared to take on everyone.

'And what impressed me about Greg was his toughness, competitiveness and determination. He'd been ranked as high as the 30s, which was well ahead of anything I'd achieved at the time, but I could see that he wanted more. That was a new slant on things – most British players in the past had been pretty excited to get into the top 100, but not Greg.

'Maybe I might have felt the same way as the others. But as it is, I can now see that Greg's arrival made a big difference to me. He was a top player, and yet he was British, so I had him in my sights.'

Another leading tennis figure who certainly did not resent what many saw as gate-crashing was Britain's new Davis Cup captain, David Lloyd, the man who first spotted Henman's talent as a youngster, and he told Britain's top players: 'If you don't want to play Davis Cup, you are a mug. Get off your backside and prove you are better than Greg. He's a hell of a player, the best we have.'

So while the likes of Petchey and Wilkinson were seldom heard of again, apart from the annual two rounds of exposure Wimbledon brings, as they struggled to scale the heights achieved by Rusedski, Henman embraced the challenge.

The pair were included in Lloyd's inaugural squad for the Euro-African Zone Group Two play-off against Monaco at Eastbourne's grass courts in July. The British team were at their lowest point in the Davis Cup's ninety-five-year history and needed to win in order to avoid relegation to Group Three, the Cup's lowest level.

Back in April, under the guidance of Billy Knight, Great Britain sank to its lowest ebb after being whitewashed on clay in Slovakia, its sixth consecutive defeat. Henman, who had played doubles against Romania in 1995, made his singles debut that day, while, at the same time, Rusedski was in Seoul winning his second career tour title.

Now Rusedski was lining up for his British Davis Cup debut, in place of Miles Maclagan, while Henman, who had won nine of the thirteen matches he had played on grass over the past two months, was retained in preference to Mark Petchey, who made up the doubles with Neil Broad.

It was the first time Rusedski and Henman had been able to get to know each other. In 1997 Rusedski recalled their first encounter in an interview with Simon Kinnersley of the *Sunday Mirror*: 'It wasn't until I joined the British Davis Cup team in 1995 that I got to know Tim. We played Monaco and it was a lot of fun. It was the first time we'd ever sat down and chatted, even though I'd seen him at lots of tournaments.

'He could have been one of the players most affected by my joining the team, but it didn't seem to upset him at all – he saw it as just another challenge. I knew when I joined the team that he wanted to get past me, that I had given him a new goal.

'There are a lot of things that impress me about Tim. He's very confident and self-assured and he has tremendous belief in his own ability. But most of all, he's not ashamed to admit that he wants to be number one in the world. There haven't been many British players who would admit to that. But he's got a chance of achieving it, and so have I. He also has the potential to have a huge impact on British tennis.'

Henman and Rusedski made a tremendous start to their first Davis Cup match together, putting Great Britain on the verge of the nation's first victory for four years, as they established a 2-0 lead for the loss of just fifteen games. And then, following a doubles straight-sets win that preserved Great Britain's modest Euro-African Zone Group Two status, the two polished off Monaco with two more singles straight-sets triumphs, to cement a 5-0 whitewash. The last time that had happened was ten years earlier, when Jeremy Bates marked his debut against Portugal at Nottingham.

The new Brit and the true Brit had given the Davis Cup team a pulse again, just months after the deathly retreat from Bratislava. And a pattern was emerging. Great Britain's previous meeting with Monaco, back in 1978, had sparked off a run of success which eventually led to its first appearance in the final since the mid-1930s. It may not have led that far this time, but it did result in the British claiming five wins, over Slovenia, Ghana, Egypt and Ukraine twice, to leave them on the verge of a return to the World Group in 1998.

Henman and Rusedski had been instrumental in the country's Davis Cup renaissance, both missing just two ties each. A virus had caused Henman to withdraw from the Davis Cup team that beat Slovenia 4-1 in1996, while Rusedski missed the 1996 whitewash of Ghana because of a back injury. In 1997, against Zimbabwe, both were out, Henman recovering from an elbow operation and Rusedski suffering wrist problems, and the British team was beaten 4-1.

The duo had played ten singles, recording nine successes each, and by 1997, in their first encounter with Ukraine, they had also displaced both Petchey and Broad as the British Davis Cup doubles team, following the latter twosome's doubles defeat by Zimbabwe. They achieved an immediate understanding as a doubles team: Henman's fast work at the net dovetailed neatly with Rusedski's familiar power game. Such a formidable pairing were they that they went unbeaten in eight Davis Cup doubles matches.

Back to 1998, and after disposing of Ukraine for the second time, Great Britain had a whiff of the promised land. The 5-0 Euro-African Zone Group One victory placed them in the draw for the World Group qualifiers, and Lloyd got the opposition he wanted: India, the only country in the hat that guaranteed him a home tie. In 1992 the Indians had been responsible for Great Britain's eventual six-year exile from the elite top 16 of the world group when they beat the British 4-1 in New Delhi.

Now the Brits were out for revenge on their own patch, but the choice of venue was an issue. Despite grass being alien to every other nation, Indian players are largely brought up on it. Therefore the best prospect was a true-bouncing, mid-speed hard court, seeing as Henman and Rusedski had just returned from America's hard-court season, and the switch was made to the City of Nottingham Tennis Centre.

The Indian challenge was headed entirely by Leander Paes, ranked 128th, and Mahesh Bhupathi, 247th. They were ranked three in the world doubles, but their singles rankings did not measure up to the British pair's.

Rusedski, who had been inactive with an ankle injury since his exit from the US Open more than two weeks earlier, opened the tie against Paes, and made a slow start as the Indian settled first, to lead by two sets to one.

On the ATP Tour, Paes beating Rusedski would be considered a shock, but the beauty of the Davis Cup is that its matches are littered with the unexpected, so this would be seen as nothing out of the ordinary.

Just then, though, Rusedski found his serve in the fourth set, and the tie was balanced at two sets apiece. The out-of-sorts Rusedski had to draw on all his reserves of courage in the decider, and among his challenges was surviving a match point. But after three hours and sixteen minutes of tense and wildly fluctuating tennis, a double fault by Paes handed Rusedski the 2-6, 6-3, 3-6, 6-2, 11-9 win to give Great Britain the vital initiative.

Henman, fresh from a successful defence of his Tashkent title, followed straight after. His match with Bhupathi was never going to hit the heights of its predecessor on the stadium court but an upset was on the cards when the Indian number two hit some incredible winners to take the first set and break Henman in the first game of the second.

Fortunately, Henman kept his cool, raised his game and began to hit with more confidence. He broke Bhupathi twice in each of the last three sets to eventually romp to a 4-6, 6-3, 6-3, 6-3 victory and give Great Britain a 2-0 overnight best-of-five lead.

The next day Henman and Neil Broad took to the court for the doubles, with Rusedski still feeling the effects of Friday's feat of endurance. The British pair had beaten Paes and Bhupathi in their previous meeting, on the way to Olympic silver, their last appearance as a pairing. But it had little bearing on this clash as the India tandem, ranked 3rd in the world, won in straight sets to reduce the British lead to 2-1.

Henman was first up in the singles the next day against Paes, knowing that victory would seal Great Britain's return to the World Group. He raced to a 5-2 lead, but an all too familiar concentration lapse allowed Paes back in for 5-5. Luckily, Henman managed to squeeze home in the tie-break. The second set was altogether more easy, as ten points in a row put Henman break up and he was soon two sets up.

But anyone who had beaten Pete Sampras earlier in the year was obviously not going to go down without a fight, and in the third set Paes revived dangerously just when he seemed devoid of energy. He broke to lead 2-0, but Henman forced a break-back, taking the set into tie-break territory again. The Indian summoned every last drop of defiance and twice edged ahead. But Henman responded and reached match point at 6-5. After four tough matches the tie was eventually decided by a simple forehand into open court from Henman that wrapped up victory for Great Britain.

At last the nation could look forward to competing in the world's top sixteen once more.

'It means a lot. It is right up there with any of my other achievements,' Henman said later. 'That is the best Davis Cup match I have played. It was a particularly high-pressure situation against an opponent who you never know what to expect from. To come through in straight sets in those types of conditions is very, very satisfying.'

For the first time in the sixty years since it had last won the Davis Cup there was now serious talk of Great Britain winning it again. Henman made it clear he believed in the possibility. 'Both Greg and I believe that on a given day we can beat anyone, so we know we could win the Davis Cup. This means so much to us and so much to the country. The stage has been set for us to go all the way.'

David Lloyd agreed. 'With Tim and Greg, I honestly feel we have got a great chance of winning.'

In fact five-times Wimbledon champion Bjorn Borg also believed that with two of the world's top ten players in their ranks, Great Britain had the strength to lift the title. He waxed lyrical: 'Tim Henman and Greg Rusedski are two great players. With the team that Britain have and the way they have been playing, they have a great chance of winning the whole event next year.'

Great Britain was drawn at home to the United States in its first match back in the World Group, a rerun of the inaugural amateur Davis Cup tie a century ago. No sooner had the draw been made than Great Britain was given a further boost with the news that the opposition's two foremost superstars, Pete Sampras and Andre Agassi, would be bypassing the tie.

Expectations were running high in the British camp, but despite their going in as favourites against the Americans, over the Easter weekend at Birmingham's National Indoor Arena, the optimism swiftly turned to disappointment. A return to the elite World Group of tennis should have been a celebration but it proved an agonising lesson. By the end of the opening day's play the British were trailing 2-0 after Henman lost in five arduous sets to Jim Courier, now ranked 54, while Rusedski sank without trace in straight sets against Todd Martin, the world number eight.

It would have taken a comeback of epic proportions to overturn the deficit, but they were back in the hunt after winning the doubles against Alex O'Brien and Martin 3-6, 7-5, 6-3, 6-7, 6-3. With Henman steering operations, the pair played for three and a half hours as if their lives depended on it, to the sheer delight of the sell-out flag-bearing crowd.

Now both men needed to win their reverse singles games to clinch a magnificent triumph. Henman got the ball rolling on the final day, coming back from a set down against Martin to tame him in four, making everything seem possible despite having been drained by more than seven hours and ten sets of highly charged combat on successive days beforehand.

He left the stage for Rusedski to go for glory against Courier. And how close he came. The son of Montreal endeared himself to the British public with a gutsy display, coming back twice from going a set behind to take it to a fifth set. There was no doubt he gave it his all, but it ultimately proved in vain after almost four hours of heart-stopping tennis, as Courier put the States into the last eight against Australia, 6-4, 6-7, 6-3, 1-6, 8-6, and Great Britain was left with the prospect of another World Group play-off.

Lloyd was philosophical in defeat: 'The boys did great and the country should be proud of them, they certainly could not have tried harder or played better. We've been in the depths of despair and come back. It hurts like hell. I'm convinced that we can still win this tournament, we are still young in this company.'

Sadly, his forecast could not have been further off the mark. In September they thrashed South Africa 4-1 to return to the summit for the 2000 season. However, with Rusedski out with a foot injury, it was left to Henman to spearhead the British charge, along with Jamie Delgado and Neil Broad, on the clay in the Czech Republic. But, despite Henman giving Great Britain a 1-0 lead, they failed to build on it and were taken apart 4-1, a result which led to Roger Taylor succeeding Lloyd as skipper.

Further embarrassment followed in the play-off with Ecuador on Wimbledon's Court One. Henman won both his singles matches, but they failed to muster another win and Great Britain was relegated.

They sprang straight back up by whitewashing Portugal at the start of 2001 and also took revenge on Ecuador 4-1. But in 2002 once again they saw their passage blocked in the World Group, this time by Sweden, who won 3-2.

Then, after another World Group qualifier win, at the expense of Thailand, at the start of 2003 Henman's shoulder and Rusedski's foot meant rookies Miles Maclagan, Alan Mackin, Arvind Parmar and Alan Bogdanovic were put into action on the Australian clay. Only Bogdanovic could collect a win, and so it was back to the play-offs. Great Britain has not returned to the top flight since.

The return of Rusedski and Henman failed to inspire Britain in the dust bowl of Morocco for its next play-off and a 3-2 defeat resulted in an Euro-African Zone revisit for 2004 and Taylor being ousted as captain by Jeremy Bates. A comprehensive 4-1 win over Luxembourg offered them another route back to the big time, but clay proved the team's Achilles heel again, as they were humbled 3-2 at the hands of mighty Austria, with Henman and Rusedski even losing their first-ever Davis Cup doubles match together, after eight consecutive wins.

It was to be Henman's final Davis Cup tie for Great Britain. In January 2005 he announced his retirement from Davis Cup action, choosing instead to concentrate on his solo career in an effort to finally get his hands on an elusive first Grand Slam title.

'I've made no secret of the fact that representing Great Britain has always been a top priority for me throughout my career,' he said. 'I've played some of my best tennis and enjoyed some of my most memorable moments while on Davis Cup duty. However, at this stage in my career, the combination of the Davis Cup format and the rigours of the ATP Tour have made it necessary for me to make this decision.

'I'm confident this offers me the best opportunity to fulfil some unachieved goals.'

Yet it is not just for Great Britain that Rusedski and Henman have made an impact. They have also had a great influence on each other.

When Rusedski joined the British ranks in 1995 he was an established ATP Tour player, while Henman was still playing predominantly on the Challenger circuit with the odd wild card coming at British-based Tour events.

One of those British events happened to be at Wimbledon, and was Rusedski's debut Grand Slam as a Brit. Both players made an impact for very different reasons. Henman's moment made him a villain, when, on an outside court, he struck a shot that landed on a ballgirl's head and so became the first player ever to be thrown out of the Championships.

In contrast, Rusedski made himself a national hero. Sporting a silly Union Jack bandanna, generously donated by the *Sun*, he broke his British duck, after first-round exits at Nottingham and Queen's, with a straightforward dismissal of world number 264 Stephane Simian of France and eventually made it all the way to the fourth round after taking two more French scalps in 16th seed Guy Forget and 44th-ranked Olivier Delaitre, before falling to Pete Sampras, Henman's slayer that year. Rusedski also finished the tournament with the fastest delivery of the tournament, measured at 134mph.

He had endeared himself to the nation with his Wimbledon deeds and come November the national championships seemed likely to be his coronation ceremony – or so everyone thought.

Crowned instead, in bizarre fashion, was Henman, ranked 75 places below Rusedski at 116 in the world.

They met in the final, and Henman had admitted to 'being worried greatly by the clock monitoring the time of the match', after Rusedski blasted his way through the opening set in under twenty minutes and then started the second set by breaking service for the third time. It looked like being a win of ignominious rapidity, the swiftest and most one-sided in the tournament's history.

But, amazingly, an hour later Henman had won, demoralising Rusedski by taking seven games in a row to capture the second set and then build a decisive lead in the third, in addition to dropping just three points in his last six service games.

'Tim deserved to win for sure,' Rusedski said, after playing him for the first time. 'He showed a lot of character and a lot of belief. I tried too hard to serve well today. When I try too hard I get nervous and tight. If he stays healthy and works hard, there is no reason why he can't make it to the top fifty. I also have no doubt that after the three Challenger tournaments coming up, Tim will be in the world's top 100.'

Rusedski's prediction was indeed right. Henman hared around the globe and scooped up two Challenger titles in the Far East, while Rusedski was into his off-season and appearing on BBC TV's *Noel's House Party*. As a result the new national champion ended the season by breaching the top 100 for the first time, at 99. As for Rusedski, he became the first Briton to finish the year in the top fifty since John Lloyd in 1985, with an end-of-season ranking of 38.

Henman had probably lost more from the arrival of his Davis Cup teammate Rusedski than anyone. But rather than moaning, like many others, he had got his head down and decided to use the ex-Canadian as a yardstick in an attempt to catch him up.

'I don't have a problem getting on with people and I'm fine with Greg, although we're pretty different,' Henman said. 'For instance, he likes the spotlight, which is fair enough, and I'm not that bothered.

'He riles some people and I'm not sure he understands our sense of humour, but he will learn. He's a very dedicated professional and his presence is very healthy. It can only be good if we're pushing each other and I intend to be pushing him soon.'

Contrasting fortunes awaited the pair in 1996, and Henman now had 'the Joker' – the smiling Rusedski's nickname among his new compatriots – in his sights.

It was Henman's first year on the full ATP Tour and he started it, along with Rusedski, by giving British tennis a fillip in the build-up to the Australian Open. Both scored unexpected first-round wins at the Peters International in Sydney. Henman defeated Mark Philippoussis, the Australian giant who went on to beat Pete Sampras in Melbourne, to progress to the last sixteen, while Rusedski beat number-two seed Richard Krajicek, en route to the semi-finals, where he lost the battle of the big servers against Todd Martin. Rusedski also broke the record for the fastest match ever seen at that tournament, with his twenty-nine-minute whitewash of Carsten Arriens.

The pair's preparations appeared to leave them in good stead for the opening Grand Slam. However, they were not afforded the best luck in the draw, being paired with two big hitters. Yet while Rusedski threw away a two-set-to-one lead to lose to 4th seed Boris Becker, the eventual winner of the Open, Henman stunned world number 26 Petr Korda by beating him in four sets, his greatest Grand Slam win to date. He was now flying the flag solo but, just like in Sydney, he failed to kick on and the next day was sent packing by Bjorkman in three.

After such a fine opening to the season for Henman, his season got progressively better, while Rusedski's got progressively worse. Standing at 85th at the end of January, Henman made three semi-finals in his next five tournaments to soar to 58th in the world. Rusedski followed up his form Down Under, which saw him go 33rd, by making the quarter-finals in San Jose, but then failed to record back-to-back wins again until the Tokyo outdoor in mid-April, where he reached the third round. As a result he fell to 45th, and now only thirteen places separated them.

But everything was about to change. Henman already held Britain's number-one berth, due to the LTA's system of national ranking, where a player is not eligible for a British ranking until they have been available to represent Britain for a full twelve months, a rule which excluded Rusedski until May.

However, after the Korean Open, where defending champion Rusedski could only make the quarter-finals whereas Henman reached the semi-final spot, he actually missed out on his first chance to take over as official British number one. Rusedski's inferior result meant that, by the start of May, Henman had overtaken him on the ATP computer. A year earlier, when Rusedski 'transferred' to Britain, he was almost 200 places ahead of Henman, but now, for the first time, Henman had nosed four places in front of him, advancing to number 54.

Henman commented at the time: 'Greg had been sort of a target of mine, a very important benchmark, someone to look up to and try and emulate in a lot of areas. There is no doubt Greg's arrival on the scene has made a big difference and most of the guys in the top fifteen in this country have improved their ranking. So there's definitely a buzz about things.'

And Henman began to sear ahead in the popularity stakes as well. He became a national treasure after defeating French Open champion Kafelnikov and going on to the quarter-finals at

Wimbledon, as well as the last sixteen of the US Open. Those two performances ensured a place at the money-spinning Grand Slam Cup, where he made it all the way to the last four.

He also managed a silver medal in the men's doubles at the Atlanta Olympics, which may not have carried any ranking points but certainly scored big back home with the British public.

Meanwhile, after Rusedski appointed Brian Teacher as his new coach in May to succeed Scott Brooke, who had decided he wanted to spend more time at home in America, it initially failed to inspire. Rusedski embarked on a disappointing end to the season, reaching merely the second round at Wimbledon, and then a hip injury forced him out of action for a month. On his return he managed only the third round of the men's singles in Atlanta and was eliminated at the first hurdle at Flushing Meadow.

He also suffered the ignominy of losing twice more to the now greater Brit. Consistent all-court skills and effective serve-and-volley tactics proved the difference as Henman took Rusedski to the cleaners in straight sets in Ostrava, their first encounter on the ATP Tour, and then inflicted another defeat in the final of the national championships for a second consecutive year. The only bright spot for Rusedski came with a promising finish to the season, when he made the last eight in Stockholm, the semi-finals in Singapore and won a title in Beijing.

Despite his reaching a ranking high of 33 earlier in 1996, Rusedski's form slumped as low as 84, before he managed to salvage 48th spot by the campaign's end. Henman, meanwhile, rocketed a total of seventy-two places to peak at 25, before ending at 28. Not since December 1978, when Buster Mottram was ranked 28 and John Lloyd 37, had Britain enjoyed having two men ranked in the top fifteen at the same time.

Henman had used Rusedski as a stalking horse since the latter roared into Britain on the crest of a wave, and now it had really paid off.

'Jeremy Bates always told me that he could have done with another British player pushing him,' Henman remarked. 'I often noticed how if Jeremy had gone through a bad spell and, say, dropped down to 120 in the world, and if another British player then reached 140, Jeremy would always play well for the next four weeks and end up back at 80.

'I think that Greg made a big difference to me when he came over last year to Britain. Without him, who knows where I'd be now. I might have sat back and settled for being the British number one. There's no doubt about it, Greg's been vital to my development. Last year I had him in my sights. He was an obvious benchmark because he was in the top fifty, and he had become a British player.

'This year the roles have been reversed, and it may not be a coincidence that Greg's played well recently to close the gap a bit between us in terms of ranking. It's inevitable that I am going to have weeks where I don't play as well as I'd like to. If at the same time Greg can have a good week, there's still going to be something positive for British tennis. I'm sure he has me in his sights. I very much hope so, and it's important to me that Greg does well because by doing so he'll push me up the rankings as well.'

He could not have been any nearer the truth. So much was expected of the British pair in 1997, and they did not disappoint as Rusedski roared back with a vengeance.

Henman started the better. Victory in January's Sydney International and a final in Doha, combined with reaching the third round of the Australian Open, increased the gulf as he rose to number 14, while Rusedski made first-round exits in Auckland and the opening slam to slip to 55.

Early in February Henman made his third final of the year, just as Rusedski found form. The British number two chalked up his first triumph of the season at the Croatian Indoor in Zagreb, and ended up making the final, before losing to Goran Ivanisevic. He built on that excellent form by achieving another final in his next tournament, in San Jose, where he took the scalps of Michael Chang, ranked 4th, and Andre Agassi, 12th.

Rusedski's resurgence brought a rise to 35 in the rankings, meaning he was now just twenty-one places behind Henman. It looked like being an epic and fiercely fought battle for the British number-one title. Yet Rusedski insisted at the time that, whatever way the see-saw ultimately tilted, their friendly rivalry would not escalate.

'It's only good for British tennis, whether it's myself or it's Tim who's doing really well,' Rusedski said in an interview with *The Independent*. 'I was really pleased when Tim did well in Doha and in Sydney and at the Australian Open and now in Antwerp. He congratulated me for a good week in Zagreb when we trained together the week leading up to San Jose. We're just both very pleased for each other, and we're not the sorts that look over our shoulder, shall we say.

'It's a friendly rivalry. It keeps the game in the public's eye, and our record so far on the ATP Tour has been good. We've had a British player in the finals every week this year besides the Australian Open, which isn't a tour event. So if we can keep that track record going I think we'll get a lot more people excited about tennis and hopefully have a few more youngsters picking up rackets and playing.'

He added, in a *Sunday Mirror* article: 'I'm sure that people like to imagine there's a big chasm between Tim and I and we don't get on. There's certainly a lot of rivalry on court; he's 3-0 up in our matches at the moment so there are some scores to be settled. But the truth is that we get on very well. I wouldn't say we're close friends; more like teammates with a lot of mutual respect.

'We're very different sorts of people. I'm very happy-go-lucky and noisy and Tim is much more reserved and quiet. You can mistake that for being shy, but he's not; he's just a little more wary, and he has a very dry sense of humour. When we're around other players I'm very chatty and he prefers to keep a distance.

'Although Tim and I see a lot of one another we don't really hang out together. We might have a bite together at a tournament but it never goes any further than that. Tennis is like that ... it's too competitive to encourage close friendships.'

Sadly, Rusedski was forced to retire in the second set of that San Jose final against Pete Sampras despite taking the first set. Britain's number two had damaged ligaments in his wrist and as a result he was forced to withdraw from several events over the next three months. But he was not the only one suffering with injury. Henman joined him on the sidelines after having elbow surgery, missing a similar period.

Their rankings suffered as a consequence of these grievances, with Henman dropping to 16 and Rusedski to 40.

The duo made their returns to the court in May for the dreaded clay season, which unsurprisingly brought with it a dip in form that saw only Henman win a single match, though both said *au revoir* to Roland Garros in round one.

But once Queen's Club opened its gates to signal the start of the grass season, both men's results vastly improved. In the build-up to Wimbledon, Henman made the third round in the Stella Artois Championships and the last four at Nottingham, but it was Rusedski who really hit the crest of a wave. He took the scalp of world number 17 Pat Rafter to progress to the last four at Queen's and failed to drop a single set at Nottingham, to become the first Brit to triumph on home territory since Mark Cox in 1975. Rusedski's name had barely been heard above the clamour for Henman over the past year, but now he had pushed him out of the limelight, if only temporarily.

'Maybe I'll get a headline now,' he said. 'Even when I played at Queen's it was "What's wrong with Tim?" and not "Rusedski's doing well." I guess the only way to do something about it is to keep winning. But I'm not really miffed about it. That's just the way it is and anyway, it takes some of the pressure off me.'

Wimbledon fever had gripped the nation with the English Grand Slam next on the calendar, and this time round Britain had two players who had a genuine chance of winning it. Not since 1977, when Virginia Wade won Wimbledon, had tennis forced its way into the same spotlight as the likes of Glenn Hoddle's England team and Manchester United's European Cup aspirations, and it was all down to Henman and Rusedski.

The knock-on effect had seen more people taking up the sport, with children for once actually wanting to emulate a British tennis star, and greater attendances at tournaments nationwide. At such events followers would be split into two distinct camps, with the girls attracted to Henman's cute looks and the boys favouring Rusedski's aggressive style and roaring service.

Rusedski carried his fine form into the main event, overcoming the 7th seed, Mark Philippoussis, in round one to go on and repeat Henman's feat the previous season of reaching the last eight, before disappointingly losing in four to the unseeded Cedric Pioline, ranked 44th. But Henman refused to be upstaged. The 14th seed also reached the quarter-final stage, by knocking out the holder, Richard Krajicek, but he, too, failed to better himself from the previous campaign, frustrated by an ageing Michael Stich. Had both won their respective matches, they would have met each other in the last four, the biggest match Wimbledon would have seen for decades.

Nevertheless, it was still the first time since 1961, with Bobby Wilson and Mike Sangster, that a British double achieved the distinction of a last-eight finish. Henman and Rusedski received gigantic publicity and rightly so. They had really put tennis in Britain back on the map. What they had achieved was very special. That year Wimbledon broke all attendance records even though eight of the fourteen days were hit by bad weather, and the massive increase was almost entirely due to the British duo. Tennis had bound the country together, just like the England football team manages every two years at the World Cup or European Championships.

They earned immediate reward for their Wimbledon endeavours, with Rusedski moving up to 24, and Henman to 18, the first time since Roger Taylor and Mark Cox in March 1974, that Britain had two men in the world's top twenty-five. There was now just six places between them, and Rusedski certainly felt the impetus was with him now. 'Tim has done really well and he is British number one, but I'm catching up and I believe I can be top man again. It's within my grasp to overtake him. Time will tell but I'm getting better with every match.'

That time was about to come much sooner than anyone expected. Henman and Rusedski both made poor starts to the US hard court season with first-round exits at Cincinnati, but after that Rusedski's form went into overdrive. At their next event, the Pilot Pen International at New Haven, while Henman could only make the last eight, Rusedski went one further and reached the semi-finals, dumping out 6th seed Albert Costa of Spain and 4th seed Richard Krajicek in the process, before losing to Pat Rafter. Rusedski's defeat prevented him reaching his fourth final of the year and, maybe more importantly, overtaking Henman in the rankings.

As it stood now, Rusedski had moved up to a career-high world ranking of 23, while Henman had fallen back to 20. Only sixty-five points separated them, and it meant that if Rusedski did well at the ATP event in Boston he would overtake Henman, who was taking a short break in preparation for the following week's US Open.

The hulking left-hander needed three sets to overcome 61st-ranked Mikael Tillstrom of Sweden, but once he overwhelmed Filip Dewulf of Belgium to book his place in the last eight, the sixty-five points he needed were all but guaranteed. Surprisingly, he fell to Jeff Tarango in the next round, but it mattered little. For the first time in seventeen months Rusedski was back at the head of the British tennis rankings, jumping three places to 20th, one ahead of Henman. 'I believe the [revised] rankings will confirm that I have reached my goal, which is a great reward for all the effort I have put into my game. It's definitely good for my confidence,' he said.

Henman had nothing but lavish praise to offer Rusedski for overtaking him. 'I think the rivalry is very healthy and probably the best thing for me. Greg deserves to be ahead of me because he's played phenomenally well but it is really going to spur me on.' But he added: 'What really matters is who ends up as number one – me or Greg – at the end of the year. That's what counts.'

However, Rusedski looked likely to extend his margin over Henman at the US Open. If Henman failed to beat world number five Thomas Muster in the first round he would lose 130 more points gained by reaching the fourth round the previous year. Rusedski, on the other hand, had nothing to lose as he had never won at Flushing Meadow and so had no points to protect. He had also been given an easier task, having been drawn in round one against world number 121 David Wheaton.

Fortunately for Henman, he did manage to pull off a shock and beat Muster, which entitled him to bonus points for beating a higher-ranked player. However, he then suffered the embarrassment of being on the end of a giantkilling when he was dismantled in round two by the unfancied Wayne Ferreira.

Rusedski did break his US Open hoodoo by beating Wheaton in three, but he was in no mood to stop there. He beat South African Marcos Ondruska, Jens Knippschild of Germany, Daniel Vacek and Richard Krajicek without dropping a single set, and all of a sudden he was facing Jonas Bjorkman, the world number 17, having become the first Brit since Mike Sangster back in 1961 to reach a US Open semi-final. He was now just two wins away from actually winning a slam.

Henman knew he would fall further behind his rival as a result. Nevertheless, he was behind him all the way, as were millions of others. He said: 'It has been a hell of an effort to get through and I really hope he goes on to win the thing, If Sampras were left in he would be clear favourite but now there is no one Greg cannot beat.'

Bjorkman became the first player to take a set off the Briton in the tournament, and even raced into a 2-1 set lead, but it still was not enough to halt Rusedski's progress as he came back to win the final two sets 6-3, 7-5 and emulate John Lloyd, the last Briton to reach a Grand Slam final, at the Australian Open final in 1977.

Rusedski went into the final against Australia's Pat Rafter, the number 13 seed, with an opportunity of becoming the first Briton to win a Grand Slam men's singles title since Fred Perry defeated the American Donald Budge at Forest Hills in 1936, in the pre-war days of flannel trousers. But Rafter was simply too good on the day, and won the title for the cost of just one set 6-3, 6-2, 4-6, 7-5. It had proved a record too far.

Some of that heartbreak, though, must have been eased with a leap up the world lists to number 11. It was the best performance by a Brit since Roger Taylor equalled that feat in 1973 – the year Rusedski was born.

Henman was full of praise for his Davis Cup teammate. 'It was an unbelievable performance. Probably since Queen's, he's really been playing a high standard of tennis. He's done it on the grass courts and in the lead-up to the US Open. He gave himself an opportunity and took it.'

Attention had certainly switched back to Rusedski, and now it was Henman who had been banished into his previous role as the afterthought of British tennis.

Rusedski returned to Britain to a hero's welcome when he played his first match since his American exploits on the clay at the Samsung Open in Bournemouth. Henman was also invited to play, but declined the invitation and travelled to Tashkent to play on his preferred surface of hard courts. It did not go down well with the LTA, who were trying to showcase the sport at the highest level outside the Wimbledon period.

Rusedski, who had only just jetted in from New York on Concorde, received a standing ovation in his first-round match against world 101 Alberto Martin, and the match was delayed for fifteen minutes while 3,000 fans squeezed into the tiny West Hants club. The longest queues generated by British tennis outside June and July are usually for the Wimbledon Museum, but there it was, a huge one snaking round the pavements on a midweek afternoon on the south coast, all for one Canadian-cum-Brit. It was the kind of attention he had craved ever since he turned British. He also received a small gift from an elderly lady supported by a walking frame who had wandered behind the umpire's chair after the first set.

Despite battling a throat infection, the after-effect of antibiotics, jet lag and exhaustion, Rusedski went on to reach the semi-finals, before losing to world number five Carlos Moya. His progress in the tournament also propelled him and British tennis to new heights, as he became the first Brit ever into the top ten.

But, thousands of miles away in the former Soviet republic of Uzbekistan, Henman was giving the perfect answer to those who had criticised his decision to miss the Samsung Open, by beating Marc Rosset to win the President's Cup in Tashkent. After that triumph, which kept Henman at 20th, he explained how Rusedski was spurring him on to greater levels. 'It's important for me that Greg's been playing well,' he admitted. 'Hopefully, that's going to lift me – now I can chase him a little bit and we'll push each other. We're on the up. Greg had a great two weeks at the US Open and another at Bournemouth. Now I have gone out and won a tournament. We're vying with each other.

'For a long time I was the number one and he was doing the chasing. I think it's great that he's overtaken me because it gives me an added incentive, it's a chance for me to feed off him a little bit, but I'm aiming to overtake him soon. Greg's broken into the top ten and he's thoroughly deserved that with his performances. And if I can continue the way I've been playing of late, then we can have two British players in the top ten. It's healthy competition.

'With the indoor season coming up, which is a good time for both of us, things are very positive. I've not had the chance to speak to Greg since he got back because I was in Tashkent and he was playing in Bournemouth. Maybe we'll get the opportunity to hit some balls at the end of this week. It's a friendly rivalry. We get on very well and practise together on the tour and in London. I know I've definitely got to pull my socks up because he's set the standards.'

But after a month in which the left-hander carved up the field at the US Open and made the semis of the Bournemouth Open and then followed it up by equalling Henman's semi-final berth at the Grand Slam Cup, he sprang a surprise on everyone by dropping his coach, Brian Teacher. Rusedski put the split down to the fact he wanted to better himself, but Teacher was having none of it, citing disagreements over money and the close involvement of Rusedski's father, who had demanding ways, and who gave Teacher sparse credit for Rusedski's rapid rise from the journeyman position of 84 a year ago to a career high of 10th.

The Californian was replaced by ex-British Davis Cup Captain Tony Pickard, Stefan Edberg's former mentor. But the move to switch coaches was controversial for more than one reason. Pickard had always been an admirer of Henman's game and David Felgate, Henman's coach, knew that Pickard had been in contact with his protégé several times in the past, ever since his Slater Squad days, and still harboured ambitions of working with him one day. Pickard had also made no secret of his concern that Felgate might not have the experience to maximise Henman's potential. Relations were polite but cool between the two coaches, and it is fair to say they were unlikely to be on each other's Christmas card list.

The tail end of 1997 saw no slow-down in Rusedski's progress, despite a change of management, as he continued to better Henman at every event they entered. He won the Swiss Open in Basle – where Henman made the last four – reached the final in Vienna – achieving his first win over Henman, in the last four – the semi-finals in Stockholm – to Henman's last eight – and the quarter-finals at the Paris Masters, compared with Henman's second-round progression.

The end result, come mid-November, was a ranking of 17th for Henman and 5th for Rusedski, who had peaked at 4th in October.

Rusedski's top-eight finish meant he had become the first Briton to ever qualify for the ATP Tour World Championship in Hanover. However, it turned out to be a torrid experience for him. He lost his first two matches in the round-robin against Pat Rafter and Pete Sampras, and then a hamstring injury ruled him out of his final match. Yet he was not the only one suffering with injury. Sergi Bruguera was also forced to pull out of his last match, with back problems. Bizarrely, after several players declined the opportunity to replace the Spaniard, Henman got the call and actually ended up winning his one-off game against Kafelnikov.

With 1997 swiftly drawing to a close, all that was left now was for the awards season to get into full swing, and unsurprisingly Rusedski won big. He pushed Henman into second place to become the first British tennis player to claim the BBC's Sports Personality of the Year Award and a week later was named as the recipient of the 'Services to Tennis' Award at the annual LTA gala.

However, the fact that Rusedski was collecting all the accolades did not sit well with Henman, and in December he was misguided enough to put his name to a ghosted article headlined 'You're really getting on my nerves, Greg', which accused Rusedski of 'sitting there grinning and collecting all the prizes'. He continued: 'The memory of seeing Greg rather than me, rise from his chair to receive award after award has made me more committed than I have ever been in my life.

'There is not a problem between us, there's no animosity although everyone knows Greg and I are hardly best of friends. You won't find us going out to dinner together and contrary to what he's been saying, I can't remember any friendly football kickabouts, either.

'It's a case of me going my way and he going his. But the fact we aren't close is only natural because such an intense rivalry has developed between us. It's just that I want to be better than Greg.

'Greg reached the final at the US Open and that was marvellous but I have to say I wouldn't have minded his draw. What he achieved throughout the year did come as a surprise to me. Never in my wildest dreams did I expect him to make number four in the world and reach a Grand Slam final.'

Although Henman later told Rusedski that the article's content had embarrassed him and that there were no hard feelings, what was clear was that the pair did not exactly get along like a house on fire. They were different personalities with different interests and tastes.

But their quarrel came to a head in February when Henman pulled out of the World Team Cup, scheduled for May on Dusseldorf's clay, the first time Britain had qualified in nineteen years. This team event is based on ATP rankings and a year earlier, when Henman was Britain's number one, Rusedski was urged to take wild cards by David Felgate, in order to try to better his ranking so they might play. Rusedski claimed it was the perfect way to prepare for the French Open, as there were no rankings points at stake.

But it was because there were no ranking points on offer that Henman did not wish to participate. His energies were centred on two things: gaining ranking points in order to catch up with Rusedski and getting Great Britain's Davis Cup team back in the World Group.

Yet it was not Henman's decision to play elsewhere, forcing Britain to withdraw, which particularly bothered Rusedski. It was more the fact that Henman had made the decision not to compete without informing Rusedski first. 'Tim talked to the press before I knew,' he said. 'I'm disappointed. This is a case of Britain's top player not making the final decision.'

Never the closest of friends, now the pair were not even on speaking terms.

Great Britain's Davis Cup captain, David Lloyd, ordered the players for clear-the-air talks, in an attempt to stop what had previously been a reasonably cordial rivalry turning into outright animosity, and managed to repair the rift somewhat in time for the Davis Cup 5-0 demolition of Ukraine in Newcastle in April, but the victory handshake was a formal one. No hugs, no high fives.

Perhaps the disharmony created should have been taken as a signal that this was not to be a happy spring for either man.

The opening quarter of the season had seen Rusedski already reach three finals, winning one in Antwerp and losing two at the Split Open and Indian Wells Masters, where he recorded the fastest-ever serve: 149mph. He had also equalled his third-round best finish at the Australian Open, achieved back in 1995.

As for Henman, after taking the scalp of world number two Pat Rafter to progress to the Sydney International semi-finals, he embarked on four consecutive ATP Tour events, starting at the Australian Open, without winning a single match. The drought ended at the Guardian Direct Cup at London's Battersea Park, where he reached the quarter-finals, and also gained a last-four berth at the Super 9 in Key Biscayne.

Spring got into full swing with the start of the clay-court season, which brought with it its regular dose of the blues for the British men, who once again struggled to find their feet on the sliding surface.

Rusedski managed just one win, in Hamburg, from five tournaments, and though Henman achieved solitary triumphs in Munich, Hamburg and Rome, he joined Rusedski on the first plane home from Roland Garros after falling at the first stage. However, Henman's defeat was forced upon him, after a back injury picked up in practice forced him to retire. No point wrecking your body with Wimbledon and greater potential for ranking points on the horizon.

And so it proved, for Henman at least. The British number two made tremendous strides in his two grass tournaments. He achieved his first-ever quarter-final at Queen's but, more importantly, he became the first British semi-finalist at Wimbledon since Roger Taylor in 1973. Henman was back as the number one in the heart of the nation.

Rusedski, meanwhile, suffered ankle ligament damage in a fall during his third-round match with Italian qualifier Laurence Tieleman at the Stella Artois Championships. The British number one was forced to retire from the match and never really recovered in time for Wimbledon. When he took to the court for his first-round match against Australian qualifier Mark Draper he lasted less than three sets before deciding his ankle could take no more and withdrew.

The repercussions were huge. His coach Pickard dropped him, blaming a total breakdown in communication after Rusedski decided to rely on advice from an Iranian holistic healer who believed he was fit to play Wimbledon rather than heeding Pickard's warning to rest his ankle. The former Great Britain Davis Cup captain also felt that Rusedski was deliberately keeping secrets from him after being unable to contact him several times the previous week. Rusedski later appointed Sven Groeneveld as his replacement.

His ranking also suffered as a result of being forced to miss seven weeks of action. While Henman surged up to 13, after his successful grass campaign, and followed that with a final in Los Angeles and a last-four place in the Super 9 Canadian Open, to move up to number ten (the hundredth player to break into the top ten since the ATP began its computer ranking system in 1973), Rusedski's enforced absence saw him drop one place to seven.

It was the first time in the twenty-five-year history of the ATP that Britain had two players simultaneously in the top ten, and only the United States could share the same boast at the time, with Pete Sampras at two and Andre Agassi at eight. More important, though, was the fact that Henman was now breathing down Rusedski's neck in the Britain number-one stakes, with just 301 points separating them.

Henman may have been celebrating his elevation into the top ten for the first time, but Rusedski was perhaps facing the toughest challenge of his career, with little time to prepare for the US Open and the danger of slipping several places down the ranking because of a large total to defend from all the points he earned for the reaching the final in New York the previous year. Yet he looked back to full power in his first tournament back at the RCA Championships in Indianapolis, making the last eight without dropping a set, thanks to tough wins over Magnus Larsson of Sweden and 12th seed Francisco Clavet. In his final pre-US Open tournament in New York's Hamlet Cup he went one further by reaching the semi-finals without dropping a set. His successful comeback from an ankle injury was rewarded by a 6th seeding at Flushing Meadow.

Henman, meanwhile, who topped up his US Open preparations with a last-eight finish at the Pilot Pen International in New Haven, was given a seeding of only 13th after he was passed by Alex Corretja, Karol Kucera and Yevgeny Kafelnikov in the rankings. But while Henman managed to justify that seeding by making the last sixteen, before losing to eventual runner-up Mark Philippoussis, Rusedski failed to get past the third round and world number 21 Jan Siemerink.

The consequence was a rise for Henman to 11th, but a drop of rollercoaster proportions for Rusedski, who crashed nine spots to 15th. It was the first time in fifty-one weeks that Rusedski had not figured in the top ten and he had also officially to cede the British number-one position to Henman after holding it for fifty-five weeks. It was time for Rusedski to regroup or face the prospect of falling out of the top twenty all together, given his great end to the previous year.

The new British number two was not the only one with considerable points to safeguard, however. Henman, after once again declining to take part in the clay-court Bournemouth Open (this time along with Rusedski), had big points, and a title, to defend in the ATP Uzbekistan Open. But, unlike Rusedski, he overcame the likes of top seed Kafelnikov and 4th seed Nicolas Escude of France to make a successful defence of the President's Cup, and as a result safeguarded his points.

Henman was now well in line to qualify outright for his first ATP Tour Finals in Hanover. He may have remained 11th in the latest world rankings, but only points won during the year count towards the eight-man Hanover finals and he was eighth, 306 points ahead of 9th-placed Petr Korda.

It was a remarkable turnaround in fortunes from twelve months earlier, when Henman was struggling to stay inside the top twenty, while Rusedski was the top Brit, sitting comfortably in the top ten and playing in the most illustrious of tournaments. Now it was Henman's turn to have that honour, and because he had progressed well in the four Grand Slams that year it meant a place in the Grand Slam Cup for a second time, while Rusedski headed to a hard-court event in Toulouse. However, Henman's hopes of repeating his last-four feat of two years earlier were swiftly blown away with a straight-sets loss to world number 13 Jonas Bjorkman.

In Toulouse, Rusedski reached his first final since March, despite having to settle for second best behind his US Open vanquisher, Jan Siemerink.

The pair now faced a frenetic round of indoor tournaments, an environment which suited their game, to finish the season, with Rusedski at this point lying just three places behind his great rival. He had rediscovered the form he had demonstrated before his ankle problems, but it was because of that lengthy lay-off that he probably had too much ground to make up for Hanover. In addition, any hopes the British number two had of leapfrogging Henman in the rankings depended largely on what happened in the next event in Basle, where Rusedski was defending champion.

But whereas Henman cruised effortlessly into his fourth final of the year, Rusedski was caught cold in round two by German qualifier David Prinosil. Henman delivered arguably the best performance of his career to defeat world number eight Andre Agassi to win in Basle and, for the first time, record back-to-back ATP Tour tournament victories. Consequently, he rose to 10th in the rankings, his second time in the top ten after hitting the heights in August for seven days, and, more encouragingly, the points he earned in the Swiss Open had taken him to 7th place in the race to qualify for the season's Hanover climax.

Rusedski's ranking, however, took a further hit as he was defending not only a title but also a major haul of ranking points and so slipped from 14 to 17. But he responded in encouraging fashion in his next tournament, the CA Trophy in Vienna, by eliminating three top-twenty-five players, Yevgeny Kafelnikov

(9), Thomas Muster (23) and Pat Rafter (2), to reach the last four, and move back up four places to 13.

Henman extended his run to twelve successive victories in Vienna to make the quarter-finals, only to feel the wrath of Pete Sampras and win just three games in a straight-sets victory for the world number one. The Briton's form appeared to dwindle after that trouncing, despite moving up to a career-high world number nine. He was defeated by 49th-ranked American Jan-Michael Gambill in the second round in Stuttgart, an event that Richard Krajicek went on to win, catapulting himself in the Hanover reckoning and leaving Henman, who had seen Karol Kucera also usurp him, at 9th.

With only two tournaments of the season left, Henman was now the underdog for the end-of-year championships, despite his place having looked assured a week earlier. And when he could manage only another second-round finish in the Paris Open hope was fading rapidly, only to flourish once more when news filtered through that Krajicek and Rafter had suffered injuries which would rule them out of the event.

Henman was now back up to 8th for the race for Hanover, and when he sealed a semi-final berth in his final tournament in Stockholm his place in the end-of-season jamboree was secured.

Rusedski also enjoyed a very fruitful end to the season, beating Rafter again, in Stuttgart, to make the last eight, reaching a semi in Stockholm and achieving his first Super 9 win, in Paris, with the defeat of world number one Pete Sampras in straight sets. He finished the year at 11th in the world rankings, two places behind Henman, but missed the Hanover boat by just one place and so was made first reserve at the event.

But when Andre Agassi was forced to retire with a back injury against Alex Corretja, Rusedski was thrust into action to complete the American's round-robin fixtures. He went on to defeat Albert Costa – another late entry, who came in when Marcelo Rios of Chile scratched – in straight sets, and then in his final group match he used his explosive serve to gun down Henman, cruising to a 6-2, 6-4 victory in just sixty-seven minutes. He may have won the battle, but the war was already lost as Henman had qualified for the semi-finals, the first home player ever to do so, after wins over Rios and Corretja. Rusedski failed to join him, however, with Agassi's result counted as his own, and so he lost his chance when Corretja beat Costa.

Henman's gallant run at the ATP Tour World Championship was brought to an end when he was beaten 6-4, 3-6, 7-5 by Carlos Moya in the opening semi-final. It meant that Henman finished 7th in the 1998 world rankings and Rusedski 9th, the first two British players to have finished in the top ten in the same year since rankings had begun.

It boded well for 1999, but while Henman started the new season by making the final in Doha, Rusedski did not win his first match until his third tournament, the Australian Open. Even then he managed only the second round before being trumped by world 187 Paul Goldstein, while Henman went only one stage further, losing to 31st-ranked Marc Rosset, as both Britons failed to justify their respective seedings of 8th and 6th.

Rusedski did not really begin to pick up form until mid-February and Rotterdam, when he looked on course to create one half of an all-British final, but world number two Kafelnikov put paid to that idea by defeating the British number two in the last four and the British number one in the final.

Henman had an instant opportunity to get over that Rotterdam final disappointment, with a chance to lift his first major title on home soil in the Guardian Direct Cup at Battersea, but his quest hardly got started. He crashed out in the first round against Slovakia's Jan Kroslak, ranked 79 in the world, allowing one of his characteristically awkward performances against lesser opposition to develop into a full-blown dismal defeat. Rusedski was left to fly the British flag, and he went all the way to the final, where he was beaten by Krajicek in three.

Yet what was momentous about this tournament was the fact that Henman and Rusedski entered the doubles as a pair, the first time they had done so outside the Davis Cup competition, in order to prepare for their upcoming clash with the United States. The duo combined well and looked comfortable in each other's company as they failed to drop a single set on their road to claiming the £35,000 first prize.

It was a remarkable achievement, considering a year earlier they had been barely on speaking terms. Their relaxed display now seemed to lay to rest the stories of ill-feeling between them. 'Our relationship has come a long way,' said Henman. 'Differences in the past were blown out of all proportion. We have sorted them out and spent a lot of time on the practice court together.'

At one point their relationship had degenerated to such a degree, owing to their acrimonious rivalry, that their contact at tournaments was restricted to mumbled greetings and nods of acknowledgements in the locker room or courtesy cars. But that all changed with the appointment of Japanese-American Kenny Matsuda as Rusedski's fitness coach at the end of 1998. He made both men realise that the stand-off was serving no purpose and that the best way for each player's talents to flourish was to work together.

'I sat down with Greg and spoke to him about this and tried to get him to take the initiative and strengthen their relationship on and off court,' Matsuda said. 'I urged both of them to act as a team when they are out on court together instead of just being out there because they have to. I told Tim that the more he played with Greg the more he would enjoy it because Greg would relax more and it would bring out the best in him, which is what has happened. Tim is a totally different character to Greg, much more animated.

'There is still a rivalry between Tim and Greg, make no mistake about that. The difference is that it is no longer so personal and tense. They have developed a mutual respect for each other which is genuine.'

Ironically, following their doubles triumph, their very next tournament pitted the two against each other in the last sixteen at Indian Wells.

On this occasion it was Henman who held his nerve, overcoming a nightmare second set to triumph 6-4, 2-6, 6-4 in a match that saw eight breaks of serve. He came unstuck in the quarter-finals, though, losing to American qualifier Chris Woodruff, who found extra reserves to overcome the below-par Brit 6-1, 1-6, 7-5.

At the beginning of April five names separated Henman and Rusedski in the world rankings, with Henman 7th and Rusedski 12th. Incidentally, Henman had also soared in the doubles rankings, reaching 70th after another doubles triumph, this time with Frenchman Olivier Delaitre on the clay courts of Monte Carlo.

It was a rather successful season for Henman on clay, by his standards, as he had won five matches in four tournaments, including one quarter-final in Hamburg, in the build-up to the French Open. Rusedski was a little slower in getting started on clay, not capturing his first clay-court scalp of the season until his third tournament, the Italian Open. Yet, by the time Roland Garros came around, the pair seemed to have overcome their apathy about playing on red brick dust. Henman won his first match there, in three attempts, and both reached the third round, the first time in twenty-one years that two Brits had done so.

Henman threw away a two-set lead to lose in the third round to Spaniard Alberto Berasategui, world-ranked 97, while Rusedski went one further before being upset in straight sets to Uruguay's world number 140, Marcelo Filippini. Their clay-court endeavours had, for once, set them up nicely for the English grass season. Henman made the final at Queen's and another semi at Wimbledon, losing both to Pete Sampras, while Rusedski made the quarter-finals at the Stella Artois Championships, a semi at the Nottingham Open and a finish in the last sixteen at SW19.

Their fine form over recent months now saw them established in the top ten, with Rusedski 9th and Henman nestled nicely at 5th. But Henman's reign as British number one was about to come under threat, as he hit a poor streak of form, helping Rusedski to rise. He won just three times in his five-tournament North American hard-court season, including a first-round exit from the US Open. Rusedski, meanwhile, played just two tournaments and managed a final berth in Boston, where he lost to Marat Safin, and a last-sixteen finish at Flushing Meadow.

Then, after Henman decided against defending his title in Tashkent, Rusedski moved ahead into 6th, despite going out in the first round to journeyman Laurence Tieleman by virtue of having no points to defend in the tournament. But that was certainly not the end of the issue.

Despite finishing 16th in the qualifying race for the Grand Slam Cup, Rusedski squeezed into last place in the twelve-man field, after Pete Sampras, Pat Rafter and Todd Martin all withdrew through injury. Henman had qualified outright for the event, but he also pulled out, in order to pursue lesser prize money in Toulouse because he was desperate for ranking points, which are not available at the Munich event.

It was ironic, then, that when Rusedski defeated Gustavo Kuerten, Yevgeny Kafelnikov, Andrei Medvedev and Tommy Haas to register his greatest success by winning tennis's richest competition, it caused a fall in his world ranking to 8th, while Henman, who could only manage the second round in Toulouse, went up one to 6th, and therefore re-established himself as British number one.

The yo-yoing for the British tennis throne continued for the final two months of the season. Henman's failure to retain his Swiss Indoors championship title in Basle – he lost in the final to Karol Kucera – coupled with Rusedski's triumph in Vienna's CA Trophy, meant a drop from 6th to 11th for Henman, eliminated in round one in Vienna, while his great rival rose one place to 7th.

The pair were stuttering to the season's end, with Rusedski complaining of fatigue and Henman a second-round casualty in Stuttgart's Eurocard Open, which ruled him out of the ATP Tour World Championship as he had now slipped to 11th in the Hanover table, and Rusedski was 13th, despite reaching the last four in Stuttgart.

Rusedski's season was about to end in the most miserable of circumstances. In the second round in Paris the reigning champion picked up a hamstring injury which forced him to default after losing the first-set tie-break against Albert Costa. The injury ruled Rusedski out for the season and as he had failed to protect his Paris points, his rival Henman now had the perfect opportunity to capitalise. But Henman made hard work of it, reaching the third round in Paris and only the second round in Stockholm, but, despite finishing the season in 12th, he had won the race for the British crown in 1999, after Rusedski slipped to

14th. It was the first time in over a year that Britain was without a player in the top ten.

It got worse for Rusedski when the season came to its close. On 22 December he had to undergo surgery to shave off bone spurs and remove a cyst from his right foot. The recovery process meant he did not open his season until February, but then a recurrence of the problem caused him to miss much of the North American summer hard-court circuit. He did not return again until the US Open, the injury having claimed a total of three months of his 2000 season.

Rusedski ended the year 64th in the ATP Champions Race, the new ranking system where every player starts the season from zero and accumulates points based solely on how they do in that particular year, and without a title for the first time since 1994. Henman ended the first year of the new century in 10th place, with titles from Vienna and Brighton (his first on home soil) to his name, as well as making finals at the Cincinnati Masters, Scottsdale and Rotterdam.

The British number two rebounded from an injury-plagued 2000 season to finish in the top thirty in the ATP Champions Race at the end of 2001 and captured his first ATP title in fifteen months in San Jose, with wins over Australia's Lleyton Hewitt, Belgium's Xavier Malisse and America's Andre Agassi, the world number one. But Henman eclipsed his rival once more, finishing 2001 with his third top-ten ranking in the past four years at 9th, as well as capturing two titles for the second straight season, both of which were indoor, in Copenhagen and Basle, where he did not drop a set.

Nevertheless, Rusedski looked like he was returning to his form of old. With hopes high of a good 2002 season, what better way to get one chomping at the bit for the year ahead than an early season head-to-head against your greatest foe?

It was to be their biggest encounter to date, their first Grand Slam encounter in the third round of the Australian Open. Rusedski was seeded 28th and Henman 6th. It was the seventh time they had played each other, with Henman holding a 4-2 record over Britain's number two. Rusedski had not beaten Henman since their Singles Championship encounter at the end of 1998. Since then Henman had won three times on the spin, at Indian Wells in 1999, and at Adelaide in 2001 and 2002.

Henman certainly went in as favourite, if their form in previous encounters was anything to go by, but he also had the upper hand in the popularity stakes. The *Sun* carried out a survey to see which player the sporting heavyweights favoured, and Henman came out on top every time.

Newcastle United boss Bobby Robson said of their impending showdown: 'I have a soft spot for Tim, and if I was pushed I'd say he's the one who is truly English. Former England Rugby Union captain Bill Beaumont suggested the same: 'Deep down I would prefer Henman to win, because he was brought up in England, and he has been so close so often.' Test cricket veteran David Gower concurred: 'I would like Henman to do it because he has a better chance of winning the tournament than the other fellow.' And Martin Offiah, former Great Britain Rugby League wing, declared: 'I want Henman to win because he is a true Brit – but it's going to be close.'

It was clear Henman was not just the British number one in tennis terms but also in the popularity stakes, all because he had been born in Britain and Rusedski had not. His greater popularity was also underpinned by the amount he had earned in sponsorships because of this fact. He was earning millions from such things as selling breakfast cereal and margarine, advertising a high-street bank and wearing an expensive Swiss watch. Rusedski once commented on their endorsement earnings: 'There's no comparison between the two of us in those terms. Tim gets a hundred times more. He's in another solar system; I'm on planet Earth.'

Such was the magnitude of the Australian Open grudge match that BBC1 cleared its schedule between 9a.m. and 1p.m. to allow full coverage of the showdown.

Each player was in prime form both technically and physically, with Henman unbeaten in 2002 thanks to his title win in Adelaide and Rusedski having won in Auckland, after losing his only match of the season thus far to Henman.

Under the lights of the Rod Laver Arena and before a record night crowd at the Australian Open of almost 15,000, the two Brits fought out an epic battle. Henman played beautifully, volleying to perfection, his selection of shots impeccable. As a result Rusedski cracked first, losing his serve in the tenth to give Henman the opening set 6-4.

The British number two shoulder's slumped still further when he lost his first service game of the second, as the frustration began to grow. However, he did manage to engineer a way back into the match as Henman served for the second. Rusedski had break point at 5-3, when Henman appeared to hit a volley long, only for the baseline judge not to call it. Rusedski was fuming. He dropped his racket in disgust and raged at the umpire: 'The ball was out! The ball was this far out. You are blind. This is fucking bullshit. You are fucking unbelievable. You should be embarrassed with yourself. How can you miss that? Are you watching a different match? I mean, that is disgusting.'

Television replays did show that the ball had actually landed on the line, but that did little to quell Rusedski's anger. He was still muttering furiously when Henman was serving at deuce. Predictably, Henman took the next two points for a two-set lead.

But Rusedski was not finished yet, as his rage gradually began to work for him. Fired up, he recovered to win the third 6-1 in just twenty-nine minutes, to put himself back in with a shout. However, not even the inconsistent Henman was about to lose this encounter from two sets up. He was too solid, too strong when it counted, and saved three break points when serving for the match at 5-3, before sealing the fate of Rusedski with a brutal backhand smash.

The two players shook hands and Henman put an arm around his rival's shoulder as they departed the court.

Sadly, Henman lasted just one more round before going the way of Rusedski, and making an exit from Melbourne International Airport after losing in round four in straight sets to world number 23 Jonas Bjorkman.

However, Henman still went on to have one of his most successful seasons. He responded to his Australian Open failure by reaching the final in Rotterdam for the third time, only to come up short in three sets against Nicolas Escude, 11th in the Champions Race. Henman went on to reach a further two more finals that year, but lost both to Australia's Lleyton Hewitt, at the Tennis Masters Series in Indian Wells and at Queen's, his third final there in four years.

He opened the clay-court circuit with his first career semi-final on clay at Monte Carlo, where he beat the then world number one, Thomas Johansson, and Argentina's world number ten, Juan Ignacio Chela, before losing in three to Carlos Moya, ranked 21st. He ended the clay season with marks of 8-5, despite only making the second round at the French Open and losing in the opening round in Rome, his solitary first-round loss of his nineteen-tournament season. After making the semi-finals at Wimbledon, where he lost to Hewitt for the third time that season, he achieved his all-time-highest entry ranking of 4th.

But disaster struck in August when Henman suffered

tendonitis in his right shoulder in Indianapolis, which forced him to withdraw from his third-round match with Dutchman Martin Verkerk. 'When my shoulder is high, that's when it becomes pretty sore. And the more you do it through a match, it deteriorates,' he said. Yet he battled through the rest of the season, and reached the third round of the US Open, despite being reduced to icing the shoulder at times, using ultrasound plus massage, to loosen up all the areas, and taking anti-inflammatories. He even played through the pain barrier in the Davis Cup tie against Thailand to ensure victory for Britain, receiving an injection to mask the pain and speed the recovery.

Henman finished 8th in the Champions Race at the end of the season, but missed out in the Masters Cup in Shanghai when French Open champion Albert Costa took the final berth as he was the highest Grand Slam winner who had not qualified automatically. Instead he underwent career-saving arthroscopic surgery at the end of the season, and was told by medical experts that, as part of his rehabilitation, alterations to his service action were required for the sake of his right shoulder otherwise he faced the possibility of his career coming to an end, just like Pat Rafter's had.

After missing the Australian Open, breaking a streak of thirty consecutive Grand Slam tournaments played, Henman returned to action in February, crowing his revival with his first Tennis Masters Series crown, in Paris, at the end of 2003, where he finished in the top twenty, at 14th, for the seventh straight year.

This is in stark contrast to Rusedski's fortunes ever since their last encounter at the Australian Open. He missed the French Open with a neck injury and lost to 38th-listed Xavier Malisse in the last sixteen at Wimbledon, despite beating world number 11 Andy Roddick in the third round. His best week of the season came in August at Indianapolis, where he beat number one Lleyton Hewitt in round three, number three Thomas Haas in the semi-final and Felix Mantilla in the final, to claim his second ATP title of the year.

However, this was followed by possibly his lowest point of the season, at the end of the month. At the US Open he suffered pain in his left foot during his third-round defeat to Pete Sampras. The discomfort resulted in surgery being deemed necessary, and as a result he missed the rest of the season. In October he flew to Munich and the operation was carried out by the surgeon who had operated on his right foot for a similar problem three years earlier.

With the injury taking longer than expected to heal, Rusedski parted company with his coach, Sven Groeneveld, as he could not guarantee him a start date for the 2003 season. He was hoping to return in March at the Masters Series event in California, but that was postponed when his injury jinx struck again, after he tore cartilage in his left knee during practice at his winter base in Florida. Further surgery was required and the Zagreb Challenger, at the beginning of May, was pencilled in as his next intended comeback. But this time a shoulder injury forced his withdrawal and so it was not until the end of May, nine months after his last match, that he finally made his return.

It came at the French Open, but he was beaten in the first round by Russia's Nikolay Davydenko in straight sets. He did manage to put together some sort of form on the grass circuit, reaching the quarter-finals at the Surbiton Challenger, the third round at Queen's and then capturing his thirteenth career ATP title and second at Nottingham, dropping just one set all week.

However, at Wimbledon, when it counted, he was out in round two, losing to 5th seed Andy Roddick in three sets, and he managed just three wins in his next five events, including losing in the first round at Indianapolis, as defending champion, to Scott Draper, number 100 in the world, and at the opening round at Flushing Meadow to Gregory Carraz, ranked 111th.

Rusedski's injury-ravaged body took a further blow in September when he aggravated a back problem in the Davis Cup defeat by Morocco, putting an end to an awful season in which he had managed just four months of action. He also slipped to his lowest ATP entry ranking position since 1994, as he dropped outside the top 100.

Nevertheless, the British number two was determined to soldier on, and returned fit and ready for the start of 2004 at Adelaide. But on 8 January his career was hanging in the balance for a completely different reason. Rusedski announced he had failed a drugs test, taken back in July at the RCA Championships in Indianapolis, for the banned substance nandrolone, an anabolic steroid which enhances muscle building in the body.

The amount of the substance found in his urine sample was believed to be only a tiny amount over the permitted limit, but if he was found guilty he was likely to face a ban of up to two years, and having already turned thirty, it would more than likely have signalled the end of his career. He said in a statement: 'I confirm that I have been advised by the ATP anti-doping administrator that a sample I provided tested positive for a low concentration of nandrolone metabolites.

'I wish to make it clear that I do not, and never have, taken performance-enhancing drugs. This is a very complex situation which once understood will clearly demonstrate my total innocence. There is a hearing to be held in Montreal on 9 February, which I shall attend. I fully expect to be found innocent.'

Rusedski, claimed he was one of forty-seven players to have tested positive for nandrolone since August 2002, with all the samples showing an unexplained 'common analytical fingerprint'.

He concluded, therefore, that the samples were contaminated or that the testing procedures were flawed. In July the previous year the ATP had admitted that supplements provided to players had been responsible for 'elevated levels' of nandrolone in a number of samples in the preceding eleven months, and it was on this statement that Rusedski's defence centred.

Condemnations of Rusedski's apparent actions came from far and wide, with journalists declaring him guilty before the case against him was proved, and numerous players refusing to back their fellow professional. Todd Woodbridge, an elected voice of the locker room, slammed Rusedski for his aggressive defence, while Andre Agassi and Andy Roddick were quick to defend the sport's anti-doping policies. In addition, ATP Players' Council boss Todd Martin said he would be comfortable if Rusedski received a lengthy ban, believing 'the onus is on us to monitor what goes into our bodies'.

But amid all the criticism and back-stabbing lay an unlikely ally in Henman, who gave robust backing to his compatriot. 'I've got to know Greg pretty well over the years, practising and playing Davis Cup, and my gut feeling is he wouldn't do something like that.

'I think he's handled an incredibly difficult situation amazingly well. He's been out in the last two tournaments playing really well and I take my hat off to him for that.

'The whole thing is a strange series of events. I don't think there has been a case where the whole story has come out before the appeal process has taken place and that is where, I'm sure, it has been difficult for him.

'There have obviously been some positive test results, and there was a large number of players with raised levels of nandrolone. You just question how that has happened. There have been a lot of people making judgements, and I certainly wouldn't want to make judgements because I think it's best to see what everybody has to say on 9 February. I'm intrigued to find out what actually happens.'

Rusedski was made to sweat it out for a month, after his closed-door hearing in Montreal with a three-man independent panel appointed by the ATP. But on 10 March he was cleared of drug-taking, with the ATP admitting that they may have been partly to blame, owing to their failure to adequately inform players of the dangers of using a specific supplement.

Henman and Rusedski: friends they may never be, but after years spent reawakening the genuine hope of a nation by constantly pushing each other to new heights, mutual respect there always would be.

8

Wimbledon

Fred Perry. There is not an English summer that goes by without that name being mentioned in conjunction with the world's greatest tennis tournament. Perry remains the man against whom all British tennis achievements are judged. He was the last Briton to win the Men's Singles Championship at Wimbledon, where he was champion in 1934, 1935 and 1936. He was also the first person to win all four Grand Slams, a feat equalled by only Don Budge, Roy Emerson, Rod Laver and Andre Agassi. He claimed the US Open three times and the French and Australian Championships once each. He won forty-five of the fifty-two Davis Cup rubbers he contested and played in the winning British teams of 1933, 1934, 1935 and 1936.

But it was his victories at the All England Club that Perry cherished above all others, writing in his autobiography: 'Wimbledon has been the scene of my greatest triumphs.' It is nearly seventy years since he clinched his third and final singles title at the All England Club. Ever since then his achievement has cast its shadow over every male player with 'GB' beside his name on the draw sheet at SW19.

Although he caught the odd glimpse of Perry wandering about Wimbledon, Henman never got to meet the greatest English player, who died in February 1995. Rather than be inhibited by Perry's record, however, he views it as an inspiration. 'When I've been growing up, coming through in junior tennis, it's almost been used as a negative against us. It's always been reported that we haven't had a Wimbledon champion since Fred Perry, emphasising how poor the standard of British tennis has been. But I think it's something I've tried to use as a positive to spur me on to try and achieve whatever I can in the game.

'People do start putting labels on your head about being the next British hope, as it were, but I've never had a problem with dealing with that. I've always remembered, with the help of people around me, that I've just got to concentrate on what I do best. If I keep working and do the things that I've done, then I'm sure that I will continue to have good results.'

If Henman needed any reminder of Perry's legacy, it is embodied in the gates named after him at the Somerset Road entrance and, more strikingly, the statue by the main Church Road gate in the shadow of Centre Court. The bronze monument to Britain's most successful male tennis player of the 20th century was erected in 1984 to mark the 50th anniversary of his first singles championship. British tennis fans are still waiting for a native son to be its next Wimbledon champion.

Roger Taylor reached the semi-finals in 1973, the year thirteen of the sixteen seeds and seventy-nine men boycotted the Championships to protest against the International Tennis Federation's suspension of Yugoslavia's Nikki Pilic for skipping a Davis Cup match.

The field was wide open, and Taylor was the highest seed left after Ilie Nastase was upset. But against Jan Kodes in the last four, Taylor choked badly in the fifth set, losing to Kodes, the eventual champion.

In the 1980s Britain had John Lloyd to cheer for. But the closest he came to the All England Club's champions' dinner was with his then wife, Chris Evert, a three-time Wimbledon singles champion in 1974, 1976 and 1981.

Henman is now the chief torchbearer of the odyssey. His love affair with the place began when he was just a child, when he sat in the stands on Centre Court admiring Bjorn Borg play. 'There was definitely a moment when I was on Centre Court for the first time – I was watching Borg play his first-round match and he'd won the four previous years – when I felt that this is where I wanted to be, and at that age I had no idea what winning Wimbledon was going to entail but it definitely wasn't a case of "I want to play out there", it was much more a case of "I want to win out there". Every time I play on Centre Court it's fulfilling a dream.

'It's the most famous court in the world. When you reflect on all the great champions that have played on Centre Court it's an honour and a pleasure every time you have the opportunity to step out there. It is what tennis is all about. It really is awesome. I love hitting balls and competing wherever I am in the world but it doesn't get any better than this.

'Looking at it now, it seems quite small compared with, say, Roland Garros or Melbourne Park, which are so huge, but it has a lasting impact on you.'

Henman made his name on Centre Court in 1996, when he defeated reigning French Open champion Yevgeny Kafelnikov, and expectation has snowballed ever since. Fans wave, or paint Union Jacks on their face, and shout, 'Come on, Tim!' like he is a one-man football team. Outside Centre Court hundreds more pile in front of a big screen on the side of Court One that has come to be known as Henman Hill.

'Just when I walk on the court and put my bags down, they start sort of chanting my name,' Henman said. 'It gives you a big lift. That's before the match has even started.'

Most fans don't care how their hero performs the other fifty weeks of the year so long as he is up for it during Wimbledon fortnight. They believe the first six months of the season are spent leading up to it and the next six are spent recovering from it.

During those two weeks in the summer when Henmania sweeps through Britain, he gets more attention than David Beckham or the royal family, and most of them are in the Royal Box watching him. He becomes the focus of national hero worship as he progresses through the early rounds. Then he is beaten and derided as a serial loser, a choker, and becomes the butt of countless needless jokes.

'I've been playing this game long enough to understand that the reaction in the press to me not winning Wimbledon was always going to be negative,' he said. 'That doesn't mean that I agree with it, but the expectation will always be there and it's out of my hands. It's something I can't control so I don't let it worry me.

'It's hard to explain to anyone who has never played a major tennis tournament what it's like out there on the main court: there's a feeling of nakedness, the crowd and the television cameras can see absolutely every emotion you're going through. You're completely exposed.

'It's always been the absolute highlight of my year, of my tennis career, playing at home. Wimbledon has always been my favourite tournament. If I was to come into this time of year not enjoying the spotlight and the attention that goes with it then that would absolutely affect my performance, but I've always thrived on it.

'If I sat and thought about all the thousands at Wimbledon who will be willing me on and the millions that will be watching on television and all the things the media were saying about me, I would be a fruitcake by the time I walked out on court. It would be difficult to play decent tennis. You have to shut that out and focus upon the task at hand. I have learnt to draw inspiration from the support without being pressurised by it. It is one of the reasons that Wimbledon has consistently been my most successful venue.'

Tennis experts have acknowledged that Henman faces the toughest pressure on the circuit when he plays at Wimbledon, because of the weight of expectation placed on him. The audience expects, nay wills, him to win every match. No player can do that.

Philippe Bouin of the French sports newspaper *L'Equipe* said: 'You put so much on Tim Henman, and you don't see what he has achieved over the last ten years. He has huge talent, not maybe enough to be the top champion you would like to have, but what he has made with his talent is great. I wouldn't bury him for not winning Wimbledon.'

Rene Stauffer of Switzerland's *Tages Anzeiger* believes that 'the Swiss have more respect for Tim Henman than the British do – he's got a great record both here and against Federer, so it's sad to see how much he's made fun of among the British public and media'.

No one understands the constant and unrelenting pressure that Henman lives under at Wimbledon better than Virginia Wade. She carried the same burden of expectation until, at the seventeenth time of asking, she won Wimbledon in 1977, the year of the Queen's Silver Jubilee.

Wade knows how difficult it is to make what the British public perceives as a simple step-up from semi-finalist to winner, having made the last four twice, as well as the quarter-finals three times, before finally bridging the gap. 'This is where the public goes a little silly,' she says. 'They seem to think it's just one more step, but it's a huge difference and it's two steps not one. They don't seem to realise that it's relatively easy to get to number ten in the world but to get to number one, it's just fine tuning, fine tuning, fine tuning, belief, belief, belief.'

Andy Roddick, whose Grand Slam triumph on home soil at the US Open in 2003 brought him an invitation to appear on all the major TV chat shows, reckons he works anonymously compared with the media circus that pitches camp around Henman. 'I'm not under this kind of microscope at the US Open,' said Roddick. 'I can't begin to relate to what he experiences here as there are a million other things people can talk about in New York, because in the States the sporting focus is so spread.'

Australia has not seen a home grown player win its Grand Slam since 1976, yet a similar level of expectation is not laid on the shoulders of Lleyton Hewitt, a player who has won Grand Slams at Flushing Meadow and Wimbledon. 'British tennis is waiting for a Grand Slam champion – and Tim is the best chance going,' said Hewitt. 'In the locker room, everyone knows the pressure and expectations that Tim has to deal with at this time of the year. And everyone respects how well he deals with it. The way he handles the pressure and comes back and plays extremely well at Wimbledon year after year is a credit to him.

'He'd fully deserve it if he comes away with the Wimbledon crown one day. Even if he never wins Wimbledon, it's pretty amazing what Tim has done there.'

Henman has come as far as the semi-final stage at Wimbledon

on no fewer than four occasions. Each time the public has swelled with pride at the prospect of a British victory, only to see it cruelly taken away.

In 1998 much was hoped of the now established top-twenty-ranked Henman. He had made the quarter-finals twice in the previous two years, and the public expected him to push on this time round.

The Championship Committee handed him a seeding of 12, four places higher than his entitlement by world ranking, after his impressive endeavours at SW19 in the past. He was paired with Czech Jiri Novak in the first round, a player ranked 86th in the world and who had arrived in the country only the day before their match, after winning a clay-court Challenger in Zagreb.

Henman was eager to end the tie in quick time so he could catch England's World Cup football match against Romania on television, due to start at eight o'clock. The pair were third on Court One, and Henman looked odds-on to witness the kick-off in Toulouse when he slogged his way to a two-set lead and then went a break up in the third. However, his concentration appeared to periodically lapse and three dropped service games later we were entering a fifth set.

He managed the vital break in the fifth game of the final set and that was greeted with understandable relief by a frustrated crowd, who had earlier been shouting out for him to finish the match quickly so they too could watch the England match. Tension was further eased when he held to go 4-2 up and then engineered another break in Novak's next service game. Eventually he served out to move into the second round 7-6, 7-5, 5-7, 4-6, 6-2, seventeen minutes into England's World Cup Group clash.

Fortunately for Henman, he was sparred a roasting in the next day's papers after failing to conjure up a comfortable win over an inferior opponent. The rags were too busy carrying out a post-mortem on England's defeat by Romania, which had left their World Cup hopes hanging by a thread.

However, two more far from convincing wins over South African qualifier David Nainkin and doubles specialist Byron Black, who both won a set off the Briton, left many in doubt as to whether he could seriously mount a challenge for the Wimbledon title.

Little did they know that a very different Henman would turn up in the second week, one that was ready to produce some of his most inspired tennis, and how he needed it. In the last sixteen he was up against 5th seed and reigning US Open champion Pat Rafter. Henman was flawlessly in control throughout, despite losing the second set on a tie-break, and carved out an impressive 6-3, 6-7, 6-3, 6-2 victory to reach his third consecutive Wimbledon quarter-final.

As the morning of the quarter-final dawned, a nation was mourning England's exit from the World Cup at the hands of Argentina the previous night. The papers were all laying the blame at the door of Beckham, after he was sent off for petulantly flicking out his right leg at Diego Simeone, who had barged him over, the Argentinian collapsing to the floor as if he had been shot.

It was up to Henman to lift the country by treading new territory and overcoming the 3rd seed and Australian Open champion Petr Korda to make his first-ever Wimbledon semi-final. The Czech was struggling with an ankle injury, picked up in the previous round against Dutchman John van Lottum, but he insisted that this would not stop him rubbing salt in Britain's gaping wounds. 'I shall stand out there and fight,' he promised. 'I will not give in.'

But even a fully fit Korda would not have been able to cope

with his opponent that day. It was easily Henman's most convincing performance of the Championships so far. Within two minutes he had already broken Korda's serve, and rammed home the advantage by dropping only three points on his own serve in the remainder of the opening set.

The Briton was similarly effective in the next set. He was serving like a demon, refusing to allow his opponent room for manoeuvre. As a result, when Korda double-faulted twice in the seventh game of the second, there was no way back for him.

The rampant Henman eased through the third set, to ensure a 6-3, 6-3, 6-2 victory in just an hour and forty minutes. It could not have been much better. A packed Centre Court erupted into a standing ovation as their hero, arms aloft, broke into a rare grin.

'It was a great match and probably the greatest result of my career,' said an elated Henman afterwards. 'I was very focused and did the job as well as I'm capable of. I don't think I could have asked for more. There wasn't a break point on my serve, which is obviously a good sign for things to come.

'When I served to go 3-0 up my confidence soared and I just seemed to go from strength to strength. In the end it was a clinical performance and I think a better one than my fourth-round win over Pat Rafter. It was strange once I broke because it occurred to me I had never broken serve in a quarter-final before, and it gave me a lot of confidence. I think I was pretty clinical in the way I took my opportunities. Every aspect of my game was really working. I was very relaxed, calm and in control of my game, and when you have that sort of feeling it makes life a lot easier. I feel I'm serving as well as I ever have in the last couple of matches.'

At last, after twenty-five long, bewildering years, Britain had its first semi-finalist since Roger Taylor defeated a callow Bjorn Borg. And what a tantalising semi-final to savour – against the defending champion and top seed Pete Sampras. The American was gunning for his fifth Wimbledon title, having yet to drop a set during this campaign and had lost just once at the All England Club in the last five years, against Richard Krajicek, the eventual winner, in 1996.

Nevertheless, Henman was confidence personified. 'To be in the semi-finals of Wimbledon is a great achievement, but I don't want to stop now. There won't be any pressure on myself. If I play the tennis that I've played and the tennis that I'm capable of, I have a good chance.'

The first set was closely fought. Henman had the first break point in the sixth game, but failed to convert it as he netted a simple backhand volley. Sampras responded by serving an arrow-like ace into the corner. But the very next game saw the roles reversed. Sampras pulled a forehand return out of the top drawer and followed it with a volley. This time it was Henman's turn to face break point. But while Sampras had replied with an ace, Henman reacted by double-faulting to drop serve. The world number one broke his opponent again in his next service game, and that was that as Sampras served out for 6-3.

'He's gone,' came the despairing whisper from one observer aching with the pain of it all. Could this be the comprehensive straight-sets defeat we all feared might happen to Henman?

How fickle we were. Henman steadied himself and cranked it up a notch. In the third game of the second set he earned himself three break points courtesy of two great lobs and a delightful backhand pass. Sampras produced an ace to save one, but when he pushed a backhand volley into the tramlines on the next point, Henman had manufactured a notable breakthrough. How the crowd cheered.

They went even wilder in the fifth game. Henman, again picking away at Sampras's serve, moved to break point with a winning forehand service return and then watched as the American netted a forehand. Henman was leading 4-1. It was the first time since his Australian Open quarter-final defeat to Karol Kucera that Sampras had lost his serve twice in a match.

Henman was producing tennis that at times was simply beyond the reach of Sampras. English hearts were bursting with pride. He even conjured up a serve so powerful that it broke his opponent's racket, which was swiftly flicked into the crowd. Although Sampras answered Henman's second break in kind, he was clearly rattled. He was reduced to ranting at the umpire over admittedly dodgy line calls and slapping himself on the leg to urge the right response. Henman dropped just one more point in the set, to claim the first set yielded by Sampras that year and make it honours even. Now we had a match on our hands.

The tennis in the third set was perhaps the finest of the entire tournament, frequently brilliant and always riveting. Henman's volleying was awesome, but some of the returns conjured up by Sampras were equally impressive, an unforgettable amalgam of footwork, touch and power.

Henman held his second and fourth games to love, and did well to stave off a break in the sixth with a low forehand volley. The crowd was beside itself, but something had to give. And at 5-6, with Henman serving to stay in the set, it did. The Briton managed to repel two separate break points, to send the game into its second deuce, but Sampras got his third with a backhand-cross court return. This time Henman was induced into an error, hitting the net with a backhand volley, to give Sampras the game and the third set. The American punched the air in jubilation as if he had just won the final.

Henman failed to capitalise on a break point in the first game of the fourth, and that was his only chance of staging a fightback gone. At 2-1 in the fourth Henman double-faulted twice and was then undone by two volleys, losing his serve. There was only one man looking like the winner now. Henman fought to the end, thwarting the champion's first match point, before succumbing to another Sampras ace.

The winning margin of 6-3, 4-6, 7-5, 6-3 did scant justice to Henman, who on another day would have earned more for his endeavours. But that was of little consolation. 'Scores are irrelevant,' he said. 'It's about winning and losing. I raised my game but it was still not good enough. He's relentless.

'That said, the experience is invaluable. I came into the game thinking I could win. And at a set-all going with serve in the third set it was anybody's game. But at 5-6 he came up with the goods. Right now losing hurts. But in a day or two I'll probably look at this and take the good things from it.'

But Henman had clearly impressed Sampras, who would go on and claim his fifth Wimbledon in the final against Goran Ivanisevic. 'One day he's going to win this thing. I'll tell you that. I don't think there are many holes in his game. He's only twenty-three and will get stronger. There was a lot of emotion out there. But that is what I play for. I had to raise my level today and when I won the third set I knew I had him. Make no mistake, this is my toughest test by far. It's tough on him but he will come back from this a better player.'

Henman was given the perfect opportunity to avenge that defeat just a year later, when he was drawn to meet the American at the same stage again. The British 6th seed overcame more early-round hiccups against world number 54 Arnaud Di Pasquale of France, before keeping his serve in tact to romp past Chris Woodruff, 126th in the world, in straight sets, and Sebastien Grosjean, listed 30th, in four.

In the last sixteen he produced a performance of raw courage against former world number one Jim Courier, saving three match points in the fifth to bring the man dubbed 'the Streetfighter' to his knees in the second-longest match in Wimbledon's 120-year-plus history. Henman showed nerves of steel to walk out the winner in a 4-6, 7-5, 7-5, 6-7, 9-7 epic, after four hours and thirty minutes of breathtaking and rain-delayed Centre Court drama.

His next match proved a far less strenuous proposition, against former Wimbledon finalist Cedric Pioline. He swept through the first two sets, at the expense of just six games, before the Frenchman hit back to win the third 6-4. But then Henman romped away with the fourth set, clinching a clash with the champion with an ace in winning his decisive service game to love.

So there he was again. A Wimbledon semi-final, with the colossal and immovable obstacle of top seed and reigning champion Pete Sampras once more standing between him and a place in the final of the greatest tennis tournament on earth.

'I'm happy with my game and if you want to win the tournament you have to beat the very best,' said Henman. 'My game has come a long way. I feel much more consistent and having played in a semi-final it's a good experience to have under your belt. I just want to continue the way I've been playing. I don't feel I've got anything to lose. I shall go out and enjoy it. When you look at Pete's record he's played forty-five matches here in the last six years and he's won forty-four of them. That record is self explanatory.'

It was only two weeks earlier that the pair had stood toe-to-toe in the final of the Stella Artois Championships at Queen's, with no more than a cigarette paper between them. On that occasion just one break of serve had allowed Sampras to emerge victorious after losing the first set to a tie-break.

Sampras had reached the last four at Wimbledon with hardly a bead of sweat on his brow. The only scare came in the quarter-finals, when Australian powerhouse Mark Philippoussis raced to a set lead, before being forced out in the next set after tearing cartilage in his knee.

That presented Henman with the ideal chance to seek retribution, but could he ram home the advantage of a partisan crowd this time?

He came bursting out of the blocks on Centre Court, holding his opening service game, and then broke Sampras to give his army of fans the chance to roar their approval early on. But the defending champion proved just why he was the world's number one by refusing to buckle under Henman's onslaught and broke back immediately.

Neither man was looking particularly safe on his own serve, and, returning so magnificently, Henman instantly restored his advantage with a wonderful backhand return down the line. This time he consolidated his lead with his first ace of the match, to make it 4-1. Sampras was under pressure again in his next service match and only just managed to stave off another break point. He was playing like a nervous wreck, his service game in tatters after a plethora of double faults.

Henman closed up the first set confidently inside twenty-seven minutes, and when Sampras had to call for the trainer to massage an apparent thigh injury midway through the second set, fans were beginning to think the unthinkable.

But it was Henman who was to slip up next. As he was serving to stay in the set, trailing 5-4, an intruder descended on the court, delaying the match and putting heavy strain on the nerves of both men. It was only a navigationally challenged pigeon, some light relief for the crowd, but Henman's concentration was consequently broken – and so was his serve, for he double-faulted on a Sampras break point. It was all-square, but the ascendancy was certainly now with the American.

He cracked Henman again in his opening service game of the third set to go 2-0 up, as the match began to rapidly run away from the Briton. Sampras was now serving more cleverly, varying his pace and angle to perfection, and when danger beckoned he had the tools to summon an ace or serve-and-volley his way out of trouble. That one break decided the third set.

By now the crowd had gone quiet, awoken to the reality of another semi-final defeat at the hands of the man they call 'Pistol Pete'. But Henman marched on gallantly, twice having opportunities to break Sampras for 4-2 and 5-3 leads. He could not exploit them, though, and as his resolve began to fade Sampras turned the screw, breaking him to love in the ninth game.

Sampras was now serving for the match, but the crowd were desperate for one more curtain call from their man. Alas it failed to materialise as Sampras whipped out the big serve to extinguish the threat and win through to the final, where he beat Andre Agassi to clinch a mind-blowing seventh crown. What Henman would give for just one!

His disappointment was plain, and as deeply felt as previously. 'Any time you lose it's disappointing. I am disappointed at the moment, but I'm sure in a week or ten days my attitude will be one that I want to go away and improve. I played OK but on the day I lost to the better player.

'The second set went away from me very quickly and he sort of went up a gear in the third. I dug my heels in in the fourth and just kept my nose in front. You create one chance and it's just a question of whether you can take that. If I could have done that it might have been different, but it wasn't to be today. I felt like I was getting on his serve, couldn't have any complaints early on. It was just a question of getting a cushion in the second, which I couldn't do.

'But I'll keep coming back. I'll give it one hundred per cent. I'll give it everything I've got.'

A change in centuries, however, did not equate to a change in fortunes for Henman at Wimbledon in 2000. In fact it resulted in a very disappointing campaign.

Despite falling a set behind in his first-round match with Paradorn Srichaphan of Thailand, ranked 104th, he rallied and eventually eased through 5-7, 6-3, 6-1, 6-3. He then brushed past world number 61 Arnaud Clement and Hicham Arazi, ranked 26th, with such ease that it seemed his time at Wimbledon had finally come, or so everyone thought.

Nothing could have possibly prepared Henman for the hurricane that hit him in the last sixteen, in the form of Mark Philippoussis. It looked like being a massacre on Centre Court, with Henman hardly having time to catch his breath during a whirlwind opening set in which he was mauled 6-1. But he refused to go out without a fight, and dug in to take the second set 7-5 before winning a tie-breaker to go 2-1 up. He failed to maintain that momentum, though, and the tide began to turn against him again in the fourth set, as Philippoussis kept hammering in his devastating serve and maintaining the pressure to crack his opponent at 4-2, and level up matters, 6-3.

There was barely a rally in sight, but the tension felt among the spectators was unbearable, and it was perhaps as a result of one of their screams that Henman's challenge was unhinged. In the seventh game of the decider, with the score at 0-30 in favour of Philippoussis, Henman was preparing to dispatch an easy volley when a female voice let out an excited 'yes' from the stands. Her actions clearly startled him and he pushed his shot long.

The 8th seed shot a vicious glance in the direction of the yelp, but it did little to ease his anguish. He managed to save two of the break points, but he could do little with the third when the Australian's mis-hit lob landed smack on the baseline. At 5-3 Philippoussis was serving for the match and a quarter-final meeting with Agassi. Three massive aces gave the 10th seed a handful of match points and, though Henman was able to save one, he was powerless to stop the final serve booming past him.

Philippoussis raised both arms in triumph, while Henman snapped his racket against his foot. It was easy to get another racket, but another broken dream would take longer to mend.

Yet by the time Wimbledon 2001 came round, it really did look like being Henman's year. The top seeds were falling left, right and centre. Eighth seed Juan Carlos Ferrero went out to Greg Rusedski in the third round, as did Yevgeny Kafelnikov, seeded 7th, to Guillermo Canas, while 5th seed Lleyton Hewitt was downed by the 24th seed, Nicolas Escude, in the last sixteen. But the biggest upset of them all came when reigning champion Sampras, Henman's scheduled opponent for the quarter-final, was upset by a little-known Swiss who goes by the name of Roger Federer, the number 15 seed.

Henman, seeded 6th, had gone about his progression with relative ease, in the early rounds. He had relative walkovers against Artem Derepasko and Martin Lee, losing just twelve games, and although he was sluggish in the first set against number 26 seed Sjeng Schalken in round three, he capitalised when the Dutchman began to lose his pace, and won through by three sets to one.

To prevent a repeat of the previous year's fourth-round exit, however, Henman needed to stage a brilliant comeback. He fell two sets to one down to Todd Martin overnight, while struggling with a stiff back, but emerged a different player on

Centre Court the next day, demonstrating his intent with an opening ace before taking the final two sets for the cost of just five games to complete a battling 6-7, 7-6, 4-6, 6-3, 6-2 win.

Then came the precocious Federer. Roared on by a 14,000-strong crowd, Henman produced some exquisite tennis at the net and, with the help of his serve-and-volley game, gained the edge in the first two sets, 7-5, 7-6. But he went perilously close to sabotaging all that fine early work when he suffered a trademark lapse in the third set.

Despite holding to love in the opening game of the third, Henman then proceeded to lose five games in a row. His game was being cut to pieces by some sustained Federer brilliance, the teenager unleashing the full range of his extraordinary groundstrokes. The Briton halted the slide, holding to love for 2-5, but the Swiss player made sure of it by serving out the set, to leave everybody in the arena on edge.

The fourth set see-sawed one way and then the other, with Henman breaking for 4-1, only to be forced into saving seven break points in two service games, and then clawed back after squandering a position two points from victory when serving for the match at 5-3.

It went to a tie-break, and as Federer racked up the points to establish a 5-2 advantage, Henman summoned the tenacity from within to come back from the point of no return and win four points on the spin. At 6-5 he was serving for the match, but he had not yet quite finished extracting every drop of emotion from the poor people at courtside and the millions watching at home.

He failed to get his first serve in on the twelfth point, but on his second the ball fizzed and leapt, Federer's return went long and the agony was finally over. Henman raised a fist, did a twirl on court and threw a ball joyously into the crowd, who drew a collective sigh of relief.

'To come through a match of that nature and that much drama feels very satisfying,' he said. 'When that last ball went long my first reaction was to make sure the line judge saw it, then an immense amount of relief. I know my games should come with a health warning. I've been in some tight situations but I don't think I have played in a match that has felt as close as that.

'I really fancy my chances and I've given myself a great opportunity to do it this time. I feel like my game has improved and that I'm a much better player than I was when I made the semis on the other two occasions. If I'm honest, I'm just pleased not to be up against Pete Sampras again. I've lost to him on both occasions. I feel I can do it now.'

In the semi-final Henman was up against a wild card who had been sending shock waves through Wimbledon and ripping through the competition. Goran Ivanisevic had come close enough to touch the Wimbledon crown but never able to take home the prize despite appearing in three finals in 1992, 1994 and 1998. Now, approaching 30, it looked like the animated Croatian's last chance had passed him by as he slumped at 125 in the world. But he pleaded with the Championship committee to give him one last chance, which they granted on the basis of his past record and entertainment value, and he thanked them by stunning a string of big-name players, including 21st seed Carlos Moya, Greg Rusedski and 4th seed Marat Safin, to steal a march into the last four.

Henman had never lost to the big-server in four meetings, including one on grass at Queen's in 1998, and he vowed to maintain that record in order to finally clinch a Wimbledon final, the first Briton do so since Bunny Austin sixty-three years earlier. 'My record against Goran is great and I've never lost to him in four matches,' he noted. 'But Goran has always had the tools to win this title and you can never count him out on grass. The pressure on me is there all the time, but I feel I am playing well enough at the moment to do it. As long as the crowd remain behind me, I am confident I can beat Goran.'

Ivanisevic started the better. His first service game took only one minute, while Henman's lasted eight, as his opponent took him to three deuces. The wild card was producing a phenomenal serving display, aces and unreturnable deliveries simply exploding from his racket.

Unexpectedly, though, the first threat of a break fell to Henman in Ivanisevic's third service game, thanks to two slices of good fortune – a net-cord winner followed by a Henman mis-hit. But it was extinguished as quickly as it arrived with a 133mph ace, already the Croat's third of the afternoon, which eased him into a 3-2 lead.

Though Henman twice managed to take Ivanisevic's serve to deuce, the set was inevitably heading towards a tie-break. Then, out of the blue in the twelfth game, Henman found his serve under threat as he attempted to stay in the set.

At 15-30 the Croat played a forehand winner to give himself two break points, his first of the match. He then flourished his racket to bludgeon another forehand winner past Henman's outstretched arm to break service and take the set. A stunned realisation dawned over the crowd as they began to fear the worse, especially when the battering continued into the second set. Ivanisevic thundered another four aces past Henman in his next two service games and by the time he took his third service game to love to lead 3-2, his ace count was already in double figures.

Dark clouds were beginning to descend on Centre Court. At a time like this Henman would probably have welcomed a break from swinging at air.

The rain never came, though, as the second set went into football's version of a penalty shoot-out. Ivanisevic created two mini-breaks for himself but squandered both as the chinks in his armour began to show. Now it was Henman's turn. After an hour and twenty-seven minutes he had his first set point and lost it. But two minutes later he closed out the set and levelled the match.

What came next can only be described as a turnaround of epic proportions. It was as if Ivanisevic had been replaced by someone else as he proceeded to lose game after game in the third set, his serve failing him time and again. He had been broken only three times in the entire championships beforehand, but in the space of fourteen and a half minutes Henman broke him three times in a row.

The three-times finalist's game had completely deserted him as he won a mere four points throughout the third set. Henman had clicked into top gear, unbeatable on his own serve and at the net, completing the set whitewash with a superb lob.

An hour later, rain was now the last thing Henman wanted, but that is exactly what happened. At 6.19p.m., with Henman leading by two sets to one, two games to one, and 40-30 down on Ivanisevic's serve, the covers were dragged on, the players rushed off and play suspended for the day.

Henman was a mere four games away from a place in the final.

'Finish Him Tim!' ordered the *Sun* the next morning. 'Come on Tim, Nothing Can Stop You Now,' proclaimed a buoyant *Mirror* back page. 'Hen on Top as Goran Loses Plot,' announced the *Daily Star*, above a sub-headline which read 'Super Tim's Set to Reign'. There appeared little doubt in anyone's mind that it was just a matter of time before Henman won.

Britain expected, but maybe not quite what they thought.

It was almost 24 hours before the match could recommence,

as the covers stayed on because of downpours until 5.38p.m. Ivanisevic produced an ace first up, to preserve his serve. It was the only thing keeping him in the match. He could hardly return the ball, as his volleys persistently found the bottom of the net.

Henman manufactured the only break point of the set, but it was saved by his opponent, setting up another nail-biting tie-break.

As Henman took a 3-1 lead, only four points separated him from a date with destiny. But Ivanisevic stunned the packed Centre Court crowd by fighting back to 5-5. Henman was now just two points away, on Ivanisevic's serve. An ace, his thirtieth of the match. Set point. Ivanisevic sent a bullet delivery over the net, but Henman's return went long. The crowd gasped in disbelief, the umpire called for silence.

It was all level, and Henman was back to square one. The fifth set started, but it didn't finish. With Ivanisevic leading 3-2 and Henman 30-15 up on his serve, the green sheets came on again. Less than an hour's play had been possible before the rain returned.

There was a slightly different mood the next morning across Britain. The *Sunday Mirror* said, 'Tim's Clinging in the Rain', while the *Mail on Sunday* believed 'Tim's Big Chance Hangs by Thread'. It was 'Water Torture for Tim' in *The People*.

Play resumed at 1.13p.m. the next day, with Pat Rafter, the 3rd seed, waiting patiently to see who he would be facing in the final. By 1.27p.m. he had his answer.

Henman comfortably won the first game of the day to even the fifth set at 3-3, but in his next service game, having seized two break points, he served a double fault to give Ivanisevic a third chance.

This time the Croat made no mistake, delivering a superbly executed backhand return winner. He was 5-3 up and serving for the match. At 40-30 it was match point. He dropped to his knees and prayed – but double-faulted. Deuce. He pleaded again. His first serve faulted, but he went for broke with his second serve and earned his thirty-sixth ace of the match. A second match point. This time his first serve stayed in, but Henman's return floated wide. Ivanisevic threw himself to the ground in celebration of a 7-5, 6-7, 0-6, 7-6, 6-3 win, en route to becoming the first wild card to win Wimbledon.

Henman looked close to tears. You simply can't get closer to a Wimbledon final than that. It was a hat-trick he had been dreading. His two defeats by Sampras in 1998 and 1999 may have been disappointing, but those feelings of despair would have been ten times as bad as he trudged back to the SW19 locker room after this one. 'I certainly did my best. But, unfortunately, it was not good enough this year,' he said. 'I have to give Goran credit for the way he played. It was a tough, tough match, but he was the one who came out on top.

'It has been a pretty long three days, but it was the same for both of us. Sometimes these breaks can hinder you or they can help. It certainly helped me against Todd Martin. In this instance to come back the following day, he obviously gets a chance to regroup, regain his rhythm and his serve. That's obviously what happened. But I can't complain.'

It was the first time Henman had gone into a semi-final where it was expected, rather than hoped, that he would win. Unfortunately, by the time 2002 came round he was once more the underdog as he headed into his fourth semi-final in five years.

He had not played particularly brilliantly at Wimbledon that year, in matches that he should have won with ease.

In the first round Henman was so superior to French qualifier Jean-Francois Bachelot there was hardly a murmur on Court One throughout the match. The Briton had to work the crowd in the next two rounds, with spectators initially sitting quietly, expecting him to win. He dropped a set against Scott Draper, a mighty 230th, and Wayne Ferreira (51), before prevailing in four.

However, he did show courage in his five-set fourth-round win over Switzerland's Michel Kratochvil (45) and quarter-final four-setter against Andre Sa (90) of Brazil. Henman was suffering from dizziness, as well as feeling sick and tired, but such is his desire to succeed at Wimbledon he ploughed on to victory in both matches.

ATP trainer Bill Norris explained: 'I massaged his legs to try to get some life back into them then I popped one of the ammonia capsules [smelling salts]. He inhaled it and it cleared his head. He wasn't dizzy after that. I think it was all down to stress. I'd be surprised if it was down to anything that Tim ate – he isn't the most adventurous of eaters. In most cases these days it's nerves when players complain of upset stomachs. I massaged his stomach a little bit because I thought a darn good fart would do him good.'

Thankfully, he was fighting fit by the time of his semi-final against world number one Lleyton Hewitt. It was the first match of the Championships that he would have been expected by the majority to lose, especially as he held such a dreadful record against the Australian. Henman had not won in five matches against Hewitt, four of which were finals, including one at Queen's that year.

If he stood any chance, he needed to produce an exceptional performance. But even though the 4th seed played his best game of the tournament he could do nothing to subdue the spirit of Hewitt. He raised his game brilliantly to attack his opponent, but was swept away as the brash Australian left Centre Court gasping with a magnificent display of passing shots and flowing tennis. Hewitt's cross-court shots were sublime, he hit the angles time and time again, chased lost causes and served well. Some of his scrambling to get the ball back was reminiscent at times of Boris Becker when he used to throw himself all over the court.

On other points played from the baseline, visions of a young Andre Agassi came to mind as the top seed passed Henman when he came to the net. In other words, he played as well as you would expect a world number one to play and thoroughly deserved his straight-sets 7-5, 6-1, 7-5 win after two hours and nineteen minutes. Henman would not have been ashamed of his performance on the day, but the defeat was made worse by the fact that rank outsiders David Nalbandian of Argentina, the 28 seed, and Xavier Malisse, seeded 27th, were battling out the other semi-final on Court One. As it was, though, Hewitt was the one to prosper, and he defeated Nalbandian, for the cost of just six games, in one of the most one-sided finals in history.

Afterwards Henman said: 'I am obviously very disappointed and the other semi makes it a bit more difficult. The person who came through the top half of the draw was going to be the favourite. I felt if I could have got through, I would have had a good chance of winning the final. But I have to give Lleyton all the credit. The better player won today, no question. My game wasn't good enough. The way he plays and the way he adapts his game to any surface, he is the best in the world and he proved that. It wasn't for lack of effort. I couldn't have tried any harder. That's good enough for me, although I'm sure that to others it won't be good enough.'

Many have been forced to accept that after that last semi-final defeat, Henman may never win Wimbledon. He has had two more efforts since, but both times bowed out at the last eight, to 13th seed Sebastien Grosjean in 2003 and the unseeded Mario Ancic in 2004. The records certainly back up this pessimism. Only four players have won their first Grand Slam over the age of twenty-seven in the Open era – Andres Gomez, Thomas Muster, Petr Korda and Goran Ivanisevic. And no player has won Wimbledon at thirty-plus since Arthur Ashe in 1975.

But despite entering his thirty-first year, Henman believes that as long as he can carry on playing Grand Slam tennis there is still every chance of achieving that dream that emanated from Centre Court when he was just five years of age.

'I think it's fair to say I've been a fairly late developer,' he admits. 'I still think I've got a lot of years in front of me, and a good chance of winning.

'I am certainly not one of the young guys any more but, injury and health permitting, I'm going to be playing for a while yet. Mentally, I will still have the desire and motivation to keep improving. Age is just a number and not something I pay a lot of attention to. As long I want to do it, I will be doing it. The desire becomes stronger and stronger once you learn about the game. I have tasted what it could be like.

'To reach four semi-finals is a hell of a record but a lot of people think of it as a negative because they feel I am a nearly man. If you said to a golfer "I've had fourteen top-ten finishes," they'd say, "That's absolutely phenomenal!" But if I lose in the quarter-finals, it's, "Oh that's not great." But that's top eight. It's the way you perceive it. Is the glass half-full or half-empty?

'Against Hewitt was the worst I played in six years but I took a lot of positives from the fact I reached the semis. It is very much an individual thing. It comes down to commitment, motivation and desire – mine is as strong as ever.'

Henman does have one complaint, though. 'The Goran match was unique, lasting over three days because of the weather. I can't say I don't look back on it and think, "What would have happened if it hadn't rained?" But maybe I'm a bit philosophical, because I say, "Tough shit. It rained." If it hadn't rained, I probably would have won, because I was in the process of dismantling his game. But we will never know that. I kind of believe in fate. It was pretty hard to swallow but in the other three semis I had no complaints.

'After each defeat the media were like, "What did you do for the next three days? Were you locked up in a room and didn't want to come out?"

'But I was arranging where I was going to play golf. Sure, I was disappointed not to be preparing for a Wimbledon final but I lost to better players.'

Nevertheless, Henman is fully aware that, after he has come so close in the past, losing in four semi-finals and three quarter-finals, it seems the media will judge him on Wimbledon alone. He accepts that he will be branded a failure if he hangs up his racket without getting his hands on the one trophy he craves most.

'The common perception of me here is that I am a good player but have yet to win the big one. Yes, I'm a good player but I've got to improve if I want to win this tournament.

'I'm not going to hide. I'm sure a lot of people will judge me and if I don't win Wimbledon they'll say I failed. That's fine, I can't control that. I've always said that if I could choose to win one Grand Slam it would be Wimbledon and I'm going to do everything to succeed.'

Tim Henman, as English as strawberries and cream, warm champagne and rain on Centre Court. A good English hero, a good player and a good loser. But it remains to be seen whether he will make a winner.

9

Classic Matches

Just midway through 2003 and Henman was already wishing it was over. A great sporting year for many, as an English national team finally won a World Cup for the first time in thirty-seven years (albeit in Rugby Union), this was certainly not turning out to be a happy one for him.

At the end of the previous season he had undergone surgery on his right shoulder, which he had injured during the North American hard-court season. The operation forced him out until February, meaning he would miss the opening Grand Slam of the year in Australia – breaking a sequence of thirty consecutive Grand Slam appearances.

He finally staged his comeback in Rotterdam at the World Indoor Tournament, a place that had given him many good memories in the past as he had made the final on no fewer than three occasions, in 1999, 2000 and 2002. However, in this instance there was only gloom on offer, as Henman failed his first test after his lay-off, losing in straight sets to Croatian world number 49 Ivan Ljubicic. His form continued to falter for a while after that, and by the end of May, eight tournaments later, he had won only six matches. Also, he had been ousted from the world's top fifty during this period.

Inconsistency ensued, with good performances at Queen's and Wimbledon followed by early exits at several Masters Series and at the US Open. Already it seemed minds in Team Henman were switching to 2004, having consigned 2003 to the wastebin. But come October and the Paris Masters, Henman's final tournament of the year, that all changed. And for once it was for the better. But it may never have happened if it were not for a twist of fate.

Henman originally had no intention of going to Paris, accepting an entry just three days before the tournament began. He came in as a late replacement for former Australian Open winner Thomas Johansson, who was forced to withdraw from the tournament with a knee injury. And after six months blighted by injury himself, Henman knew how the Swede was feeling.

Despite the fact that he was unseeded and knew he was likely to face a barrage of top-twenty players in order to make headway in France, the omens were good.

Henman's first-round opponent was twenty-two-year-old Nikolay Davydenko, whom he had also beaten en route to winning the Washington International Series Gold event in July, his first title of 2003. He had gone into that event after a month's break from tennis, having been knocked out in the quarter-finals at Wimbledon by Sebastien Grosjean. He explained at the time: 'I'm going to take some time away to recharge my batteries. I'll continue to do my shoulder strengthening exercises, but I won't hit too many balls for the next couple of weeks. The last few days have been a bit painful as I felt I had an excellent opportunity to progress further than I did at Wimbledon – and losing always hurts. But I think if I can continue the improvement I've seen in my game over the past few weeks, then it can be a successful trip for me.'

At first the decision to take that break appeared to be vindicated by his performances at that US-based International Series, which opened his summer hard-court season, and began his preparations for the US Open.

Seeded 10th, he recovered from going a set down to American Paul Goldstein to win 5-7, 6-4, 6-3, before dispatching Davydenko in straight sets in the second round.

Then came stiffer opposition in the form of Paradorn Srichaphan in the quarter-finals. He won that taxing encounter 7-6, 7-5, to set up a gruelling semi-final against big-serving Andy Roddick. It was the pair's first-ever meeting, but certainly not their last of the year.

The American, with home advantage, swept Henman aside effortlessly in the first set 6-1, and an easy win looked on the cards for the 2nd seed.

But Henman refused to be undermined, and recovered his composure to level the match 6-3 in the second set, and then seal victory in the third in a tie-break, to reach his first final since losing to Lleyton Hewitt in the 2002 final at Queen's.

This time Henman was determined to finish the job. 'It's been a tough twelve months. My shoulder problems have been well documented but I'm glad to put that behind me and concentrate on tennis. I felt happy in the third set. There were no breaks of serve. I lost the first point of the tie-break to an ace but then won the next seven points so I can't complain about that.

'It's going to be a tough match whoever I play in the final but I'm looking forward to being back in a final.'

Twenty-eight-year-old Henman was pitted against Chile's

Fernando Gonzalez, who had beaten world number one Andre Agassi in the semi-finals. But that failed to deter the Brit and he overcame the 4th seed in straight sets to lift the Legg Mason Tennis Classic trophy.

Preparations for the US Open, which was in less than a month's time, could not have started any smoother. But, rather than push on from his Washington triumph, Henman's preparations went into freefall and he failed to make it past the second round of the Masters at Montreal and Cincinnati.

When the US Open came round, at the end of August, he didn't fare any better. He was sent packing in the first round in straight sets by world number one Andy Roddick.

Many critics argued that Henman's serve was still paying the price of the shoulder surgery he had undergone in 2002. This was encapsulated in the final game of that US Open match, where he needed to cause Roddick real problems to stay alive. Instead, however, he proceeded to deliver a 100mph serve, followed by an 85mph effort, to hand the American two match points. Roddick required only one, however, when his opponent fired a forehand wide, and the Briton was out.

Henman had to wait until October to win consecutive matches again. He advanced to the last four in Vienna, before losing to world number seven Carlos Moya in straight sets.

The season was almost at its end but it was not until its final two weeks that Henman showed any form of consistency. He made the last eight in Basle, and then came Paris. All of a sudden, 2003, from being Henman's most gruelling season ever, was also to mark his greatest tennis tournament triumph.

He beat Davydenko 6-3, 6-4 in the first round before coming up against 7th seed Sebastien Grosjean, who had broken Henman and English hearts twice that year by beating him at the Stella Artois Championships and Wimbledon.

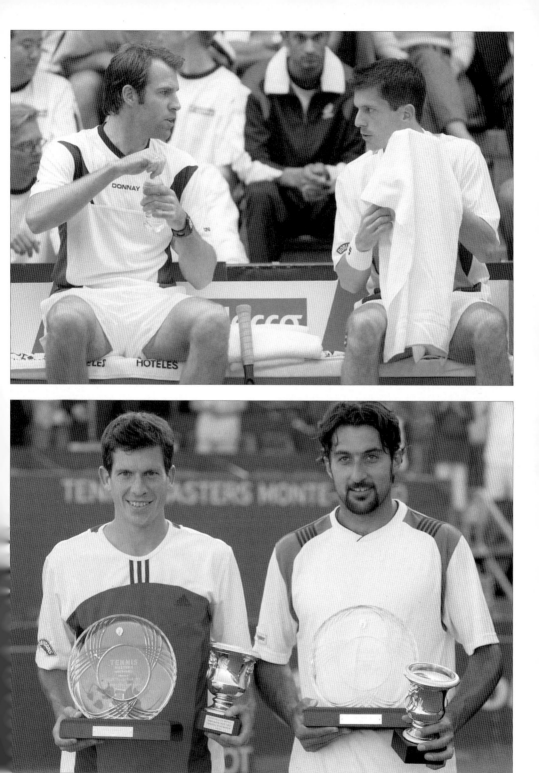

Above: In the mens doubles quarter finals against Luxembourg, Henman and Rusedski discuss tactics.

Below: He was crowned champion in the mens doubles with partner, Nenad Zimonjic of Serbia at the ATP Tennis Masters in glamorous Monte Carlo.

Posing with a medal of a different kind, Tim was awarded an OBE in 2004.

Playing on a rather different surface, Henman and Lleyton Hewitt play street tennis in front of the Eiffel Tower in Paris.

Above: At the Tennis Masters Cup in 2004, he was introduced to Former US president, George Bush.

Below: Prior to the same tournament, Tim and the other competitors for the mens singles title took part in a photo call. *From left to right*: Guillermo Canas, Gaston Gaudia, Carlos Moya, Marat Safin, Tim Henman, Guillermo Coria, Lleyton Hewitt, Andy Roddick and Roger Federer.

In 2004, Henman was chosen to help carry the Olympic flame through the streets of London. He is seen here, proudly holding the torch on the steps of the All England Lawn Tennis and Croquet Club.

Henman in action in the Masters Series in Hamburg, *above left*; the quarter finals of the Stella Artois Championship, *above right* and at Wimbledon, *below*.

Although Tim is extremely dedicated to his tennis career, he still finds time to relax with his family too.

Above: Going for a spin on a jet ski in Miami during a break from the Lipton Championships in Florida.

Below: The beautiful English home that he shares with his wife and two daughters.

Tim Henman displays his trademark clenched fist celebration. The victory was short lived though as he went on to be defeated by Roger Federer in the Kooyong Classic in Australia at the beginning of 2005.

Henman sensed retribution. 'I suppose this is a good opportunity to try and get some revenge on his home turf.

'He's played very well here in the past and I think in all honesty there's a lot more at stake for him than me. But I've got to try and use that to my advantage because I want to continue to play well, and there's probably that little bit of added pressure on him.

'I certainly don't think there's too much for me to lose, but lots to gain.'

Indeed, this attitude of nothing to lose was a theme running throughout his Paris campaign. Spending parts of 2003 absent from the courts, for one reason or another, had obviously given Henman a chance to reflect. Coming into the final weeks of the year fresher than most and regarding the season as a write-off, he really did have nothing to lose.

This outlook was truly exemplified in his game with Grosjean. He had lost the first set 6-3, but realising the Frenchman could not hurt him any more than he had done during that English summer, he fought back to finally vanquish some of those demons to claim the next two sets 6-4, 7-5, and the match.

He explained afterwards: 'It is pretty evident that my demeanour, my attitude on court, was pretty relaxed. I was down a set but I still felt I could win. This attitude of nothing to lose is something I have got to develop a little bit more.'

Brazilian Gustavo Kuerten, in the last sixteen, was the next to feel the force of Henman's new-found carefree style of play. Looking relaxed in his strokes, Henman took control after breaking the three-times French Open champion for 3-2 in the opening set. He attacked at every opportunity, regularly deceiving Kuerten with his changes of pace and the direction of his returns.

In addition, Henman served with speed and placement, breaking Kuerten twice more in the second set to lead 4-0. He also saved four break points at 4-1, before going on to strike an ace, followed by a superb forehand half volley pick-up and then another ace to win the match after seventy-five minutes in straight sets.

His morale high and confidence brimming, it seemed nothing could deter Henman from the prize at stake – not even Roger Federer, who was to be the next obstacle in his quest for Paris glory. He demoralised the Wimbledon champion by winning in straight sets 7-6, 6-1.

Henman had begun slowly, but was holding on to his own serve, saving two set points at 5-6, after failing to make an impression on Federer's serve. The set went to a tie-break. This allowed Henman time to launch an assault of his own. He rallied to a 6-3 lead in the tie-break before offering the Swiss youngster a route back into the set with a double fault. However, after steadying himself at 6-5 he lured Federer into hitting a forehand over the baseline on his own third set point, to obtain a set advantage after fifty-five minutes.

The second set was not as lengthy, lasting just twenty-four minutes, as Henman produced some of his greatest form in years. Federer's resistance was broken after he lost his serve for 1-3, double-faulting twice. Henman then broke to love for 5-1 and served the match out with an ace. The victory was greeted by a chorus of whistles and jeers from dismayed locals eager to see a Federer win, which was made unattainable by the rampant form of Henman. Job well done.

Awaiting Henman at the semi-final stage was Andy Roddick, the man responsible for his first-round demise at Flushing Meadow, on his way to winning the tournament. But Roddick was soon to realise to his cost that this was a different Henman to the one he had faced in August, or the one who had beaten him in Washington.

'I have the capabilities of serving a lot better because I am serving more aggressively, and I also feel I am playing better,' Henman told a crowded press room before the game. 'To play matches as consistently and consecutively, it's the best I've played. I am in a relaxed frame of mind and feel pretty confident.'

It certainly wasn't a case of confidence being misguided. From the first point he hit with precision and superb length to leave Roddick scampering all around the court. Arguably, it was an even more impressive performance than that in the previous round against Federer.

Henman's brand of serve-and-volley tennis consistently foxed the tousle-haired American, and his blocked returns against the world number one's serve, which yielded just nine aces, enabled him to break to fifteen in the opening game. It was only the third time Roddick had conceded break points in the tournament.

He reacted by attacking Henman, who was forced into saving a break point in the sixth game and three more in the eighth.

Fired up, Roddick stubbornly refused to give in and allowed Henman a miserly two points in the next three games, including finally breaking him to love when Henman was serving for the set.

As they went into the tie-break it seemed the impetus was certainly with Roddick. But Henman refused to buckle and clawed his way back into the match. The tie-break was delicately balanced at 4-4 until Roddick whipped a backhand into the net to hand Henman the initiative and a mini-break. Then some acrobatic volleying, followed by a nerveless service winner, guaranteed Henman the set, to the utter frustration of Roddick, who earned himself a code-of-conduct warning for banging his racket into the ground.

Henman appeared to have him just where he wanted. The second set was tense, with Henman continuing to play with authority but failing to convert any of the six match points put before him, and the result was a second tie-break. Henman netted a forehand with the first point of the tie-break but his recovery was swift and he won the next five points as Roddick's game turned ragged. Henman was in touching distance of the final, creating three match points at 6-3. But he was unable to convert any of them, as Roddick brought himself back into contention at 6-7. Anxiety could easily have set in, but Henman refused to concede, and finally completed victory, 9-7, when Roddick sliced his return to a slower serve into the net.

Tim Henman was in the final of the Paris Masters, and not even Roddick was going to begrudge him that. Taking defeat gracefully against the only man to have beaten him during the hard-court season in 2003, he described Henman as an extremely underrated athlete who stands out as one of the sport's best volleyers and boasts one of the most skilful sliced shots. 'It's almost like he can hit dimes out there on court, he has such great control. He stuck to his guns, played aggressive. That's what won him the match,' he said.

It was only the third time Henman had made a final in a Masters Series. His first was at the turn of the millennium in Cincinnati, where he was edged out 7-6, 6-4 by Sweden's Thomas Enqvist. His second experience in an ATP Masters Series final was not as tight. Indian Wells in March 2002 was the scene, as Henman's game was completely dismantled by Lleyton Hewitt. It is certainly a match he wishes had never happened.

That day Henman made too many unforced errors against the feisty Australian and was punished every time. He was broken in the opening game, but, despite breaking back straight away, he failed to hold his serve once in the first set, which ran away from him in almost embarrassing haste. Taking only six points from the last five games, he lost the set 6-1.

In the second set he fared only marginally better, holding serve just once as he succumbed to the awesome Hewitt 6-2. Never before had Henman had his own serve broken seven times in two sets.

No matter how relaxed he claimed his attitude had been in Paris in 2003, there is no doubt that after reaching the final, visions of that humbling by Hewitt must have come flooding back.

The opposition this time, however, was certainly no Lleyton Hewitt, but an unseeded Romanian, who was also a late entry into the competition. Ranked 191st, Andrei Pavel, too, had spent much of the calendar recuperating from injury.

There was no doubt that Henman was regarded as the favourite after being cast as the underdog in the four previous rounds. However, he knew he could not assume he merely had to turn up to beat Pavel. After all, his opponent had beaten Guillermo Coria and Germany's Rainer Schuettler, seeded 4th and 5th respectively, as well as Jiri Novak in the semi-final, in order to earn his date with Henman. Complacency was not an issue.

'The job is not done,' Henman insisted. 'If I start saying what an opportunity because I've never won a Masters Series title, then I'll suddenly put so much pressure on myself, and that's not what I want to do.

'It's going to be a big day and it's important I approach the final with the same attitude I have shown all week. If I do that, then I have a good chance.'

Besides, he had a history of faltering at the crucial hurdle, if his record of previous final appearances was anything to go by. In twenty-five final outings before Paris he had managed to hold aloft the winner's prize just ten times – less than half the number of times he had played a final.

'I'll work hard on staying loose on my serve while being aggressive and looking to move forward when I get the opportunity,' he said, 'then I won't be focusing on the outcome but hopefully starting to play good games. You win games, you win sets, and then, hopefully, you win the match.'

Henman was in no mood to slip up in this final and virtually bypassed the first set with ease, playing every point with great assurance. He broke for 3-2, and then Pavel aided his cause further by double-faulting to 5-2.

When the Romanian surrendered his serve again in the opening game of the second set, Henman grabbed the initiative and got himself into a position, leading at 5-4 and needing only to hold serve to take a two-set lead.

But errors crept in and he was broken. Another choking session looked on the cards, as the second set eventually went into a tie-break.

Henman took a 5-2 lead in the tie-break, but then double-faulted on his first set point at 6-4, which gave a route back in to Pavel, who pulled back level to 6-6. The pressure was certainly on, though it wasn't just getting to Henman, it seemed. After the Briton won the next point, Pavel threw down his racket in frustration. And when his backhand smacked the net on Henman's third set point, he threw the racket all the way to his chair.

But after taking his drinks break Pavel managed to regain his composure to really threaten his opponent's supremacy for much of the third set, and almost earned himself a break on Henman's serve, though he was unable to convert it.

That was the closest either man came to winning a break in the third set. As a result it eventually had to be decided by another tie-break, which Henman won in quick time.

He swept to a 5-1 lead, and won the title on his first match point with a powerful serve which Pavel could only return into the net.

The twenty-nine-year-old Romanian had been outclassed, hard though he had fought, and he knew it. 'I tried my best, but he was the best,' he said. 'I have no regrets because I had no chance.'

Henman's triumph was greeted with a standing ovation from the 14,000 capacity crowd inside the Palais Omnisports.

'Merci beaucoup,' Henman said over the microphone after receiving the Arbre Fanti trophy along with his first Waterford Crystal Masters Shield and a cheque for £420,000. The applause he received had been thoroughly deserved after his cool, assertive campaign to win a tournament he used to dread, having previously not advanced beyond the third round there.

'It's been an unbelievable week for me,' said Henman after the match. 'If you'd have told me six months ago that I'd win this title I'd have probably thought you were smoking something. When I came into the first round, I didn't have a particularly good record and I was a little unsure of the conditions. I'd never won a Masters Series title and I could count the matches I'd won here on one hand but from the word go I was in the right frame of mind and playing the right type of tennis. But then, after getting through to the final – having lost in two previous Masters Series finals – suddenly I really did feel the emphasis was in me.

'I got my tennis right this week and I don't want it to be an exception. The challenge for me now is to do it more often. I felt totally in control; I was playing the level of tennis where I had no reason to panic. Even so, the third set [against Pavel] was the most difficult of the whole week for me. I had to stay in the same relaxed frame of mind, and that is when he became more aggressive. The match point was the end of the nerves and tension. It was a great test of my mental strength and character to make sure that I went out there and played the same way.'

The Parisian fairy tale was complete, and no one was going to deny Henman his moment of glory. He had won this trophy the hard way, taking a collection of scalps that would satisfy even the most demanding of critics. Roddick, Federer and Kuerten were neither powerful nor adept enough to take even a set off him.

It was the most prestigious title win of Henman's10-year professional career, and helped propel him to an end-of-year ranking of 14th in the world. Only a month earlier he had been languishing in 40th spot and looking forward to 2004 in hope and back at 2003 in disgust. But the Masters win in Paris had changed all of that.

'Wimbledon is obviously at home and the most beautiful tournament in the world, but that tournament has always finished with a loss,' he said. 'This one's finishing with a final and a win, so right now this is definitely my greatest achievement. This had been my toughest year as a professional because of the shoulder injury. So when I beat Andy Roddick in the semi-final I thought no way am I going to let this chance slip through my grasp. It's been an incredible atmosphere this week and I look forward to defending my title. I am confident I can win a Grand Slam, and snatching a tournament of this stature can only reinforce your belief about that.'

Although in 2004 Henman demonstrated that his performance at the Paris Masters was not a one-off, his crusade to defend his Paris crown ended disappointingly. After receiving a bye into the second round, Henman, seeded 3rd, beat Paradorn Srichaphan in straight sets and appeared to be in fine form going into the next round against the unfancied Mikhail

Youzhny. He had put on a flawless performance against the Thai world number 26 and produced some of his best shots.

However, it was a completely different Henman that took to the court against the Russian. Despite being 5-4 up in the first set and holding a 0-30 lead after Youzhny missed two forehands, Henman failed to take advantage and seize the set. Consequently, Youzhny raised his game to recover and claim the first set 7-5.

The defending champion appeared completely deflated in the second set, his serve started to stutter and his forehand flapped aimlessly. Youzhny took full advantage to romp home 6-1 and win the match in an hour and 17 minutes.

With the elite Masters Cup in Houston just two weeks away, Henman was not happy. 'I wasn't very sharp on the court. I don't think my movement is particularly good. I wouldn't say I'm picking up the returns particularly well. I'm just a little bit sluggish. Physically, I'm not injured, I'm not ill, but I need to get a little bit more sharpness back.'

It was not the first time he had failed to make the later stages of a competition in which he was the title holder. Then again, since the turn of the century he has defended only three of the seven titles he has won, usually because injury has played its part in denying him the opportunity to do so.

Of the three 21st-century titles – Vienna (2000), Basle (2001) and Paris (2003) – he has attempted to defend, the furthest he has gone is the last eight in Basle's Swiss Indoor tournament in 2002. The Swiss carpet courts of Basle have been one of his most successful venues, where he has a 26-6 won-lost record. Since making his debut there in 1997 he has never failed to make the quarter-final stages in eight consecutive appearances. 'I've had a lot of success here and that's given me confidence coming here,' he said.

His debut tournament saw him edged out 7-6, 6-4 against big-hitting Mark Philippoussis in the semi-finals despite dropping serve just once in twenty-four games at that tournament. Sadly, it came against the Australian in the third game of the decisive second set.

After that match Henman said: 'You have to make one or two returns on his big serves and if you don't do that it comes down to the tie-break – and there is always the chance that he will play one or two great points which he is entitled to do.

'I can't have too many complaints with my own performance. I played a good match but it boils down to a few key points – and he won them.'

Henman appeared to heed his own lesson, as a year later he won the traditional October event, beating Andre Agassi in the final and claiming it to be the most impressive scalp of his career at the time.

His service was emphatic, his groundstrokes impressive and his volleying as incisive as ever.

'That was probably the best match I've ever played,' he explained. 'It wasn't just that the level was high, it was also consistent. Agassi's stature is of the highest pedigree, and to beat him in a four-set match is a really good feeling. From the first round my standard has just got better and better and to win a tournament of this stature is great for my career. This win is right up there with Wimbledon this year [where Henman lost to Sampras in the semi-finals] if not even greater. There were so many great players taking part here and to come away having won the tournament is one of my best achievements so far.'

Despite being seeded 8th, Henman had to beat players ranked in the world's top forty in every round in order to make that final, among them Sweden's Thomas Johansson and Nicolas Kiefer of Germany.

Against the shaven-headed Agassi, Henman had it all to do at 3-3 in the first set and with the American holding three break points. But he showed great bouncebackability to win five points in succession and then break the 8th-world-ranked player at 5-4 to win the first set. He carried that superb form over into the second set, surging into a 4-1 lead, breaking the American twice, before running out a 6-3 winner.

The deficit was reduced in the third set, when Agassi, who had been 122nd at the beginning of the year, found his best tennis. In the fifth game he chased down a lob to play a stunning cross-court forehand winner on the turn, which clearly unsettled Henman and allowed Agassi to break and eventually win the set.

A fifth and final set looked on the cards, but Henman clawed his way back from a break down early in the fourth set, to take successive breaks and give himself some breathing space at 4-2. But while Agassi fought back to level at 4-4, Henman broke crucially at 5-4 and displayed a killer instinct to round off the match in two hour and sixteen minutes and claim his first Swiss Indoors title.

Agassi was full of praise for his conqueror: 'I thought he did everything real well, the guy's a great indoor player, he plays well on a lot of surfaces but best when the ball stays low like grass or here. I had to get a shovel to get under his backhand slice, he served really big and didn't miss too many volleys – he impressed me very much.'

Henman made a stout job of attempting to defend his Swiss title in 1999, beating Roger Federer (then just 106th in the world) and Goran Ivanisevic in straight sets in the quarter-finals and semi-finals, respectively, to make back-to-back Basle finals. However, he was to experience how Agassi had felt a year earlier, for he lost to Karol Kucera in an epic four-hour, five-set tie-break decider.

It couldn't have started any worse for Henman as he was broken in the opening game by the Czech, who held on to that advantage to take the first set. The match then fell into a rhythm, with Kucera working primarily from the baseline and Henman attacking the net. Neither was able to carve out an opening, forcing the second set into a tie-break which the challenger won 12-10, to Henman's dismay. The Briton had held a set point at 9-8 but simply couldn't live with Kucera's serving, which had seen him persevere in the opening two sets. It looked as if he was having his title taken away from him with little ceremony.

But then the fightback ensued, which almost resulted in an astounding victory for Henman. After almost two hours he finally got the break he had been searching for, to open up a 2-0 lead in the third set. Signs of fatigue began to show in Kucera, who had only recently returned from a two-month lay-off after injuring his right wrist, as Henman broke him for a second time to take the third set.

In the fourth set Henman continued to apply pressure, once again recording the early break to even the match up at two sets apiece, sending the bout into a deciding set. The reigning champion was in supreme control and with his opponent looking drained and concerned, he appeared to be a clear winner. But, surprisingly, it wasn't to be.

Although he snatched an early break in the final set to lead 2-1, Kucera suddenly dug deep into his reserves and broke back immediately to send the match into another tie-break. Now it was the Czech who held the upper hand. He dominated the ensuing tie-break, establishing a conclusive double break. This time there was to be no comeback, as Henman surrendered the all-important tie-break with surprising ease, 7-2.

'It was a tough one to lose,' he recalled. 'It was disappointing to lose a final in that nature – a fifth-set tie-break. But I felt like I was hitting the ball well.

'I thought I had turned it around, I could have won. But it's difficult against a guy who returns serve as well as Kucera does; you can take nothing for granted. I don't think it's anything I did wrong; I think he just raised his game. I don't think there was a lot I could have done differently. I have no regrets, I couldn't have played better.'

Henman took another step back the following year, falling at the semi-final stage when he was thrashed in straight sets by Thomas Enqvist, despite not dropping a set in any of the previous rounds.

Struggling with his service game throughout the match, Henman lost his opening serve and then, just as he had made a break-back, he carelessly lost it again, and with it the set 6-1. In fact he only held his serve for the first time when he was 2-0 down in the second set, and, despite managing to hold on to his next three service games, it wasn't enough to slow his opponent, ranked 9th in the world, who broke again at 5-3 to wrap up the set and match.

The 2001 Swiss Indoors was Henman's most successful year in Basle, as he raced to his second title without dropping a single set, losing just twenty-three games in total.

Not even the likes of the 2001 French Open champion Carlos Moya or the home favourite, and Henman's opponent in the final, Roger Federer, could halt the number-two seed.

It was the accuracy of Henman's serve that was decisive against Federer, but he also executed his volleying with purpose and control. He needed just a single break in the sixth game to take the first set 6-3 from the twenty-year-old, who had ended Pete Sampras's Wimbledon dreams that same year.

Then a poor service game by his opponent in the next set gave

Henman an even greater advantage. From 40-15 up, Federer managed to drop his service to give a 4-3 lead to Henman, who never looked back. Federer was in disarray, unable to land a backhand to save himself, and the more his shots flew out of the court the more panic-stricken he became.

Although the Swiss youngster managed to hold his serve in the first game of the third set, Henman reeled off five straight games to go 5-1 up. And despite failing to seize his first match-point in the next game on his own serve, he didn't have to wait much longer to claim the match. He broke Federer in the following game and after just two hours he had secured the winner's cheque for £95,000. Federer, grief-stricken at the margin of his defeat in front of his home crowd, was reduced to tears at the closing ceremony.

'It was a very satisfying result. I didn't put a foot wrong all day,' Henman enthused. 'This week all my hard work paid off, and the end result was plain to see. I'm very pleased to have won my second title of the year [he had won in Copenhagen in February] but, more importantly, I'm delighted with the way I've played all week. My serve has felt great and it makes such a huge difference to my overall game. I mixed it up well and used both the body serve and the kick serve to great effect. When I'm volleying so well behind it, it's a very good combination. I expected a very difficult match but I didn't expect to play quite as well as I did and quite as consistently. I wasted very few opportunities.'

Holding back tears, an emotional Federer paid tribute to his superior opponent on the day. 'Tim just played very well and there was nothing I could do about it. He didn't leave me any chance.'

The 2002 event saw Henman produce his best title defence since the turn of the century, but it still turned out to be his poorest run in the Swiss Indoors, as he bowed out at the quarter-final stages, and fared no better in 2003 and 2004 by also failing to surpass the last-eight phase.

David Nalbandian was the opponent when Henman was defending his trophy in 2002 and the Briton, despite claiming the first set, lost the second on a tie-break and surrendered the third 6-2. It was yet another loss dished out by Nalbandian, against whom Henman had enjoyed little success over the years. From their five encounters he had only emerged victorious once, and that was in 2003 in his favourite Grand Slam of them all – Wimbledon.

Henman has always performed admirably on London's famous grass courts. However, the same cannot be said of his progress in the other three annual Grand Slams. Before 2004 he had never progressed further than the last sixteen in Australia, France or America.

Many observers have been surprised that Henman has failed to make it to the later stages of the Australian Open, given that he has always performed so well in the hard-court tournaments in the build-up to the southern hemisphere centrepiece. Henman himself has said: 'It's a tournament I should do well at. The conditions are favourable for me. It's a pretty quick court and the ball is lively. I think it does help the aggressive players, the serve-and-volleyers and the guys who are moving forward.'

In Qatar's Doha Open, which Henman entered three times between 1997 and 1999, the only time he did not make the final was 1998, when he was knocked out in the quarter-finals.

Henman has also played in the Sydney Outdoor final both times he has participated, in 1997 and 1998. In the 1998 final he lost to an unseeded Karol Kucera, despite beating number-one seed Pat Rafter in straight sets and Thomas Enqvist en route. A year earlier he had won the tournament as a non-seed, beating Carlos Moya in the final in straight sets as well as top seed Goran Ivanisevic in the last four.

Since the turn of the century Henman has opted to play Adelaide, as preparation for the Australian Open, and he performed commendably there, too. He made the quarter-finals in 2000, losing to 8th seed Nicolas Escude, reached the semi-finals in 2001, where he lost to Chile's Nicolas Massu and won the event in 2002, beating Mark Philippoussis.

Yet, despite normally having a good build-up to the main event, he has never made it past the last sixteen in the Australian Open, and he never made it that far until 2000.

It had been a lot worse before then. In 1998, ranked 18th in the world, Henman crashed out in the first round after enduring a ding-dong five-setter against French qualifier Jerome Golmard, a player who was eighty-three places below him.

Henman double-faulted on ten occasions throughout the match. The first, at 0-30 in the seventh game, effectively cost him the first set 6-3. His serving in the first three sets was erratic, and almost cost him the second set as well, when at 0-1 and deuce he delivered his third and fourth double faults consecutively to gift-wrap another break for Golmard.

Fortunately, Henman recovered, after trailing 3-0, to take the set on a tie-break 7-2, but then immediately lost his serve at the start of the third, and with it the set 6-2. Yet he still did not learn, as his sixth double fault put him break point down in the opening game of the fourth set. However, he did manage to recover straight away to eventually take the set 6-3 and drag the match into a decisive fifth.

In the penultimate game of the final set, Golmard was struggling and needed to call for a trainer to burst blisters on his feet. But still Henman could not take advantage, and trailed 10-9 on serve. This was when he committed his greatest sin of the

day. After shoring up his serve at the start of the fourth set by
no longer serving to Golmard's heavy forehand, he won fourteen
successive service games. But then, in the final game of the
match, he directed two serves at Golmard's venomous forehand
and found himself facing two match points at 15-40. It proved
too big a mountain to climb and ultimately sealed his fate.

Henman was seething. He pulled no punches as he ripped
with blistering ferocity into his four-hour and nineteen-minute
flop show against Golmard. 'That was the worst performance of
my life – watching a tape of that match will be like seeing a
horror movie. There is no way I can let myself play like that. I
thought things were going well but to come out and put in a
performance like that is just not acceptable. I could not have
made life more difficult for myself just with the standard of
tennis I played. I just cannot explain what happened. There is no
satisfaction in it going to a fifth set. He is a good player and has
beaten people like Jim Courier, but I wouldn't say he had a great
deal to play against today.'

But Henman appeared to regroup and come back a better
player the following year, achieving a career-best third-round
berth.

Having been seeded 6th at Wimbledon, he bypassed the first
round in straight sets over Morocco's Karim Alami, and then faced
Australian Sandon Stolle, who was placed 240th in the world.

After experiencing so many years as the crowd favourite at
SW19, Henman was about to get a taste of how his opponents
had always felt, as the Australian crowd attempted to roar their
own on to a famous victory. The wave of spectator enthusiasm
appeared to rouse Stolle, who broke Henman three times to lead
5-1 in set one. Henman did manage to recover some pride to
make a contest of the first set, but eventually lost it 6-4.

Stolle may have had the fans on his side on Centre Court, but

Henman certainly had the luck. In the second set a seemingly legitimate ace from the wild-card entry was called out and then a Henman backhand was judged to be in when clearly long. Henman took the set 7-5, but it still did nothing to ease his tension. He continually missed shots that he would normally have put away with ease, and his volleying was particularly inept.

His frustration boiled over in the opening game of the third set, when he hit a double fault and then missed a simple overhead, which led to his losing his serve. He slammed his racket to the floor and actually got it to bounce over the net, which was more than he could manage with a ball.

Stolle held serve five times to claim the set 6-4 and lead two sets to one.

But then it all changed. Henman started to play more bread-and-butter shots, and all of a sudden it was Stolle who was feeling the heat. He gave up the fourth set with little fight 6-1, and then the fifth 6-4.

It should have been a routine win for the 6th seed. But his dire display, against a player not even in the top 200, made the match far more difficult than anyone could care to have imagined.

However, he searched for the positives, saying afterwards: 'This was a scare for me and it does build confidence when you can win when not playing your best tennis.'

The same could not be said, though, in the next round, against his former doubles partner Marc Rosset. The five-set win over Stolle had obviously taken too much out of Henman and he was downed in straight sets. It was a major shock for him not to have made the last eight. To make matters worse, he would not have faced a seeded player until the final, and even then it was Russia's Yevgeny Kafelnikov, who was seeded four places below him and went on to win the title. It was definitely a golden chance blown.

Even though the tournament was played on the Rebound Ace surface, which is favourable to Henman's game, he had never survived the first week before. But that almost changed a year later, when, seeded 11th, he progressed to the last sixteen, the furthest he had ever been. But again, despite his reaching this landmark, it was tinged with disappointment. After exacting revenge over Jerome Golmard and overcoming tricky obstacles in Rainer Schuettler (forced to retire hurt) and Sebastian Grosjean, he could not overcome 51st-ranked Chris Woodruff. The American may not have dropped a set before coming up against Henman, but he had also never previously made it beyond the third round of any Grand Slam event.

The blustery conditions made play difficult for both competitors and no doubt contributed to the fifteen breaks of serve seen throughout the five sets. The first of them was in Henman's favour in the fifth game of the first set. But, from leading 4-2, he lost five of the next six games, including at 5-5, when he held four break points. Woodruff won the set 7-5, and in a moment of sheer frustration Henman gave a bottle of water a whack with his racket as he returned to his chair.

It served a purpose temporarily as he went out again to roll off six straight games, including breaking Woodruff three times, and promptly won the second set when the American double-faulted on Henman's set point.

As had been the case so many times in the past, the impetus was with Henman and he looked on his way to his first Australian Open quarter-final when he led 2-0 in the third set. But instead he was broken straight back, and then lost his serve again at 4-4. The situation worsened when a bad forehand return into the net handed Woodruff a two-sets-to-one lead. But Henman was not done with yet. In the fourth set he broke his opponent at 2-1 and then dropped only two points in his next three service games, to win the set convincingly 6-3 and set up a tense finale.

Of course, there should have been no need, had Henman taken his chances early on, in addition to those offered to him in the fifth set. After four successive breaks of serve he should have broken again for 6-5, when Woodruff fell 15-40 down. But he failed to capitalise and in the next game he netted his final volley to end matters in Woodruff's favour. Another Grand Slam dream faded into the distance.

What made matters worse was that Woodruff had committed eighty-two unforced errors and served fifteen double faults, yet had still won. He also admitted: 'I feel pressure from the very first point whenever I play Henman because I know he is going to come after me, so I'm surprised he didn't serve-and-volley more against me.'

On throwing away yet another glorious opportunity to make an impact at a Grand Slam, Henman stated: 'It's very frustrating to play for such a long time and to be so close. Irrespective of the nature of the points, it's the winning and losing. Although I came second, I definitely wouldn't say I played badly. I felt like I was competing extremely hard and I'd like to have taken a few more of the chances I had. This is my best performance here [in five visits], but to lose like that is very disappointing. I would love to have won and it's difficult to talk too positively because you've just lost, but I can't question myself or second-guess myself. I don't think we could have had much more difficult conditions, I was out there for nearly four hours, I gave everything I had for every point and, you know, I lost 7-5 in the fifth.'

Despite making additional progress three years in a row in Australia, he has yet to break through the glass ceiling that is the fourth round of the Australian Open. The two years that followed 2000 saw Henman again thwarted at that same round, both occasions in straight sets. In 2001 it was Pat Rafter who won through, despite Henman not dropping a set in the competition leading up to that clash, and in 2002 Jonas Bjorkman was Henman's conqueror.

Up to 2004, the last sixteen was something Henman could only dream of reaching at Roland Garros. Clay is arguably his most challenging surface and he has always struggled to get to grips with the unique slow, looping bounce of clay-court tennis.

'I don't expect my best results to come on clay, but I think the work I put in is an investment which should take my game further on all surfaces,' he said before the start of the clay-court season in 1998.

'I can dominate people on clay. But the problem I have is that it is very difficult to keep playing aggressively if my consistency isn't quite there, and that is the challenge for me. I think when I am being dominated on clay that is when I struggle. I do find it difficult to turn things around, but I am definitely capable.'

It is certainly not serve-and-volley tennis, something Henman has been used to on other kinds of court. Clay is a thinking player's surface, where every point has to be earned through sheer physical endurance. It means dragging your opponent in, forcing him back, using and extending every muscle and sinew your body has to offer, in the quest for glory.

British tennis players have been renowned for struggling to get to grips with clay, possibly because they are no longer laid in England any more. Fred Perry is the only British male player to have won there in the past 100 years, in 1935 against Germany's Gottfried von Cramm. Henman, by contrast, failed to win a single game at the French Open until 1999, his fourth attempt, and even that was a struggle, against a player ranked 56th in the world, Karim Alami.

Such was Henman's determination to finally break his Paris duck in 1999 and prove himself on his least favourite surface that he embarked on a relentless build-up which saw him taking in clay-court events in Barcelona, Monte Carlo, Hamburg, Rome and the World Team Cup in Dusseldorf. He played a total of eleven matches and came out victorious on five occasions.

Henman felt ready. Before the tournament in Paris he said: 'I have a really great feeling about the next two weeks and that gives me such a lift. I've never been better prepared for the French Open, I couldn't have asked for a better build-up and I feel very upbeat.'

Despite his optimism, the 7th seed couldn't have started any worse against Alami, losing the opening three games of the match. His poor start looked like perpetuating his unremarkable French record, until he broke twice to rally and take the first set 6-3. Yet this early revival proved illusory as he began to spray shots wide and allowed the muscular Moroccan, sporting dyed blond hair, to dictate the proceedings from the baseline.

There was nothing Henman could do right, as Alami let rip to take the next two sets. For a while it looked like all his hard work over the past few weeks had been for nothing, until in the fourth set he found another gear and saved three break points from 0-40 at 1-1. Now with a more consistent service, he won the set 6-3, to take the match to a crucial fifth set.

Alami appeared to be becoming distracted by influences outside the court, particularly a mobile overhead camera, which he waved at. Henman, though, held his nerve and performed with skill and determination to see the job through. He broke for 2-1 and even managed to hold serve despite double-faulting twice from 40-0. He then stormed into a 5-2 lead, when the Moroccan missed a routine backhand volley. So angry was Alami with himself that he belted a ball into the crowd, which was ruled a code violation by the umpire.

Victory was there for the taking, but Henman failed to serve out the match at 5-2, and had to wait for his serve to come around again at 5-4 to finally dispose of his opponent.

'It was a great relief finally to win a singles match here,' Henman said. 'I didn't fancy the idea of having to come back next year to try to make it fifth time lucky. I think I used to be a bit intimidated playing on the clay against some guys. But now I feel I can take on anyone on any surface and my self-belief is really high.

'At 6-4, 3-3 I felt as if I was totally in control, and I was disappointed with the way I allowed him to dictate the play after that. I got defensive and was erratic. At two sets all I had to start again. I'm just happy with the way I finished it off.'

To play five sets on tennis's slowest surface is a monstrous and agonising experience. But to make matters worse, Henman put himself through another nine sets in his next two matches. In round two he played Jiri Novak, coming back from a set down to win in four, and then endured a needless five-set epic against Alberto Berasategui. At two sets and 3-1 up Henman required only to hold serve to wrap the match up in straight sets. The clay specialist had been unable to cope with Henman's aggressive game for two and a half sets, but then he began to find his range with his contorted backhand once the Briton lost consistency on his first serve. 'I was thinking that the match was over,' said the Spaniard, 'but then I realised he was not serving as well.' Indeed, Henman was broken three times and Berasategui went on to win the set, to get back in the match.

The fourth set was also a disappointment, with Berasategui pummelling his forehand to telling effect, as Henman handed him the set on serve again.

None of this would have mattered had Henman taken his chances in the final set. Suddenly and thrillingly, he rediscovered his form to establish a 3-1 lead, and with Berasategui struggling at 15-40 on serve the stage was set for Henman to make it into the last sixteen for the first time.

'But then I missed a forehand by an inch or two,' said Henman ruefully. A double break at this point and Berasategui would surely have had no way back into the game. 'It was the worst moment of the match for me,' admitted Berasategui. 'I had a little bit of luck on that game and that gave me, confidence.' The Spaniard preserved his serve.

Henman wasn't done yet, though. Despite losing his next service game, he broke back immediately to go 4-3 up. But if you're thinking it was a case of third time lucky, you are sadly mistaken.

The match was well into its third hour and on-court temperatures were surpassing 27∞C. Henman wilted. A combination of heat, understandable fatigue and his opponent's rejuvenation saw him start to react a fraction too slow as he charged the net, and he saw a number of volleys go astray. He succumbed on serve in the very next game and at 4-5 in the final set surrendered the lead for the first time since Berasategui held serve in the opening game. The game was up, and the Briton had been robbed of a berth in the next round.

Afterwards a dejected Henman said: 'Although I was delighted with the way I played in the first two rounds, to come so close in the third round and not go through hurts. There has been progress on clay for me and I feel I should have been in the fourth round, especially with the way I played in the first two sets and the opportunities I created. Not to finish him off was disappointing. As soon as I started to miss a few serves he started to get a few more opportunities and the momentum changed. Every time we got into rallies the angles he created from the back of the court did not give me many chances. I had to keep playing and believing in my own game. I did that, but at the end of the day it wasn't quite good enough. It's a tough match to swallow.'

It was a painful experience, but one that Henman certainly appears to have learnt from. Since his exploits in 1999 he has never been eliminated in the first round at Roland Garros again, and he even repeated his 1999 feat three times in the next four years, though a fourth-round place still eluded him.

But, then again, he has not always been particularly lucky with the draw for the French Open. Each time he has made the third round he has been paired with opponents from Spain or South America, renowned for their clay-court skills.

The red dust of Roland Garros is their territory. They are brought up to spend hours sliding and top-spinning their way to success on clay, whereas Henman had struggled to come to terms with it.

In 2000 and 2001 he was the victim of yet more five-set defeats in the third round, losing to Spain's Fernando Vicente and Guillermo Canas of Argentina, respectively, while in 2003, even though Henman won the first set, it was 3rd seed Juan Carlos Ferrero who emerged victorious in four sets on his way to winning his only Grand Slam up to now.

The US Open was a relatively happy hunting ground for Henman while he was attempting to make a mark on the senior tennis circuit. In his first visit, in 1996, he upset 12th seed and home favourite Todd Martin, on his way to reaching the fourth round, and in 1997 he took an even greater scalp by beating Germany's Thomas Muster, seeded 5th, in round one, but then fell disappointingly at the next hurdle to the talented but unpredictable Wayne Ferreira.

Henman had certainly made an impression at Flushing Meadow, and bigger things were anticipated in 1998 as he was handed his first seeding for the tournament: 13th.

'The other guys in the locker room do seem to be expecting better and better things from me,' Henman said at a press conference in the build-up to the US Open. 'I like my chances here.'

He kicked off his campaign at Flushing Meadow by emphatically defeating Australia's Scott Draper, winner of the Stella Artois Championships at Queen's that year, in straight sets.

In round two he saw off Felix Mantilla, positioned at 18th in the world, in four sets, before coming up against German qualifier Michael Kohlmann. He was determined to see off the underdog, especially as the game was scheduled for 6 September – his twenty-fourth birthday.

Henman began the match, on the Louis Armstrong Stadium's Court Two, in perfect fashion, by producing a booming ace to win the first point, and was in control as he adopted tactics similar to those that had helped him defeat Draper and Mantilla in the first two rounds. He was rushing the net at every opportunity and swarming over Kohlmann, in order to pile on the pressure, with pinpoint approach shots and decisive volleys. The result was that the twenty-three-year-old German conceded the first break in the sixth game, and eventually the set, 6-3.

It was all going too smoothly for Henman, and so it proved. At 30-all on his serve in the second set he sprinted towards the net to collect a drop shot, but ended up tumbling on to the concrete floor after losing his footing. It certainly took a lot out of him, and even though he managed to maintain his service game, he was broken in the next, to trail 4-1.

It was nothing less than you expected of Henman. After all, no match against a lesser-talented opponent would be complete without Henman losing concentration when on top of his game and offering a lifeline to his rival. And it continues to blight his performance.

Fortunately, Henman did manage to break back straight

away for 4-3, but then the plucky German broke him again. Only some spectacular volleys in the next four games, which yielded consecutive wins, allowed Henman to scrape through with the set.

But the shakes from that fall were still evident, as Kohlmann broke Henman twice in the third set to race into a 5-0 lead. Despite every stroke Henman could do no wrong with earlier, he was now struggling. The set was a lost cause, and although he avoided a whitewash by coming back from two breaks down in the sixth game, he lost it 6-1.

His embarrassment over his loss of confidence having ebbed away, he was now clearly irritated; and he didn't waste time in letting the umpire know it. At the beginning of the fourth set, after struggling to win his service game, he lost his cool and launched into a verbal tirade at the official, who, he felt, was the reason for his having such a bad birthday. 'Wake up and concentrate, you've done nothing in this match!' he yelled.

It was unmistakably an outpouring of anger at the way he had allowed his opponent back into the game with some sloppy errors, after mastering him early on. Yet his tantrum appeared to have a therapeutic effect on his tennis. Previously hesitant and exposed on the baseline, he was now back to his aggressive self, and broke the German early in the fourth and finally shook him off 6-4 to win in two hours and thirty-one minutes.

Henman put his lacklustre performance down to the swirling wind, 30∞C heat and a lack of concentration; these were the most difficult conditions he had ever played in. 'Mentally, it was painful out there,' he said afterwards. 'They were really difficult conditions, but I had a game plan and always felt it would pay off. It was a bit of a relief to get through. It was really hot, the wind was coming from all directions and the wheels came off for a while. I needed to get more fired up and make sure the umpire was concentrating. I got the job done in difficult conditions and playing pretty ordinary tennis, pretty ugly tennis at times. If the conditions are the same on Tuesday then it won't be easy. But I think I learned from this match and can hopefully use that on Tuesday. But I'd like it to be a bit calmer.'

The weather did alter in time for his fourth-round clash. However, against Kohlmann he had used too much energy for comfort and that had a detrimental effect on his performance against Mark Philippoussis two days later.

'The Scud', named after the famously unreliable missile, chose this match to produce three excellent sets of tennis, and Henman was simply too drained to be able to do anything about it. Despite whitewashing the Australian in the second set, he had already lost the first set 7-5, and then the weather intervened once again, with showers forcing play to stop. Philippoussis was fortunate to gain the half-hour breathing space offered by an unseasonal shower, and then enjoyed further luck when play resumed.

Henman was still in command until 2-2 and 40-30 in the third set, when a crucial line call went against him and abruptly ended his best spell of the match. Philippoussis broke him, and after that the Australian became largely unplayable, winning the next two sets 6-4, 6-1, to end Henman's Grand Slam aspirations for yet another year.

In the five years following that defeat Henman never again scaled the heights of the fourth round of the US Open, putting pay to the promise he had shown in his early years at the tournament.

In 1999 he suffered the embarrassment of being one of the first seeds to be eliminated from the US Open, when, seeded 6th, he was thrashed in straight sets by 64th-ranked Guillermo Canas.

In 2000 Henman came out unscathed in the first and second rounds after straight-set wins over Fernando Vicente and Fernando Gonzalez, respectively, only to fall against a 46th-ranked Richard Krajicek in five sets, after throwing away a 2-1 set lead.

Henman, seeded 9th, repeated the trick in 2001, by reaching the last thirty-two, only to lose again in five sets to an inferior opponent in 37th-ranked Xavier Malisse. Another opportunity at Flushing Meadow squandered.

This prompted former Wimbledon champion Pat Cash, in the build-up to the 2002 US Open, to launch a stinging attack on Henman's form, accusing him of being a huge disappointment in the American Grand Slam. 'Tim's got a reasonable draw being seeded so high and he should be able to get through a few rounds. But the US Open hasn't been a good one for him – it's always been a disappointment. It should be his second-best tournament after Wimbledon, but he's been a big let-down.'

Henman appeared to take note of the criticism aimed at him by Cash. He responded by getting through the first two rounds of the tournament without losing a set, and dropping just fifteen games. But then the curse of the third round struck again. This time it was the turn of 26th seed Juan Ignacio Chela to emerge victorious over Henman, seeded 5th. It all seemed a little too easy as Chela tore Henman apart and conceded just eight games on his way to a straight-sets win.

After the match it turned out that Henman was struggling with a right-shoulder injury, which he had picked up in the RCA Championships in Indianapolis, earlier in August. 'I bluffed my way through the first two rounds with my shoulder but you cannot do that against a guy like Chela,' he said. 'It's a different type of disappointment. When you go out and you're healthy and you're one hundred per cent, that I feel is the most disappointment. I gave it a try and it wasn't successful.'

It was that same shoulder injury that looked set to destine Henman to an entire twenty months of exasperation and dismay, come 2003.

Thank goodness for Paris.

10

Changing Faces

There are not many tennis coaches whose names have the honour of being synonymous with a player. It's like in football. Manchester United have a face in Sir Alex Ferguson, Arsenal have a face in Arsene Wenger and Charlton Athletic in Alan Curbishley. But, apart from these, there are very few others around.

Tennis is exactly the same. Greg Rusedski and Boris Becker have seemed to change their coaches as often as their shirts, but there are a few exceptions. Pete Sampras and Paul Annacone, Stefan Edberg and Tony Pickard and ... Tim Henman and David Felgate.

Henman and Felgate teamed up in 1992 when the Lawn Tennis Association put Felgate in charge of a group of four young players. Previously he had been coaching privately in America before returning to England and becoming involved with the LTA as their assistant manager of men's national training.

The choice of Felgate, still in his twenties, was an intriguing one. An all-round sportsman, he first became interested in tennis after watching the memorable Stan Smith–Ilie Nastase

Wimbledon final in 1972. He chose to pursue the game rather than his other great love, football, after breaking a leg twice in the same year. His highest singles ranking was 250th – he competed just once in the Wimbledon singles, in 1988, when he lost on the opening day to Ivan Lendl – but he believed he was always destined to become a coach.

'When I watched football as a youngster, I wasn't one of those who barracked someone when he made a mistake,' he said. 'I tried to work out what he was trying to do. It intrigued me. Then as a tennis player I always liked analysing matches and enjoyed talking to the coaches.'

In July 1992 the LTA's national development officer and former British number one, Billy Knight, wanted to set up a squad system in which a group of three or four leading young players would be assigned to a particular coach. 'I was never keen on one-to-one coaching for young players,' Knight said. Felgate was entrusted with Nick Gould, Barry Cowan, Dan Sanders and Tim Henman.

Though Knight was concerned about Felgate's lack of experience, he was struck by his knowledge of the game and his contacts within it. 'David was very professional,' he said. 'The way he read players impressed me. He saw quickly who had potential, what their strengths and weaknesses were. That's a gift, I think. The players liked him, but he could be very tough with them.'

One time Felgate was away training with the Henman group and was frustrated as he felt they were not giving 100 per cent, so he drove back to the hotel on his own. The players had to run back.

When Felgate first saw Henman as a youngster he thought him 'unremarkable, not even among the best of his age group. There were some good signs – you would see a shot now and again that looked like one from a top player but I certainly couldn't see him progressing to where he is now.'

Henman was crowned National Junior Champion swiftly after joining Felgate's national squad, and ended 1992 as the British number 18. However, it was another member of the group, Nick Gould, the British number nine, who began as the outstanding player. But in a comparatively short space of time Henman was number two in the group and by 1993 he was number one.

Under Felgate's tutelage all four improved rapidly, but Henman's transformation was remarkable. 'He obviously had more talent than other people,' Knight said. 'He knew and felt the game much better. And he understood what he had to do to get better. He could understand what David Felgate could give him, and more. He knew what he had to do to become a better player.

'They clicked very quickly. On David's side, he's young and very with it. He really knows the game very well. He's been a player himself, mixed with a lot of top players, and knows what's needed. Tim's very smart, and he's a very quick learner. And the other thing is they are both very ambitious. They know where they want to go.'

For a while it had seemed the young Henman's potential may have proved limited, but Felgate put paid to that idea. He was a calm guiding influence who kept the player relaxed but focused, and who also had the tennis brain to improve his game.

Having made his impact as a junior, the next step for Henman was the satellite circuit, an arena which has proved an insurmountable hurdle for many. His former Slater Squad colleague James Baily, for instance, made an earlier impact than him when, at seventeen, he became the first Briton to win a junior boys' Grand Slam title for twenty-eight years at the

Australian Junior Open. Eighteen months later, though, he was out of the game, the satellite scene proving unbearable.

Buoyed, perhaps, by his profound love of the game, Henman, with Felgate at his side, sailed through. By 1994 he had become Felgate's sole charge. By this time Felgate had also succeeded Knight as national development officer.

'I think it was very important that the one-on-one partnership evolved,' Felgate explained. 'I don't believe in, "OK, this player's great. Here's a coach. Off you go." Our relationship was allowed to develop.

'Tim's body still looks only that of a seventeen-year-old but that could be a big plus; it suggests he will be in full mature prime between around twenty-three and thirty, which is ideal. But already Tim displays a marvellous feel for the game. He has really good "hands" and an excellent "head"; on court he observes and absorbs, which are two crucial attributes. But he has enormous potential and has already turned more than a few heads, and in the nicest way. There was never any question in his own mind that he would be a good player. But it all had to come together.'

Felgate would set his protégé targets, in terms of rankings and physically, in order to push him on to the full ATP Tour and realise that potential that both of them knew he had.

'When Tim recovered from his broken leg [suffered against Chris Wilkinson in Singapore in 1994] we set him the target of going into Wimbledon '95 with a ranking of around 200. He was well ahead of that schedule and the next step was to get him to bulk up a bit in the gym. An extra half-a-stone of muscle would make a huge difference to his game.

'When I started working with him three years ago he was as thin as a rake. He is still very slightly built for a man of six foot one and we will start him pumping iron next, then apply to the LTA for a fitness trainer to accompany him on tour.

'Tim will never be a Boris Becker-type blaster but he has great touch and a good all-court game. He just needs a bit more strength to compete with the big guys.'

Henman spent hours in the gym bench-pressing, doing leg-extension exercises and strengthening his upper body and shoulder muscles. His increased strength made a remarkable difference to his serve, which regularly touched 125mph.

Everything flows from the serve. If it is going well, the rest of a player's game tends to go well too. With Henman's, the raw materials were already in shape, but Felgate managed to improve his rhythm and get his timing right, which meant a harder and more accurate service.

'It was always a perfectly good service action,' Felgate said. 'So we didn't do anything technical to it. It was just a question of making Tim aware that he does have the strength to hit the ball hard, and consistently hard. It's still not there yet, but there are times when he does serve very well and it can be a weapon. There's a tendency when you try to hit harder that you lose the timing. So it's important to get the balance right. And that isn't so easy when you're in a match situation. It's mainly a case of going on to the practice court and just keep hitting serves so that you don't have to think about it.'

By the time the 1996 Wimbledon Championships were approaching Henman had experienced almost a year of uninterrupted progress, in which the development of various weapons, especially his serve, had continued apace and he had begun to make a mark on the ATP Tour, having moved up to 61 in the world. He said at the time: 'There's a big difference in it between now and a year ago. I can put a lot of the better results I've had down to my serve. I'm probably hitting it ten per cent harder, and it's a lot more consistent. That's pretty important in a serve.

'I've spent far more time in the gym in the last year than I did before. It's also an endurance thing. In a five-set match you need to be able to serve as well in the fifth set as you do in the first.'

This stood Henman in good stead for Wimbledon that year and no doubt contributed to his five-set win over French Open champion Yevgeny Kafelnikov, the upset of the tournament, as he made the quarter-finals. Throughout the tournament Henman would constantly look across to try to gauge the reaction of his guru, who would respond with a firm, reassuring nod.

'I wanted to leap out of the players' box and run across the court,' Felgate confessed, after that ground-breaking match against Kafelnikov. 'It was just unbelievable.

'You go through every emotion in a match like that. There's disappointment, relief, the dread of impending defeat, the absolute elation of victory, incredible highs and lows

'I find it hell to watch Tim. People say I look calm, but my stomach aches so much that I need to go for a run afterwards. There are times when I feel physically sick, it's that bad. A football manager can scream and shout. I can't. It's agony and there are times when I'd love to leave.

'Yet there is nothing more professionally satisfying than to see Tim hitting winning shots, especially on Centre Court.'

At Wimbledon there was always a fixed order among Henman's closest supporters inside the players' box. To Felgate's left would be Knight, whom the duo would insist on being there, then Henman's girlfriend and eventual wife, Lucy Heald, then Felgate's wife, Jan (Henman's agent) and then Henman's parents, Jane and Tony.

By now Henman and Felgate had forged a strong working and personal relationship, and as Henman continued to improve, so Felgate spent more and more time with him, a progression that reached its natural conclusion when, at the beginning of 1997, he became Henman's coach full-time, with Jeremy Bates taking on his duties at the LTA.

'David's a hell of a lot more than just a coach,' Henman emphasised, after finishing 1996 in the top thirty. 'He's a great friend who I can talk to and discuss virtually everything about my career. He's been the most important person in my career, so long may it continue. David should take a huge amount of credit for what's happened. Some of the top guys do seem to switch coaches quite regularly and it doesn't seem to matter so much to them. The reason why they do that I don't know, but that's not the way I'd work.'

With Felgate's wife Jan, who worked for the IMG management agency, Henman's agent and David his regular backgammon partner during those rainy days at Wimbledon, the Felgates had become like a second family to him. The teacher-pupil days were long gone.

Felgate revealed: 'We've become good friends, which isn't what I set out to do. I set out to coach him and make him a better player, but it evolves from there. I think that is very important and a key factor in being successful is to have the right people around you.

'We live close by, train together and eat together. It's got to a stage where we can communicate without talking. When I watch him at Wimbledon I get all my emotions from him. He may be losing, but if he is playing well, then I'm still confident. I can tell what he is going through by the little things he does, like touching his hair or tugging his shirt.

'Obviously the down side of living in each other's pockets every day is that we have our share of disagreements. We both get pissed off with each other from time to time about various things. But when it comes to tennis matters we talk about it and that's it over and done with. As soon as we're away from the court it's a different story.

'I don't mind when we disagree. I wouldn't want everything I ever said to him just to be done without question. I don't mind him not doing it then finding out I'm right and vice versa – it's more important we do it as a team. And there's plenty of graft goes into it. If he's not in a tournament he plays three to four hours' tennis a day and does an hour's training. We work on speed, flexibility, all these things.

'But it's his mental strength that will take him to the top, no doubt. I have to admit I get excited when I watch him. He has the potential to be the best British player for sixty years. He listens well but he's got a stubborn streak which is a great trait. He's shown everything I've known he's capable of since I started coaching him. I sense that Tim has that something extra, that desire, it takes to go on from here. The good thing about him is he can handle the attention, enjoy it and then go and have a beer afterwards. That's important. He should have a life outside the game.'

Within a month of Felgate becoming Henman's full-time coach, the Briton won his first ATP Tour title at the Sydney Outdoor. He finished the year with a second title at Tashkent and a ranking inside the top twenty. The duo were gaining credibility within the ATP. In August Felgate was elected European representative on the six-man board of the ATP Tour, outvoting Guy Forget of France, Dutchman Jacco Eltingh and Emilio Sanchez of Spain, while Henman was elected to the Tour's player council.

Henman continued to progress in 1998, finishing the year in the top ten and qualifying for the end-of-year Singles Championships. But though it is true that the player takes the plaudits when things are going well, the moment things take a turn for the worse it is the coach who takes the flak.

This problem surfaced towards the end of 1999. Until that stage the duo could point to a continued progress, but it appeared Henman was now beginning to drift backwards. Expectation had grown among the fans, so both men lived under constant scrutiny. Henman's talents were never in doubt, but at this point his results had failed to live up to the hype after, as the 6th seed, he was dumped out of the US Open in the first round by world number 68 Guillermo Canas, a result which saw him drop out the top ten at the end of the year and finish potless.

For years he was talked of as being a 'late bloomer' and he has always been 'ready to take the next step', but when those steps were more of a stumble after Flushing Meadow, Felgate bore much of the criticism.

The consensus was that as a coach Felgate was inexperienced and limited and his input needed to be supplemented or even replaced if Henman was to win the big matches and not remain a mere journeyman.

Henman's former teacher in the Slater Squad and now Davis Cup captain, David Lloyd, believed Henman's friendship with his coach was a bit too close and was preventing him from hitting the heights. 'I think Felgate has done a very good job but he is Tim's very best friend,' he said. 'Henman needs someone who has been there and done it, been to the very top – someone that, in a given circumstance, could say afterwards, "Why did you play that cross-court shot?"'

John McEnroe was another who joined the clamour to have a cheap shot at Felgate. He described Henman's performance against Canas as 'shocking, really awful', suggesting that he had reached the most crucial phase of his career and maybe needed a different coach.

'Ultimately it's got to be Henman's decision,' McEnroe said, 'but I think a new voice, with new ideas, is never a bad thing.

He's been with David Felgate a long time and they might know something I don't, but at the very least they should be going to someone else, even if it's just to pick their brains.

'Felgate has a big choice to make as well. If a player believes in his coach he'll probably want to stay with him. But if you care enough about the player and you think it's time you weren't around, you have to be man enough to make that choice.'

But Henman remained steadfastly loyal to Felgate, refusing to oust him in favour of a more experienced operator and trying to take some of the flak when he had been performing poorly.

'He will always be my coach for as long as he wants the job,' he insisted. 'When I have a bad run of form people always seem to blame David, but I've said all along that I'm the one who goes out there sometimes and plays like an idiot.

'Journalists are happy to write week in and week out that I should get a new coach, but if I suddenly reversed the roles and said I should speak to their editors all hell would break out.

'Those who say he should bring other people in to help me have no understanding. They don't know he talks to all sorts of people about my game. I find it quite amusing now, though I am sure he doesn't.'

Meanwhile Felgate refused to allow the criticism to affect what he was trying to achieve with Henman. 'Everybody can keep criticising, they can say what they like, but they don't really know what goes on,' he said. 'I've been accused of just being Tim's buddy and not saying the tough stuff, but nobody really knows. It's just speculation and it's not something I really worry about.

'What would you regard Pete Sampras and Paul Annacone? What would you regard Brad Gilbert and Andre Agassi? What would you regard Tony Pickard and Stefan Edberg? Were they not mates? So that argument's dead. I get sick and tired of it. It's an old chestnut.

'Tim's happy with what he's got, I'm happy with what I'm doing and if I didn't think I was doing a good job I would walk away. The sad thing is, nobody ever walks up in the changing room and confronts me or Tim or asks the questions. They just go on air and get paid their money at this time of the year and then walk away.'

With the added help of Kieron Vorster, brought in to help structure a new fitness programme, Henman returned to the top ten, winning autumn titles in Vienna and Brighton, temporarily quashing any talk of Felgate leaving.

But at the Australian Open in January 2001 Henman was beaten for a second successive year in the fourth round, this time by Pat Rafter in straight sets, and despite his earning a brief reprieve with victory in Copenhagen, his seventh title from eighteen finals, two tactically inept defeats – at Indian Wells against Nicolas Lapentti, ranked 102, and in his first match at Key Biscayne against 48th-ranked Fabrice Santoro – once more fuelled the calls for change.

In April that year, after nine years, seven titles and not a little turmoil, Henman and Felgate parted company. They did so with the minimum fuss, Henman leaving the deed to IMG, his agent. A brief statement stated: 'After serious consideration, David and I have made this decision. David has been instrumental in helping me to find success as a player and naturally this has been very difficult for both of us. But in analysing my situation, we came to the conclusion that for me to make that next step, it was necessary to make this change.'

Felgate had little to add. 'While Tim and I have had a very successful partnership over a long period, sometimes change is necessary,' he said. 'I wish Tim every success.'

However, he later told BBC Radio Five: 'It's a shame, because it is something that has gone on for nine years – but it's also a sense of relief because he won't have to keep answering the questions about should I or shouldn't I be his coach any more.

'Have you ever had that feeling in the stomach when you know something's right? Well, it was like that. Look, Tim and I got on really, really well. Still do. It is a very intense relationship between a tennis player and a coach; we probably saw more of each other than we did of our wives. But we had been talking for more than six months and, although the subject of a break wasn't actually raised, we knew that was what was on each other's minds. It was right.

'There were some extremely high points and hopefully he can go on now and get back to those high points.'

Henman travelled the globe without a coach throughout both the clay and grass circuits. But, after his devastating three-day Wimbledon semi-final loss to Goran Ivanisevic, he turned to Californian Larry Stefanki. The pair knew each other well, having played golf together regularly.

Stefanki's coaching CV makes impressive reading. He has coached Marcelo Rios and Yevgeny Kafelnikov to the world number-one spot, taking Kafelnikov to the Australian Open title in the process. Both men are, at best, challenging characters and, at worst, almost impossible to deal with. Not that it seemed to stop Stefanki. A hard taskmaster, he spotted the talent and managed to harness it to produce the required results.

Before stints with those two, he also oversaw the revival of an ageing John McEnroe. McEnroe enjoyed Stefanki's straight-talking assessment of his game, as he succumbed to the emerging power-players such as Boris Becker and Jim Courier.

Stefanki sat down with McEnroe and played a videotape of the player in his pomp. 'I think he was frightened to remember how good he was,' the coach recalled. 'As a friend, over a beer, I told him that he was selling himself short, that his game was not the same as it used to be and I wanted to know why. There was no bravery in it. I could see what he was going through and I didn't like to see it.'

The 43-year-old player won two titles on the ATP Tour and reached a career-best 35 in the world rankings.

With Henman, Stefanki would initially fly over from his home in California to help prepare him for the American summer circuit and then travel with him to tournaments in Montreal, Cincinnati, Indianapolis and, ultimately, the US Open, after which the relationship would be reviewed to determine whether to continue on a long-term basis.

Henman said: 'I felt Larry and I had a lot of similar ideas, the timing was right and I was ready to give it a try. Larry came to London last week and then obviously travelled over here and I am pleased with the way things are going. He has a great deal of experience with the players he has worked with and hopefully I can benefit from that.

'It's another exciting time for me. It was different before Wimbledon when I was working things out for myself. I really enjoyed that and I think it was good for me but I wanted to get some input and I'm happy with the decision I made.

'It certainly takes some adjusting to listening to a different sort of input. But that's what I'm looking for. If I employed a coach, he gives me advice and if I say, "Hang on a minute, I don't want advice", then what's the point? It's taking Larry a bit of time to adjust to the way I prepare for matches, the times I like to practise – it's a learning process for both of us.

'From a tactical and technical point of view he is very good. He's got some very good ideas, some very basic ideas about strategy, just playing a smart type of tennis that is playing to my strengths and trying to put my opponents into more difficult situations.'

After only two weeks in the job Stefanki pinpointed two key weaknesses of Henman's game: the forehand and the first service. Both, when they work, can be real match-winners, but in the past they had been problem areas which had let him down on so many occasions. Stefanki was encouraging Henman to try using his forehand cross-court shot more often, while he felt his first service needed tightening up to make it more consistent, with an emphasis on placement rather than power, in the manner of classic serve-and-volleyers like Pat Rafter and Stefan Edberg.

There were definite signs that Henman was listening to the advice on offer from his tutor. Writing of Henman's second-round straight-sets win against South Korean Hyuing-Taik Lee, in Cincinnati, in what was only his second tournament under the guidance of Stefanki, Alix Ramsay of *The Times* said: 'Throttling back slightly on the pace of the first service, Henman is trying to use a little more brain than brawn, with the result that the percentage is moving up gradually and the tactics are becoming clearer. Yesterday he succeeded with 71 per cent of his first-service attempts – a marked improvement on recent days – and whenever a break point presented itself, he took it with glee.'

Henman was certainly impressed with what Stefanki had brought to his game, and likewise Stefanki had been impressed with Henman. Stefanki was so convinced that Henman could still win a Grand Slam that the deal, which was meant to be reviewed after Flushing Meadow, was made permanent weeks before the start of the event.

'Tim has been an absolute breath of fresh air,' Stefanki enthused. 'In the weeks I have been working with him I have been very, very impressed. Tim listens and wants to improve. For a guy in the world's top ten to accept that he needs to make a change is unusual.

'What I look for in taking on a job is talent – what their athletic talent is, what their level is, and basically their ability. Can they get to that next echelon of being in the top five in the world?

'He can do it because his style is a dying breed. And that style, with the way the guys play, is a good style to counter what they do well.' (Which, translated, means serve-and-volleyers have an advantage over baseline players as the majority of players are not used to playing them.)

'I was not going back on the Tour for a job,' Stefanki said. 'It would have to be something very special and Tim happened to be that special guy for me to do that. I knew that he wanted to be solo for a time. I think that has helped him an awful lot to develop as a person and as a player and, like I say: he is the horse. He has to hit the balls. No one else can do that for him.

'Tim's fluctuated in the style of play he wants to play on a consistent basis. He's sometimes vacillating on whether he going to be a serve-volleyer or a baseliner: kind of a combination of both. I've always envisaged him as an aggressive player, not just a guy sitting and waiting for something good to happen. It's something that I'm trying to impress on him: serve – volley; any short ball, be all over it, get to the net, end the point.' The bottom line? 'He's not a baseliner.'

Henman was playing confidence-filled tennis. His forehand could not have looked more solid, and although his ace serves were few and far between, he was now losing a minimal number of points from double faults.

In the space of a year, thanks to his remodelled game, Henman had reached his highest-ever ATP Entry Ranking of 4th, winning forty-nine of his sixty-five singles, including four finals, triumphing in two at Basle and Adelaide, as well as a first semi-final on clay in Monte Carlo. That equates to an impressive 75 per cent win rate.

However, as yet Henman had still failed to make an impact at a Grand Slam outside Wimbledon, managing only the third round at the US Open, the last sixteen at the Australian Grand Slam and round two at Roland Garros, compared with yet another semi-final at SW19.

Many experts within the game believed he would struggle to win a Grand Slam because of his new style of first serve. Darren Cahill, the coach who guided Lleyton Hewitt to the world number-one spot, said: 'If Tim keeps playing in this new way, he won't scare any of the big guys. He's taken far too much off his serve. He is just asking for the top players to smack it straight back past him. If you are going to beat the very best, you can't hold back on anything and that's what Tim is doing.'

Henman had lost to inferior opponents in all three Grand Slams outside Wimbledon. In Australia Jonas Bjorkman, ranked 64th in the world, repeatedly punished the Briton's serve as he cruised into the quarter-finals with a 6-2, 7-6, 6-4 victory. And at Flushing Meadow and Roland Garros, Xavier Malisse, lying just inside the top fifty, had feasted on Henman's serve when eliminating him from both events. 'Tim hits a lot of first serves in but they're not the fastest,' said the Belgian. 'I always feel I can break him, so I have an easy time of it. I like playing against Tim.'

The technical changes in Henman's first serve were also causing him physical stress. The altered serving motion was putting too much pressure on his right shoulder, and as a result in August it became inflamed. He stuttered to the end of the season before being forced to have arthroscopic surgery to repair the damage.

Henman admitted at the time of his operation that he had not protected his shoulder well enough after Stefanki advised him to alter his service action at the beginning of the year. 'It's tough enough to compete when you are one hundred per cent fit because the standard is so high. I could point to four or five things – changing my serve slightly, practising that serve a lot more, lack-of-strength-work and the time I spent in the gym. If I had one negative I might have been OK, but four...'

Henman did not return until February, by which time he had dropped out of the top forty. To make matters worse, he was advised by his doctor to redesign his serve again or face the prospect of the injury resurfacing and a premature end to his tennis career. He made an attempt to rediscover his once-imposing first serve, but he was not getting the right results on matchdays. In his first seven events after his return he won only four times.

The next tournament was the French Open, where Henman made a conscious decision to go it alone. Stefanki would not go with him to Roland Garros and they agreed that they should concentrate their time together on working outside tournament play.

Henman said on his website: 'The vast majority of time Larry is with me is spent at events and sometimes it becomes difficult to work on various aspects of my game while I'm competing.

'I don't feel I need somebody with me day-in, day-out, so we've slightly changed our working schedule. That means that for some events in the future Larry won't be travelling with me.

'Larry has gone home to spend some time with his family and is due to return for the second week here in Paris. He will then stay in Europe to work with me until the end of Wimbledon.'

Henman went on to equal his all-time best at the French Open, with a place in the third round, and was hitting the ball well in wins over Vladimir Voltchkov and Todd Martin, serving with more power and authority. There was evidence that his serve had become a real weapon again. He admitted he could not remember the last time he had played so well in back-to-back matches.

'When I'm out there on my own it doesn't seem to faze me,' he said. 'Some people would say they would like to have someone with them week-in and week-out. I don't think that is necessary for me. I don't want it that way, and neither does Larry.

'We both feel it's kind of horses for courses. Todd Martin no longer has a full-time coach for example and I certainly view it in similar circumstances.

'One of the aspects that Larry and I talked about was that when we are working at these aspects, I find I try to implement them in a match and when they don't work, I get frustrated.

'I say to myself: "I've been working on something for the last three days and now it's useless in the match and it's getting worse." I tend to dwell on that a lot more.

'I have to look back a long time to find when I played so well in successive matches. There is a lot of satisfaction, just by the nature of what has happened to me over the last nine months. To play that type of quality tennis after a long period of time out does fill me with a lot of confidence, and it certainly does bode well for the future.'

Henman continued to fly solo throughout the grass season, winning seven of his nine matches, and then, when he went on to lift his first title since surgery at Washington, taking such notable scalps as Andy Roddick and world number 23 Paradorn Srichaphan, the end was looking nigh for Stefanki.

In September Henman announced he would be parting company with his coach and said, after his successes alone, that he had no plans to replace him. 'It's been a fantastic experience working with Larry, who has been a good friend as well as my coach over the last two years. We've worked together on some effective technical and tactical changes, which have given my game an extra dimension.

'I feel now that I simply need to concentrate on competing and winning matches, which is something I think I can do on my own. I have already had the experience of travelling without a coach and enjoyed the freedom of that very much.

'Over the last couple of years, Larry has become a very good friend, which I hope will continue into the future.'

Now completely independent, Henman came out of his next three events with a quarter-final from Vienna, a first-round defeat in Madrid and a semi-final in Basle.

But he was by no means satisfied. He felt he needed someone to talk to for advice, and so turned to a friend called Paul Annacone, whom he had got to know well when he was coaching Pete Sampras, one of Henman's closest pals on the tour.

'I played very poorly in my loss to [David] Nalbandian in Basle and I decided to give Paul a call to talk through a few things about my game,' said Henman. 'Paul has always been a good friend. I have got to know him over the years with him working with Pete Sampras and he knew my game really well.

'I called him out of the blue and we had a really good chat. I said to him, "Give me the honest impression you have about my game, and what you really think about it." From my point of view it was a really fascinating conversation. He said a lot of really encouraging things about my game and pinpointed a few errors, and where he thought I could do a lot better and wasn't maximising my abilities.

'It was food for thought, and I put the phone down and had a really good think about the direction I wanted my game to go in. This was probably two or three days before the Masters series in Paris [his last tournament of the season].

'And out I went with not a great deal of expectation, not a great deal of thought and it's funny how the week turned around. I beat Federer in the quarters, Roddick in the semis and finished the tournament really nicely.'

Henman went on to win that event in Paris, his first triumph in a Masters competition. That success brought the curtain down on a topsy-turvy season for Henman, but he still had a lot of thinking to do. He had been mightily impressed with the advice handed down to him by Annacone, and as a result they reached an agreement whereby the American would become his part-time coach.

'I've played well and enjoyed considerable success when I've had the freedom to make my own decisions on the couple of occasions in my career when I haven't been working with a coach,' said Henman. 'On the other hand, I've also learnt a great deal from both David [Felgate] and Larry [Stefanki] when I worked with them. It's always nice to have somebody to be able to talk things through with whenever the need arises, so this time I want to try and get the best of both worlds by working with a coach part-time.'

In his own playing career Annacone had reached a career-high singles world ranking of 12 while his highest doubles ranking was 3rd. He won three singles titles, at Brisbane, Los Angeles and Vienna, and fourteen doubles titles, including the 1985 Australian Open with South African Christo van Rensburg.

Sampras's former coach saw things very clearly and simply when it came to how best to fulfil Henman's potential

'I believe Tim has to play his game and not care what the other guy does,' he explained. 'My aim will be for him to keep it simple and play to his strengths.

'He is a great athlete, a great mover with a classical game and he shouldn't be worrying about the consequences of any result.

If he wins or loses, it has to be on his terms, playing the way he wants to play.'

'He has done well, but he can do better. Tim is such a class act with a tremendous amount of talent and integrity and it's going to be real exciting to see what unfolds.

'He knows that one win doesn't mean he can stand on the mountain top beating his breast and equally, if he loses in the second round of his next event, he has to swallow the disappointment and move on.

'He should expect to win because he can win, but he is going to lose matches as well and the idea is not to get too emotional about anything. My job is to say what he needs to hear and say it in the way he wants to hear it.'

Within weeks of the start of their new on-court relationship Henman was already delighted with the way they had been progressing. 'Paul and I have been friends for a while but this is the first time we've actually got out on court and worked on specific aspects of my game and it's been great,' he explained on his website.

'It was obvious right from the start that we viewed the game similarly and whilst there's been no huge overhaul of my game we've been working on some subtle changes that will hopefully help me on the match court.

'I think in the past I've perhaps got too caught up in how my opponents play and I've tended to worry a bit too much about how I'm going to change my game plan to counter that, rather than having the mentality that if I execute my game plan to the best of my ability then that will be good enough to get the job done.

'Paul has been great at getting me to concentrate on my own strengths and I think that having worked with Pete Sampras so successfully for a number of years he has a very good understanding of how to get the most out of a player that likes to play the way I do.

'We've worked hard at trying to use my serve as a real weapon, and that's helped my confidence a lot. Of course, I'm never going to break any world records in terms of speed but my ace count is definitely improving and, more importantly, the average speed of my first serve has increased a lot since I started thinking differently when I step up to the line to serve, which has certainly helped my cause.

'Paul has also been very keen for me to try and use my second serve much more effectively, and now I'm not so worried about throwing in the occasional double fault as long as I go for the serve and commit to the shot I'm trying to execute.'

With Annacone by his side, Henman was about to have his most successful Grand Slam year.

11

The Slams

'Can I win a Grand Slam title? I don't see why not. I've just beaten six of the best players in the world in consecutive rounds and there's no reason I can't bring that into a Grand Slam. I've come relatively close at Wimbledon and if I improve my game, which I know I can, I don't doubt I can go one or two stages further. There are so many opinions out there. If I worried about them, I'd just be wasting my time. It's my job to prove things to myself. I know my capabilities. People talk about age and whether my best tennis is behind me, but it's all a load of crap. Agassi is 33 and supposedly playing his best tennis. I'm 29 and done. It's nonsense. I've never stopped believing that my best tennis is still to come. I'm stronger and fitter than ever. I'm also mentally more mature and able to handle things on and off the court. What really encourages me is that I know there's more to come. That's exciting because I know there is every possibility the next three or four years are going to be my best.' (Tim Henman, Paris Masters, November 2003)

At the beginning of the 2004 season it seemed it was now or never for Henman. No longer was he Britain's bright new hope, assigned the task of one day emulating Fred Perry's Grand Slam feats, set way back in the 20th century. With Henman well into his 30th year, 'one day' was now.

But, rather than feeling intimidated at this prospect, he was raring to go. After taking some time off he was relishing the start of the new campaign and the chance to get back on the court, having finished 2003 with his best-ever tournament win, in the Paris Masters.

'I've enjoyed my time off and had a great Christmas but I can't wait to get a bit of sun on my back and compete again,' he said. 'Hopefully, if I can start this year as well as I finished last year I've got a great chance to improve my ranking still further. I've put in some quality time on the practice court and I can't wait to get back on to the match court.'

Henman began his preparations for the Australian Open as 7th seed in the Qatar Exxon Mobil Open in Doha, where he would be competing with the likes of world number one Andy Roddick and the previous year's Australian Open runner-up, Rainer Schuettler, for the $1million winner's prize.

He was determined to start 2004 the way he finished the previous campaign, and adopt his new mantra of 'Play the ball, play the point'. 'The thing that I tried to learn from Paris was how calm and relaxed I was on the court, and that I had a clear game plan. In the past I have been guilty of trying too hard. I've just got to say, this is the way I want to play, this is the right style of play, and I'm just going to let it happen. However, if you get involved in a big match, it's not easy to stay relaxed.'

His warm-up for the opening Grand Slam of the year began in ideal fashion with the first-round straight-sets hammering of David Sanchez, who ended 2003 ranked 50th. It was a confident display by Henman, who broke the Spaniard twice in the first set and then whitewashed him in the second.

Next up in Doha was Henman's US Open slayer from 2003, Juan Ignacio Chela. Henman heaped revenge on the Buenos Aires-born right-hander with a straight-sets 6-3, 6-4 win which was forged with impressive conviction.

He followed that with yet another comprehensive straight-sets win over Armenian baseliner Sargis Sargsian, 6-3, 6-1, to book his berth in the semi-final.

It had been an ideal start to the 2004 campaign and Henman was now widely being tipped to pick up the $1million prize, especially considering 8th seed Agustin Calleri was the only other seed left in the draw. With the Australian Open also looming, Henman looked a genuine bet to make a huge impact on the opening slam.

It was the best run of his career. He had not dropped a set in eight matches, the last being against Sebastian Grosjean during that glorious Paris Masters campaign, and he was now unbeaten in nine competitive matches. If he could reach double figures against Ivan Ljubicic, the big-serving Croatian who beat him in his comeback match after shoulder surgery last February, he would have reached his third Doha final.

'I am really pleased,' Henman said. 'The conditions over here are pretty tough; it's windy so serving can prove a bit difficult and it can throw the timing of other shots off a bit.

'It is always nice to get a few matches under your belt early on in the year and I am pleased that I have made it this far but the job is not done yet.'

Alas, it was not to be a case of third time lucky as Henman's chances of striking gold in Qatar dissipated into the desert air. Ljubicic dispelled that dream, as Henman paid the penalty for failing to serve out the first set when leading 6-5, and losing two tie-breaks against the Croat, who booked his place in the final against wild card Nicolas Escude with a hard-fought 6-7, 6-3, 6-7 win.

'It would have been better if I could have beaten Ljubicic and got off to a winning start in the first tournament of the year,' admitted Henman. 'It was a disappointing loss, but in the context of what I'm trying to do, it has been a very positive week. There are definitely lots of positives to take into the practice week and, hopefully, into the Australian Open.'

Indeed, one of those positives was a boost in the ATP Tour rankings as he rose three places to 11th, in addition to receiving an 11th seeding for the forthcoming Australian showpiece.

After exiting Qatar Henman opted to avoid further tournament tennis and instead headed straight to Australia to undergo some warm-weather training on the outside courts at Melbourne Park, in order to acclimatise to the 100°C heat likely to await him on court.

Before Australia he had also been spending much time modifying his first serve by getting back to basics, in a bid to produce a much more aggressive delivery. He said: 'I was getting far too analytical about my ball toss, where my weight was and how long my weight was staying back. At times it was a little bit paralysis by analysis. It's amazing how you clear your thoughts when you get back to basics. I definitely understand my serve a lot better now. There's been continued work on my serve to make sure that I'm more aggressive than I have been. I felt like I served pretty well last week [in Doha], and I feel much more positive about the whole thing.'

The success his new service approach had yielded in Paris and Doha had left him with increased confidence as he went into the Australian Open.

'The preparations have gone really well. Now, it's time to put it together on court and I am looking forward to my first match after a good build-up. I would love to have a great run here. I've never been past the sixteens and I don't think that's good enough for someone of my ability and the way I can play on these courts.

'It's no good just winning in Paris and playing well in Doha, I've got to be able to sustain that for a long, long period of time. That's why I'm looking at the next twelve months as a massive opportunity because I know I'm playing better than I've ever played.'

His first-round opponent at the Australian Open was likely to inspire further confidence. Jean-Rene Lisnard was France's 13th-best tennis player and held a modest world ranking of 113. Henman had only met him once previously, on the hard courts at Adelaide in 2000, and had beat the Frenchman in three sets.

He was chomping at the bit. 'The last few months have been a very positive time for me and I'm looking to extend that here in Melbourne. I always enjoy coming here and I'm looking forward to getting started.'

'We played a few years ago in Adelaide and I managed to get the better of him in three sets. There's been a lot of water under the bridge since then so I'm not sure how much significance that result will have. I'm focusing primarily on my own game. If I can execute my game plan I'm confident I can get the right result.'

And the right result he got.

Having prepared to play in sweltering temperatures, Henman was shunted on to an outside court for an evening session, which tends to attract those fuelled by beer and too many hours in the Melbourne sun. It proved to be the case. The crowd showed little etiquette, forcing delays as they stood and shouted at inopportune moments. One spectator chatted constantly on his mobile phone during rallies, and later dropped a tray of beer all over those around him. Cries of 'Go back to England!' could also be heard from the Australian crowd, obviously still sucking on lemons from that Rugby Union World Cup final defeat at the hands of England at the end of 2003.

But Henman stuck to his guns, and had few problems in defeating his opponent. Lisnard could do nothing right, even turning up four hours too early for the match, and it got worse for him once play got underway.

Henman was irresistible. Dominant to the net, following in his own serves and playing an effective chip-and-charge game, he took Lisnard to deuce in the opening game with a clever volley and broke him to love in the third after he had served two double faults. He broke again for a 5-2 lead when he converted the second of three break points after chasing a return from Lisnard's second serve and feathering a deft volley. After that he comprehensively served out the set 6-2 in just twenty-eight minutes.

Henman carried his rich vein of form into the start of the next set, and broke Lisnard immediately. At 4-3 up Henman saved two break points as he out-thought his inferior opponent, and sealed the second set 6-4.

He then closed out the third and final set 6-2 with a pinpoint winner for an emphatic victory, which was greeted by the English contingent among the crowd with a rendition of the rugby anthem 'Swing Low, Sweet Chariot'.

A delighted Henman said after the match: 'There is a whole feel-good factor from the World Cup win down here and it has had a massive impact. From my point of view, the tone I set early on was very positive, chip and charge and not giving him the rhythm he needs to play his game. That tempo was to my advantage and I was able to maintain that for all three sets. Committing to that style of play and being aggressive, whether you're winning or losing the point, I knew that was the right way to play. I was very aggressive from the outset and set the tone and made sure I was playing the match under my terms. Early on, I put him under a lot of pressure. Even in the first game, I could have broken him. When you put a little doubt in your opponent's mind early on, it's going to put extra pressure on. I've probably been guilty in years gone by of not doing that enough.'

In round two Henman faced Czech number two Radek Stepanek, who had rallied from two sets down to win through against Italy's Davide Sanguinetti. Henman and Stepanek's only previous meeting had come at the Paris Masters in November 2002, shortly before Henman had an operation to cure his long-standing and painful shoulder problem. 'I ended up winning that match, I played pretty well but I can't say I remember so much about it because I was probably concentrating so much on my shoulder,' he said. 'I think I won in straight sets [6-1, 7-5]. He's a dangerous player. I think he's got a pretty good serve, plays with a lot of feel. Good volleys.'

Looking relaxed, Henman started strongly and swept through the first set 6-2, with three service breaks in twenty-eight minutes, chipping approaches at Stepanek's feet and cutting off the angles, to the delight of the vocal English fans decked out in flags of St George inside the windswept Margaret Court stadium.

However, after an uncertain start, Stepanek was beginning to grow in confidence, holding serve three successive games before pulling off the crucial break of serve for a 4-3 lead in the second set as Henman missed a couple of forehands that had previously been serving him with distinction.

It was Henman's poorest game of the match and Stepanek took full advantage, cementing his lead by holding his own serve to love. But the pressure appeared to be getting to the Czech. His frustrations built after three consecutive line calls went in Henman's favour, and he was questioning, pouting and generally miffed at what he felt was the umpire and line judges ganging up on him.

'I hit a return out that didn't get called,' Henman said. 'He hit a shot down the line that was in and got called out. Then, the next serve he hit was in and it got called out.

'I thought that was pretty humorous but I don't think he did.'

With Stepanek serving for the set, Henman earned himself five break points. But he squandered all five opportunities and lost the set 6-4.

'That was pretty horrendous,' he said. 'There was one 20-30 shot rally in the middle of the game where it was perfectly feasible to keep the ball in and I missed a forehand 12 feet long. It is hard to say that was a good miss.'

Better players may have punched up a gear after this but Stepanek instead allowed Henman to break away to a 3-0 lead in the third set.

The number 11 seed was now back on song, allowing the Czech just three more games in the entire match. Henman rounded off the third set by holding his own serve to love and then pressurising Stepanek's to cruise through 6-3.

The final set was even more resounding. Once again Henman forced break point early in the set with an emphatic drop volley, before holding his own serve to love for the sixth time in the match.

From then on it was a stroll in the park, as Henman produced a flurry of thrilling tennis to break Stepanek twice and complete a fourth-set whitewash, and with it the match.

He said afterwards: 'I got off to a really good start. I felt like in the first set and a half I was dictating a lot of the play and to a certain extent dominating the match. At the end of the second set he started to play much better. He served better and took the initiative away from me a little bit. We had a tight game at 5-4 in the second set but it didn't go my way. That said, I still felt very confident and comfortable about the way I was playing. To then go and win the third and fourth sets three and love, it was very good for my confidence.'

Such was his form now that even the top players in the world were beginning to sit up and take notice of him, including Wimbledon champion Roger Federer, who said: 'If Tim can win Paris then he can win this event. I haven't seen any of his matches but I am not surprised he is winning. He is playing well, is a dangerous player for anybody and is a contender for the title. I'm not going to face him until the quarter-finals. That's OK. We'll see how he goes.'

Thinking of quarter-finals against Federer was certainly premature. After all, the fourth round was likely to produce a clash with 8th seed David Nalbandian, and even before that he had to overcome his Grand Slam bogeyman, Guillermo Canas, in round three.

The unseeded Argentinian had beaten Henman in their last three clashes, including a bruising third-round encounter in the 2001 French Open and the first round of the US Open in 1999. Canas was unseeded because he had missed eight months in 2003 with a wrist injury. Before that he was ranked 15th in the world. He appeared to be back to his best in the second round, after disposing of compatriot and 22 seed Agustin Calleri in five gripping sets.

Henman was well aware of the threat his rival posed. 'Canas is a class opponent and he's capable of beating some great players. He's given me some trouble in the past and we've had some really tight matches. I know I must play at a really high level otherwise I'll come up short.'

Things couldn't have started any better for Henman. He took the first set on a tie-break 7-6 and the second with a solitary break for 7-5.

But, from two sets up, Henman was hauled back as Canas ran himself ragged in pursuit of every ball and hit back with a 7-6 tie-break success in the third set. The Argentinian then won the fourth with a break in the eleventh game for 7-5. A familiar pattern was beginning to emerge.

Henman had to be sure of himself when he came forward or else Canas, officially ranked at 258th in the world, would pass him, lob him or try to drill the ball right through him.

For the impartial observer it was a cracking match. The longer it went on the better it got, as each player pushed the other to a higher level.

In the deciding set Henman charged into a 4-1 lead. He was playing positively and showed a steely determination to commit himself to every shot. He was within a whisker of the next round. But then Canas began to throw himself more into his shots, running, rallying and passing Henman when it mattered most. He battled back and broke to tie things up at 4-4. Games then went with serve as the match was delicately balanced on a knife's edge, until the fifteenth game. Henman double-faulted twice and consequently dropped his serve. Once again, when it had mattered most Henman had slipped into reverse gear and Canas kept his nerve to serve out for 9-7 and win the match, after four hours and fifty-three minutes of sheer drama.

Despite playing well throughout a very tight match, Henman had been beaten by someone who, even though he had missed eight months of tennis, was fitter, faster and stronger than him. It was the third time Canas had destroyed Henman's Grand Slam dreams, but this one hurt more than ever.

Nearly five hours of sweat, hard graft and some of his best

tennis he has played at a Grand Slam outside Wimbledon, striking a remarkable 100 winners but committing seventy-four unforced errors, and still Henman couldn't win.

'It is a pretty bitter pill to swallow,' a dejected Henman said. 'After such a positive finish to 2003 in Paris and a relatively good week in Doha to start 2004, I was really looking forward to improving my record in Melbourne, which unfortunately ultimately proved a very disappointing experience for me. Losing is never easy at the best of times but to lose such a close match after leading for the vast majority of the contest is hard to take.

'The first couple of sets I was able to win a couple of important points and that was probably the difference. In the next two he won a couple of critical points and that's the difference. It is very easy to over analyse something like this. We played a good match and unfortunately he was the winner. There is very little difference between us, as the scoreline suggests.

'Although Grand Slam events are all about winning and losing, it's also important to try and keep one eye on the big picture all the time and in that regard I'm pleased with the progress. So, after a couple of days rest, it's back to the practice court for more hard work on the areas of my game that we've highlighted in the hope for even more improvements before I compete again.'

All that was left now was the prospect of a long flight home and twenty-one hours to ponder more missed opportunities.

Former Wimbledon champion Pat Cash was scathing in his criticism of Henman's campaign in Australia. In his *Sunday Times* column on 25 January he wrote: 'Reports had been favourable, and initial sightings seemed to back up the optimism. Maybe there was a new Tim Henman ready to do what he'd promised for years and win a Grand Slam title.

Sadly, after his match with Guillermo Canas, the 2004 model seems much the same as all the others, and that simply isn't good enough.

'There are many things to praise about Henman. Give me his serve and volley any day ahead of the predictable and ugly power-hitting from the baseline that so many of today's top players employ.

'Sadly, there are also several crucial things to bemoan about Henman's game, and it's too late to change them now. The bad habits have been ingrained. Worst of all is his chronic lack of concentration. Yesterday he was cruising at two sets to the good, and for a player of his experience, that should be enough. He knows he shouldn't take his foot off the gas, but time and again I see him lose his focus – and back storms the other guy.

'As long as I've been watching Henman, I have been amazed by his flimsy attentiveness and sloppy shot selection. It seems he almost goes to sleep just when he should be really pushing home, and that's not a smart game to play.

'It has tended not to happen so noticeably at Wimbledon because he's got the whole country sitting on his shoulder there. Consequently, he's reached the quarter-final or better in all but one of the past eight years. That's not a bad record, although he should have done better.

'Look what he's done elsewhere at Grand Slams. A few fourth rounds at the Australian and US Opens and a third round at the French. To me, that is nothing short of gross under-achievement.

'Against Canas, all the bad old signs were there to see. His second serve is just not strong enough, and was punished time and time again. He failed to finish off points he had won, and there were whole games that he seemed to happily let slip.

'Every time I see Henman go out of a Grand Slam, I am reminded of Billie Jean King's words. A player can count his or her career in ten points. If players grab those points, they become famous; if they don't, they are easily forgotten.

'I fear that Tim Henman has let too many of those points slip through his hands.'

John McEnroe, a former Wimbledon and US Open champion, offered a more sympathetic approach in his *Sunday Telegraph* piece.

'I was hoping that the name of Tim Henman would figure among those intriguing match-ups with a fourth-round appointment against David Nalbandian, but it is not to be. It's frustrating for me, never mind him.

'I've always liked Henman, I like his professionalism. It's just too bad he can't win a couple more matches at a major other than Wimbledon to prove he is a legitimate top-ten player. Guillermo Canas is a tough competitor, but it looked to me like a match Henman should have won. But my disappointment will be nothing compared to his.'

Henman's next opportunity to silence his critics was to come at far and away his least productive Grand Slam, the dreaded red clay of Roland Garros. He had never progressed beyond the third round in eight visits to the venue, but had had a decent clay-court season, winning six matches on clay, including reaching the Monte Carlo Masters quarter-finals and the third round of the Rome Masters. He had also swept to his first title of the season, winning the Monte Carlo Masters doubles. Henman and his Serbian partner, Nenad Zimonjic, beat Argentinian pair Gaston Etlis and Martin Rodriguez in the final 7-5, 6-2.

After receiving a seeding of 9th, and a tough first-round draw against Cyril Saulnier of France, whom he had beaten in three tight sets in their only previous meeting, at the Stella Artois Championships at Queen's a year earlier, the main objective for

Henman was to go beyond the last thirty-two for the first time at the French Open. He said: 'The transition to clay from any surface is tough for me and hitting on it for the first time in ages was a bit of a shock to the system. It's not my least favourite surface – I love playing here – but it's the hardest for me.

'I've felt as comfortable as I have ever felt on clay this year, which is very encouraging. I had a lot of tennis in Monte Carlo, and then played very well in Rome in trying conditions, so I don't see any reason why I can't do better than I've ever done in the past in Paris. The third round being my best performance here is just not good enough – I am a better player than that. To reach the fourth round would be a big boost and the way my game has progressed over the last months, I feel it is now at a different level. I feel good about the way I'm hitting the ball and I feel I've won enough matches to be confident of doing well as long as I'm fully fit.'

But that was the problem. He was not fully fit.

A virus that had felled him two weeks before the start of the tournament, leaving him with a feverish cold that robbed him of energy during the Hamburg Masters, had still not completely cleared from his system. And although a blood test to discover the cause of the problem came back clear, he still did not feel on top form after a couple of heavy training sessions.

It did not bode well for the battles ahead on a surface which always demands maximum effort and concentration.

Feeling rotten and playing just as badly, Henman fell two sets behind to Saulnier. The effects of whatever was troubling him had taken the edge off his movement and he could generate little power off the ground. So long as Saulnier could keep the ball inside the lines, he always had a great chance of winning the point.

But then two unrelated events helped Henman find his way

back into the match. First, at 4-3 to Henman in the third, Saulnier took a medical time-out after complaining of cramp in his right hand. Then a computer engineer walked on court just before the start of the third-set tie-break to deliver a laptop to the scorers and Henman gently hit a ball in his direction, which unsurprisingly missed. Warned by the umpire for unsporting behaviour, he snapped back: 'It's 6-6 on a tie-break and you're blaming me?'

The incidents appeared to galvanise the Briton for the tie-break, which he won 7-2. After that, though groggy in some games and sweating buckets, Henman looked the more likely winner. Slowly the edge came back and his slices found the angles of the court rather than those of the net, and his lobbing began to pay dividends. Saulnier tried to dig deep, but Henman had more in reserve than he could possibly have imagined and broke the 79th-ranked right-hander twice to land the fourth set 6-4.

However, the commotion was not over, as Saulnier broke first in the deciding set. But Henman recovered yet again, discovering a level that he had been nowhere near at the outset, before Saulnier double-faulted on Henman's second match point, to give the Briton the match.

Henman was still white-faced and perspiring at the press conference. He said of his first win from two sets down at a Grand Slam: 'I got through on guts and determination, that's about it, but if I can play for four hours and come back from two sets down I must be doing something right. I never want to turn down winning. Funny things can happen. There was no point penalising myself with a poor performance mentally.

'I still don't feel one hundred per cent. I was just very frustrated that I perhaps wasn't feeling my best. I had a blood test last Monday and that came back negative. It's a little strange and I will definitely speak to the doctor again and see what he thinks. It must be a virus of some sort. The doctor probably doesn't recommend five sets. The bizarre thing is that my energy level was the same from four games into the match as it was in the fifth set. I didn't feel like it deteriorated, but I just felt pretty tired after four games.'

There was further cheer for Henman when news filtered through that Andre Agassi, a potential opponent in the fourth round, had been upset in round one by French qualifier Jerome Haehnel.

Now Henman had to ensure this shock result would be of benefit to him by reaching that elusive fourth stage. Despite still feeling lethargic, which led to his having regular check-ups, blood tests and a precautionary ECG (electrocardiograph), he made light work of 91st-ranked Lars Burgsmuller of Germany in round two, 6-0, 6-3, 6-3.

Now only Spain's Galo Blanco stood in the way of his making that giant stride into the second week of the French Open.

Henman had bitter-sweet memories of Blanco having lost to him in the first round of the Monte Carlo Open in 1998, when he was still struggling to come to terms with clay. 'At the end of the match I basically had had my back against the fence and was just moon-balling to see whether that did any good,' he recalled. By 2002, however, he had become wise enough to adapt his attacking style to clay, and in round one of the French Open he defeated Blanco in straight sets.

'It took a while to really understand what my assets were on this surface,' Henman said. 'My game is not particularly demanding on my body. I'm moving pretty easily, trying to keep the points fairly short.'

Blanco was certainly beatable, having lost in the first round of the four clay events he played before these championships;

however his five-set win over Luis Horna of Peru proved that he was in good shape and willing to go the extra miles required.

Henman knew he faced a challenging encounter, having still not fully recovered from his viral infection: 'The attitude I have has to be just to get on with it,' he said. 'You can't always feel your best, whether you've got a niggle or just don't feel great. If I can play the level of the last three sets of my first and second matches, why can't I progress?'

It arguably turned out to be Henman's most accomplished performance on clay. He served beautifully, smashing nineteen aces, and played with a controlled aggression that Blanco simply could not cope with.

Henman took the first set on a tie-break 7-3, and was then 5-0, 40-0 up in the second set before Blanco had time to draw breath. The Spaniard was allowed a momentary reprieve, during which time there were five breaks in six service games, before Henman got himself back into the groove. He eventually blitzed Blanco in just an hour and fifty-two minutes, 7-6, 6-1, 6-2.

It was the first time since Roger Taylor back in 1973 that a Briton had advanced to the fourth round at Roland Garros.

Blanco was so spellbound by Henman's performance he even tipped him to steal in and nick his first slam. He said: 'If Tim plays like that next week, he can win Roland Garros. I have no doubt about that. At the end, I congratulated him and said, "How much do I have to pay for the lesson?" He played unbelievable tennis. As he proved out there, he is one of the best players in the world – and that includes clay. He may not be a natural clay-courter but plays his normal game and it can work as he has the serve and all-round ability.'

With Andy Roddick and defending champion Juan Carlos Ferrero joining Agassi on the French Open casualty list, Henman now had a great opportunity to make the semi-finals as a minimum.

A grinning Henman said: 'I've spent plenty of weekends in Paris – normally the weekend before the French Open, but not normally the middle weekend! I was down two sets to love on Monday [against Saulnier] and now I'm in the fourth round. I'm enjoying myself. It's another positive. In the past when I got to the third round here, I was really excited to have won a couple of matches at the French. But the way my game is now and the way I am playing, I want much more out of it. But now I think my game's much better than that. I'm pleased to be among the last sixteen – but I want more. I don't believe just getting to the third round of the French Open is satisfactory for my ability. To look back and think I didn't explore every avenue here would be a bad situation. I'm pleased to be in the last sixteen but I want more.'

So into week two of Roland Garros, and uncharted territory, Henman went. Michael Llodra of France was his fourth-round opponent, a player noted more for doubles than singles. Before this year the 94th-ranked player had never even won at Roland Garros in four attempts, and lost to Henman in straight sets in the second round at Wimbledon in 2003, though his mind was hardly at ease that day as his mother had just passed away.

Even so, Henman was regarded as so much of a better player than Llodra that a place in the quarter-finals of his first Grand Slam outside Wimbledon seemed a formality, especially now he had finally rid himself of the virus.

But of course no potential victory would be complete without the first rule of Henmanism being further established – namely, if something is simple, then make it more complicated. He made a dreadfully weak start and could easily have been beaten in little more than two hours. Despite breaking first, he fell 5-2 down in the opening set, before recovering to force the tie-break. But he lost his way when he double-faulted to go 4-2 behind and Llodra served out the shoot-out 7-2.

Things continued to go downhill as Henman lost his serve at the start of the next set, while also being forced to save one set point in the ninth game and another two in the eleventh. It was no surprise when Llodra eventually served out to take the set 6-4.

Henman was now faced with coming back from two sets down, just as he had done in the first round against Saulnier.

It looked unlikely, but slowly the Frenchman began to lose his edge. At 3-3 in the third Henman saved two break points, before striking a wondrous inside-out forehand to take his opponent's serve, and the set in the tenth game. Henman then levelled matters by winning the fourth set 6-3, when he saved three more break points at 2-2 before moving ahead in the next game with a backhand lob that landed smack on the baseline.

Surely he couldn't pull off another miraculous comeback? Well, if he was going to, it would have to be even more breathtaking than his remarkable recovery against Saulnier.

After forcing the match into a fifth set, the fist-waving Frenchman, egged on by the entire France Davis Cup squad, started to look solid again as Henman produced three double faults and missed a backhand volley when trailing 5-4. Llodra had match point.

He chose to chip and charge behind a backhand approach, but Henman ran around his backhand and somehow found a tiny opening. Henman survived.

And then, after three successive love games, Henman played a brilliant game at 7-7 to secure the crucial break, with one forehand down the line and a backhand cross-court which left Llodra on the edge.

The extraordinary comeback was completed with Henman serving out to love. It was only the second time he had recovered from match point to win a Grand Slam encounter, after beating Jim Courier in 1999 on Centre Court at Wimbledon.

After saluting their man, French fans rose to give Henman an ovation, such was their admiration for him. He had kept calm throughout, despite playing badly, and finally showed his class to turn a forgettable encounter into a classic.

'For an hour and fifty minutes I was playing the wrong way and it wasn't a great sign,' he said, 'but to find a way to win is character-building. I didn't really dictate with my style enough. Llodra tried to do the same thing as me and for two sets he did it much better than me. He was dictating the play, serving more aggressively and getting forward. I had to find a way to turn it around. I take a lot of positives out of it – determination and the sort of mental strength I showed to get through somehow. I've certainly lost a few of these in Grand Slams but it adds to my satisfaction. It couldn't have got much closer, although I won some important points at the end. In terms of the atmosphere and the drama, that ranks pretty high.'

It may have been the first time Henman had won through to a Grand Slam quarter-final outside Wimbledon, but at least he had the experience of a series of Grand Slam last eights under his belt. For his adversary in the quarter-final stage, Juan Ignacio Chela, this was his first ever. The 22nd seed had met Henman twice on clay previously, and they had picked up one win apiece, each time at the Monte Carlo Masters. Both had been tight encounters, decided by one set, but that had little bearing on the result this time.

Henman battered Chela into submission with his attacking play and produced a string of the stunning shots that had become the hallmark of his progress through the tournament.

The match did not start until shortly before 7p.m., and many believed bad light or rain, which had interrupted much of the play earlier, would bring the proceedings to a premature end. But once Henman started it was obvious that there was no need to carry this over to the next day. He looked confident and kept the game at a high tempo with the quality of his serve-and-volleying, as well as looking equally good from the back of the court.

Before the clock had struck nine it was already over. Henman had ruthlessly defeated the Argentinian 6-2, 6-4, 6-4, using aggressive tactics that also saw his second serve turn into a platform and had served him so well on faster surfaces in the past. It may not be the conventional way to win matches on clay, but it was certainly doing him no harm.

After all, he had just become the first Briton to reach the last four of Roland Garros since Mike Sangster in 1963. But who was to say it had to stop there?

Certainly not Henman: 'I imposed my style from the word go. I never gave him the chance to settle into a rhythm. I played my own tennis, and made it look relatively straightforward. My demeanour on court was very good. It was relaxed and calm and I'm getting better mentally at playing the same way. There is a good sense of achievement. I am so pleased with the way I am playing. If you said I was going to be in the semis of a slam again and it was not Wimbledon, then I would probably have not chosen here. But that adds to the satisfaction. And why stop now? I feel good about my game and in good shape. I will be ready to come back on Friday and try to go through again.'

Not everyone shared Henman's optimism, however. The day after Henman romped past Chela, American tennis legend John McEnroe felt it was so unlikely that he could actually win at Roland Garros that he offered to honour an unusual promise if he managed it.

'I saw Tim in the locker room earlier in the week and he said, "What these clay-court players hate is when you force them to come to the net when they don't want to." You knew that was going to be part of his game plan and it worked to perfection. He looked great, fabulous. But as well as he's played to get this far he's going to have to play even better to win it. If Henman pulls this off, I will stand on my head for the entire first set of the first match I cover at Wimbledon.'

Realistically, McEnroe was right. Henman's semi-final opponent was a considerable step up in class. Guillermo Coria had lost just one clay match in thirty-six, and that was to world number one Roger Federer at the Hamburg Masters. He had also won the 2004 Monte Carlo Masters, which in recent times had been a good indicator of form for Roland Garros. He may not have been a big hitter or server, but he had wonderful control on clay and, more importantly, infinite patience. He was the red-hot favourite to win the whole thing and was yet to drop a set in his run to the last four.

Nevertheless, it was Henman who enjoyed the blistering start against the 3rd seed, and for an hour McEnroe must have been practising his balancing act, for the unthinkable looked possible. His serve was good and his return even better as he put Coria in all sorts of trouble. He broke him twice in the first set to lead 5-3 and clinched it with a thunderbolt serve that flew past his opponent and hit someone on the head.

The Argentinian was clearly rattled, smashing his racket and questioning line calls. The 3rd seed then lost his serve at the start of the second set and looked like facing the prospect of falling two sets behind.

But in the eighth game came the turning point, as Coria managed to take Henman's serve. Then, in the tenth game, with Coria 5-4 up, Henman was left fuming when he served an ace on set point, only to have the umpire call a let, claiming the ball had touched the net cord. Henman raged: 'No one else in the stadium heard it and you think you're right! It's not a very good day for the umpire.' Coria eventually won that game to level the match at one set apiece.

After his outburst Henman's game became more ragged and he fell away completely, as Coria began to flourish, halting the Henman tide by embarking on a mammoth thirteen-game winning run to whitewash the Briton in the third and lead 3-0 in the fourth.

This time it really did look all over.

Henman refused to believe he was beaten, and once more rallied and rediscovered his form to string a run of games together himself. He won five games in a row and was leading the fourth 5-3. It would have been one of sport's greatest comebacks, even eclipsing his previous fightbacks in the tournament.

However, it proved a false dawn as Coria regained his composure to break Henman in the tenth game and level 5-5. He needed to be positive, but looked just a little too weak. Serving to stay in the match, Henman lost his delivery again when a backhand slice went long; the match was finally Coria's.

Philosophical in defeat, Henman said: 'For some of the time, I made the best clay-courter in the world look pretty ordinary. After such a good start, my level dropped fractionally and that gave him a chance to pick his level up. The bottom line is I wasn't good enough to do it for the amount of time necessary.

'But I still have some fantastic memories of my two weeks here. I still reflect on that first Monday afternoon when I was two sets down and feeling pretty awful against Cyril Saulnier. Just to take away the wins that I had, the confidence from performing well at a Grand Slam outside Wimbledon, there's a lot to build on.

'I'll be looking forward to hitting some balls on grass on Sunday or Monday. There is no down side to these championships at all. I still have over two weeks and it doesn't take me any time to adapt to grass. I'll be going to Queen's next week with a lot of games under my belt and a lot of confidence.'

There was no doubt that Henman's run to the last four had been anything short of astounding, pushing him up to 5th in the world rankings. It was a truly magnificent effort. Clay is meant to represent the most unrewarding surface for fast-court players like Henman, but instead, after becoming the first British male semi-finalist at Roland Garros in forty-one years, in addition to testing the finest current exponent on the crushed red brick, it had turned out to be arguably the greatest achievement of his career.

Despite this, many were concerned that with Wimbledon just two weeks away his impressive feat on clay may have taken too much out of him, especially as he had just recovered from a virus. He refuted such suggestions, believing his exploits could only be of benefit to him. 'The transition is so much easier going from clay to grass than the other direction,' he said. 'There is just something very special for me about playing on grass, it suits my game. With my attitude change in the last six or seven months I'm particularly excited about the coming tournaments. I'm a far better player, I've had a lot of experience and I will try to use those things to my advantage. If I can play this style of play on clay, where my opponents have more time against me, then on grass it should be even easier.'

If only that were true.

Henman prepared for Wimbledon by aiming to win the Stella Artois Championships for the first time, but it was over almost before it began. Having received a bye into the second round, by virtue of his 4th seeding, he surprisingly lost to world number 79 Karol Beck of Slovakia in three sets. He was completely outplayed in the opening set and after recovering to take the second he was unable to convert his solitary match point in front of a stunned Queen's crowd.

'I'm obviously disappointed right now, but in the context of my Wimbledon preparation, I don't think it will have any bearing because I'm playing very, very well,' he said. Henman may have believed what he was saying, but he certainly wasn't demonstrating that kind of form on the tennis court, as his French Open hangover appeared to carry over into the first round at Wimbledon, where he was afforded a 5th seeding.

His opponent was a little-known Spaniard, Ruben Ramirez Hidalgo, who had never played at Wimbledon before and never progressed past the first round of a slam. Like most of his countrymen, he was a self-confessed clay-court specialist, and he had played his last eighteen matches on the stuff. It was unlikely that he would relish the transition to grass and so he seemed the ideal first-round opponent to get Henman back on song.

Then again, it wouldn't be a Tim Henman game in the first week of Wimbledon if it wasn't a bit of a struggle. And on Court One a struggle it certainly was. Appearing tight and anxious, Henman stuttered past a player not ranked even in the top 100 in four hard-fought sets, after battling back from a set down and then falling 6-4 behind in the second-set tie-break.

'I've been playing here for the past ten years and been in pretty tight matches,' he said afterwards. 'I'm sure the crowd are getting the hang of things by now. But I never felt the result was going to be in doubt.'

That was easy for him to say.

Thankfully, he refrained from a repeat in the second round against Swiss qualifier Ivo Heuberger. The world number 137 was dispatched in straight sets, as Henman attempted to lift the gloom of a nation mourning the exit of their football team from the European Championships the night before, beaten on penalties by host nation Portugal, after England had a controversial goal disallowed by Swiss referee Urs Meier.

'I was very much aware of our disappointment and the disappointment of the team,' admitted Henman, who had stayed up late the previous night to watch the drama. 'It was such a tough game to lose, and certainly in the circumstances, not only the penalties but a pretty dubious decision. It was nice to get a bit of revenge on the nation – Switzerland, that is.'

England's Euro 2004 exit had ensured that Henman had the summer limelight completely to himself. The pressure was on to deliver.

His third-round clash was against Morocco's Hicham Arazi and was scheduled for the normally sacred middle Sunday after the match was rained off on the Saturday. However, come People's Sunday, Henman had returned to his first-round form, as he struggled for any kind of progressive form and made life very difficult for himself. He did not serve particularly well, dropping serve first in each of the four sets, and was simply not at his best.

But, as he learned from his epic run to the last four at the French Open, the key to success is to win matches when you are playing badly, and despite struggling against the 32nd seed he managed to step things up when it was most necessary and eventually prevailed 7-6, 6-4, 3-6, 6-2.

It was the ninth time in succession that Henman had made the last sixteen at SW19, but never before had it been as much of a struggle. This time he was up against Mark Philippoussis, who had sent him spinning to defeat at the same stage in 2000. Coincidentally, that same year Henman lost in his first game at the Stella Artois Championships, something he had not repeated until three weeks before.

Philippoussis had come into these championships without a single tour win since the third round of the Australian Open in January – a drought that equates to seven straight first-round defeats – but returning to these grounds had acted as a restorative, and he planned to sustain that against the home favourite.

Henman knew he had to bring his game back in line with the heights he had achieved in Paris little less than a month ago, or face extinction.

Thankfully, he took his game to a higher level against the 11th seed and, after a week without conviction, demonstrated the sort of form which could take him all the way to the prize. It was a display of clinical ruthlessness, accompanied by a serve so solid that Philippoussis did not win a single point on Henman's first delivery, until the Briton was already two sets in front.

Henman also demonstrated steel, in order to repel a spirited fightback by Philippoussis, fired up by an encounter with the umpire when disputing a line call after Henman's serve was not called out in the third set.

'Fuck the cyclops,' the Australian screamed at the umpire. 'You should have been all over that. Open your eyes. What's wrong with you?' When the umpire responded with a warning, he hit back: 'I should give you a warning because you suck. What are you looking at? I am not accepting this, man.'

Philippoussis eventually sneaked the third on a shoot-out, and as tensions mounted in the fourth set some spectators buried their heads in their flags rather than watch. An air of tension hung over Centre Court as Henman wasted two match points at 5-2, but then with dusk falling Philippoussis hit a backhand service return wide in the fourth-set tie-break, and ended the agony of nearly 14,000 spectators in the arena, thousands more on Henman Hill and a TV audience of millions.

Henman was in the quarter-finals for the eighth time in his career.

'It was such an intense match and the quality of play was so high the whole time,' he said after the match. 'Mark had to stick in there after I got off to a great start. Then he started to hit the corners and I had to be patient. I knew I was playing some good stuff. It was tough on him, but it went my way today. There were some tight calls, but that is the nature of the game. I am just relieved to get through. The fourth set was just an incredible atmosphere and I had to keep fighting and eventually I finished it off.'

The talk soon switched to a possible semi-final encounter between Henman and Andy Roddick. The prospect of Henman struggling in the last eight, on his favourite surface, against a player ranked 63rd in the world, seemed laughable. But Mario Ancic was certainly a danger. The Croat had defeated every seed he had ever come across at Wimbledon. In 2002, in his debut Grand Slam, he beat 7th-seeded Roger Federer (his last defeat at Wimbledon) and in this campaign he had already disposed of Luis Horna (33) and Dominik Hrbaty (27).

So what chance of him doing the same to Henman on his own patch? Very likely in fact.

Millions of Henmaniacs watched in horror as the twenty-year-old annihilated their hero in just three sets. Ancic served with a devastating combination of speed and accuracy, and Henman simply could not cope. Apart from a high-quality opening set from both players, which was settled 7-5 on a tie-break, Henman was hardly in it, as his opponent grew in confidence shot by shot.

In the second set Henman's form dipped alarmingly and despite recovering from a break down, he lost his serve again at 3-3, and as Ancic piled on yet more pressure, he cracked. Ancic was bigger, more accurate and displayed a cool, calm persona throughout. The gathering quality of his return against Henman's weak and predictable serve proved decisive.

The third set verged on humiliation, with Ancic producing

some of the best tennis seen at the 2004 Championships, taking a 5-1 lead, to his opponent's sheer embarrassment. Henman managed to hold serve in the next game, but then Ancic pounded down two aces before clinching the match with a 131mph effort which Henman could merely send ten feet long.

The end was a blessed relief for the subdued spectators, and as he shook hands with his opponent over the net, Henman looked on the verge of tears. He admitted afterwards: 'This is a massive disappointment for me. But there's no question the better player won on the day. Losing here gets worse each time. My hopes and desires were to win this tournament. Having lost, it's a tough one to swallow. I've never hidden the fact that this is the tournament I'd love to win the most and this was a good opportunity. Now I'm going to get away. There's no reason, no incentive to pick up a racket for a while. I need to step back and let time heal but it will be hard. He won it – I didn't lose it. Yet I still believe in myself and I'm going to keep working hard.'

The Wimbledon fantasy had ended unfulfilled for another year. Disappointed and dejected, Henman spent a month away from tennis practising his golf and took his family away for a week, before the busy few months that lay ahead. Yet he was remaining optimistic about his future in the game.

'I felt I was playing some of the best tennis of my career going into Wimbledon and I had high hopes of winning the tournament, but obviously the fortnight ended in disappointment for me earlier than expected.

'Having had a few days to reflect not only on the tournament itself, but also on the last eight months or so, I still feel very positive about my tennis. I am looking forward to getting back on court during the North American hard-court season, which this year is sandwiched neatly either side of the Olympics, so there's a lot of exciting tennis ahead of me this summer.'

With over half the season behind him, and lying inside the world's top eight, Henman also had one eye on a possible place in Houston's end-of-season Tennis Masters Cup, an amalgamation of the Grand Slam Cup and ATP Singles Championships created in 2000.

'I have made no secret of the fact I want to qualify for Houston and the next few weeks may prove crucial,' he said. 'There are a lot of ranking points at stake in Toronto and Cincinnati, and I want to try to take the pressure off myself at the end of the year by doing well at both of the Masters Series events as well as at the US Open.

'I would then be able to go into the European indoor season in a very strong position. However, it is never easy going into Masters Series events without any matches under your belt because there is never anywhere to hide in the draws and there are no easy matches. But I needed the rest after Wimbledon, so my aim is to take it one match at a time.'

Besides building up to the US Open at the end of August, Henman also used the North American hard tournaments to prepare for the Olympics in Athens.

However, his preparations did not go as well as hoped. He could manage only a second-round berth at the Masters Series event in Toronto, where he lost to Gustavo Kuerten in straight sets, and went just one step further in the Cincinnati Masters, winning a mere five games in a straight-sets loss to Lleyton Hewitt.

It was not turning out to be the best of summers for Henman, and to compound matters he was having problems with his back. It was not injured, but it was stiff, and meant he was struggling to serve.

'I feel like I'm serving off one leg,' he explained. 'It's more on my right side, my right hip. And that's where a lot of your momentum going up into your serve comes from. So I'm relying on my left leg. It's a bit frustrating. I don't feel that it's injured but it is very stiff and very tight. I need to get that sorted out. I've just got to do a lot of stretching, a lot of massage, to try and loosen it up. If I have a few days' rest, hopefully it will be better for the Games.'

Henman declared himself fit for the Olympics just three days before his first-round match with Jiri Novak, a former top-ten player, now ranked 27th. But he needn't have bothered. Despite being seeded 4th, and tipped as a genuine British medal prospect, he demonstrated no such form to back up those claims and was beaten at the first hurdle in straight sets. So embarrassed was Henman by his lacklustre display that he went out of his way to apologise to British Olympic Association chief executive Simon Clegg, and stayed on for a couple days to encourage his British teammates in various sports.

The summer was turning into a long, painful haul.

An exceptional display was needed in the US Open to keep his Houston flame flickering. But despite receiving a 5th seeding and being handed a rather fortuitous route to the last sixteen, he needed to carve out gritty performances, to see off three players not even ranked in the top fifty.

In the first and third rounds he required five sets to see off world number 52 Ivo Karlovic of Croatia and Czech qualifier Michal Tabara, ranked 149, respectively. He also needed four sets to fend off French qualifier Jerome Golmard, placed at 339 in the world in round two.

He had been on court for almost ten hours in order to complete three matches, and not once had he been in complete control.

His back problems had also resurfaced, after an incident in a sushi bar on the eve of US Open, and almost forced him to withdraw from the tournament before it began. 'I was sat there having some sushi,' he recalls, 'and when I got up to leave the restaurant I could barely walk. My back was absolutely screwed. I was in such a bad way.'

Fortunately, he had been showing few signs of it on the court. But then again he was not the only one suffering, as his second- and third-round opponents had expressed similar complaints, even calling for treatment in the middle of their matches.

In stuttering to the fourth round, Henman had equalled his all-time best at Flushing Meadow, but the chances of making the quarter-finals for the first time were remote, as he was up against the in-form player of the tournament. Nicolas Kiefer was having a tremendous hard-court season, having won twenty-eight of his thirty-seven matches and taken scalps such as Carlos Moya, Marat Safin and Sebastian Grosjean along the way.

Many believed the 19th-seeded German was playing as well now as he was when he reached his career-high number four in the world in 2000, and was yet to drop a set at the US Open that year.

Henman could not afford, against Kiefer, the extended lapses that could have been exposed by his first three opponents.

But at least he had persevered to get this far. In the past he had generally lost matches against opponents he should have beaten comfortably. This run was uncannily like the French Open, where he ground out results when not at the top of his game, as well as harnessing a less than perfect physical state. Could history be repeating?

The match was scheduled for the day of Henman's birthday, and there was nothing more he would have wanted that day than a win, and a place in his first-ever quarter-final at Flushing Meadow.

'It would be some present to reach the quarter-finals,' he said.

'My performances at Grand Slams outside Wimbledon haven't been satisfactory. This is a good opportunity to put that right.

'Given the way I felt on Sunday before the tournament with my bad back, it is good how things have turned around. It's only when I stop that it comes on. I found that when I was sitting down between games, my back was getting stiff. We sit down for sixty to ninety seconds and I find that for the first couple of serves when I come back out I feel so stiff that there isn't any flexibility.

'It is obviously going to be a very tough match against Kiefer. He is playing as well as anyone this summer. But he can be beaten. I have played some good stuff and competed very hard – although I know I can play better. I'm optimistic.'

But when Kiefer burst from the traps to lead 4-0 in the first set inside fourteen minutes, such self-belief appeared misplaced. Henman slowly edged himself back into the contest and broke back twice, only to lose a tie-break that he should have won, 7-5.

Henman was also the first to lose his serve in the following set, as Kiefer led 3-1. But once again the Briton snatched straight back, starting a run of ten successive games unbeaten, which demoralised the German, whose game fell apart. Henman had finally settled to his task and started feasting on Kiefer's second serve, which is one of the weakest in men's tennis.

He won the second and third sets as Kiefer struggled to find an answer to his superbly executed chip-and-volley tactic. The German also exploded mentally. When he was foot-faulted, he hurled German obscenities, earning a code violation warning from the umpire. Later, with Henman serving at 5-4 down in the fourth set, Kiefer erupted again, furiously launching a ball high into the upper deck of the giant Arthur Ashe Stadium, after netting a volley. As a result he had a point deducted and another outburst could have cost him the match, but it never got that far.

Kiefer miraculously took the fourth on another dramatic tie-break, and the pair looked destined for a battle royal. But then, in the fourth game of the decisive fifth set, with Henman storming into a 3-0 lead, a tendon in Kiefer's right wrist popped. A trainer was called to assist him but it was to no avail. He was forced to retire and that meant Henman had done it. He had made his first-ever US Open quarter-final.

The end was not the way Henman would have wanted it, for no one likes to see an opponent hurt and having to give up, but he still deserved an enormous due. Henman had played thirteen hours and thirty-one minutes of tennis across eighteen and a bit sets, while enduring terrible pains in his back. And after all, it was his birthday.

'I'll go out for dinner and have a few drinks, definitely. I hope I've got enough puff left to blow out thirty candles,' he joked. 'Coming on court I felt very fresh. I'm sure as long as I don't have any complications with my back, I'll be ready to go. Not long ago I could barely walk on to court. But I'm playing good tennis and that gives me confidence.

'I've been making slow starts, so I am wary of that. He was playing great and I wasn't quite at my best but I picked my game up quickly and dominated. I felt the momentum was with me in the fourth but I had nothing to show for it. But I kept fighting. It was tough but I felt very good about my game and there was no need to panic. I'd made a good start to the fifth and it's a strange way to win a match. I thought he had cramp in his hand, which some of the guys do suffer. He sat down and Per [the trainer] came on and they were just talking, whereas often he would have a massage. Then it crossed my mind that it might be more serious. It was a weird feeling at the end.'

Derided by his critics as a loser after his failings at Wimbledon and the Olympics, Henman was now standing on the brink of his second Grand Slam semi-final of the year.

He was certainly the favourite going into his last-eight match with Slovakian Dominik Hrbaty, who had also come through three five-set matches to get this far. Hrbaty may have had three tour tournaments to his name that season, but Henman had won both their previous encounters and had never dropped a set against the 22nd seed.

He looked set to continue in his rich vein against Hrbaty, as he made a flying start in the opening exchanges. He won the first five games and looked confident and relaxed. Hrbaty finally got off the mark in the sixth game, but Henman held his serve comfortably to close out the first set 6-1.

The Briton was serving well when he had to and got himself out of trouble twice in the second set – coming back from 0-30 down in the fourth and eighth games to restore parity. Hrbaty's serve was far more erratic. In the seventh game he followed three unreturnable serves, including a 133mph ace, with three double faults.

A significant turning point came in the tenth game, when Henman saved three set points. Hrbaty responded to missing those chances – his first break points of the match – by dropping his serve in the very next game.

There were a few nervous moments as Henman served for the second set at 6-5. He netted his first set point and double-faulted on his second, but made no mistake with the third, to move within one set of a last-four place.

When Henman took a 2-1 lead in the third set, following a double fault by the Slovakian, the finishing line was in sight. But then came the much-anticipated glitch.

Needing just two games to win, Henman dropped his serve for the first time. Hrbaty then held serve and took the first point of Henman's next service game. Fortunately for the 5th seed, at that point rain stopped play and in the process halted a potential Hrbaty revival.

When play eventually resumed the next day, with the after-effects of Hurricane Frances still blowing through the air, Henman held his serve at 4-5. But just two games later a netted approach shot gave Hrbaty the set and a glimmer of hope once more.

However, Henman quickly put the setback behind him to regain control and rip his opponent to shreds with some outstanding tennis. Hrbaty was helpless to stop Henman's game plan in the strong winds, and he was broken twice in the fourth set. After a total of two hours and thirty-seven minutes, Henman finally put him out of his misery, serving out the match with a forehand volley to the corner of the court, to book himself a semi-final date with world number one Roger Federer.

Henman was in bullish mood ahead of his showdown with the Wimbledon champion. 'There's no point in stopping now. Beating Federer is the toughest job in tennis but I've got nothing to lose and everything to gain. I'm playing good tennis and I'll see what I can do over this weekend. I've beaten him a few times in the past and, hopefully, I can beat him again. I'm very excited about reaching my first semi-final in New York – and playing Federer will be a pretty special match.'

Despite holding an impressive 6-2 record over Federer from previous encounters, it seemed it would take an extraordinary performance for Henman to go any further. Federer had won practically everything put before him so far in 2004, having already lifted silverware at both Wimbledon and the Australian Open, as well as beating Henman in the Indian Wells Masters final, on the way to three Masters titles.

If Henman was to beat Federer in a confrontation of such importance everything would have to be working perfectly in his favour. But on the morning of the match it seemed the elements were already against him. The wind that had been buffeting New York, ideal for hitting passing shots against a net-rusher like Federer, had been replaced by benign and partly cloudy conditions, a perfect environment for Federer.

The first set would also be crucial, and Henman's first serve needed to be flawless. But a return of just six first serves staying in play in the opening set tells its own story. While Federer was winning his first three service games to love, Henman was constantly struggling. So it was no surprise to anyone when Federer took the upper hand and secured the first break in the sixth with a ripping forehand pass. Although Henman immediately broke back, he dropped his serve again in the next game, allowing the Swiss star to serve out for the set, and he duly obliged.

Henman attempted to lift his game at the start of the second set, keeping Federer off balance by mixing sneaky forays to the net with fierce groundstrokes. But the world number one was in imperious form and had an answer for everything. Henman's first double fault in the seventh game gifted him the break and effectively the second set.

Unlike Henman, Federer rarely slips when in pole position of a tie. Everyone knew the match was over as a contest, and despite Henman managing a late break in the third set with Federer already leading 5-2, he was only delaying the inevitable. Federer made no mistake second time round.

For the sixth time, on the threshold of a Grand Slam final, Henman had been denied.

But no shame could be attached to his latest failure. He had been beaten by the world's best player at the top of his game. 'I think he showed why he is number one,' said the defeated 5th seed. 'He's playing phenomenal tennis and he's so complete in every area. This game is a lot about confidence but when you have as many shots as he has, there is so much to fall back upon. He's setting the standards for everyone to catch up right now. Roger was too good on the day. I tried a whole lot of different things but all credit must go to Roger.

'It's been an unbelievable fortnight for me. My desire and motivation and my fitness in general I think is getting better. That is very, very motivating. If you go back fifty-four weeks I was ranked around 40, and all of a sudden I've won a Masters Series, I've been in a Masters Series final, and in the semis of two Grand Slams outside Wimbledon. In the context of this year it puts me in a great position and I have got some great opportunities coming up.'

Henman's exploits in New York meant he had climbed up to 4th in the ATP world rankings, equalling his all-time best. With just two months left of the season there was still everything to play for if he was going to qualify for the end-of-season Masters Cup.

He spent three weeks resting the back he injured during the US hard-court season, before heading to the Masters in Madrid, where he was top seed, for one of the three tournaments left before the season's end. At this point he had dropped to 6th in the rankings but a berth in the Madrid final would rubber-stamp his place at the ATP Tour's year-end finals. There were just four places left after Federer, Roddick, Hewitt and Gaston Gaudio had already reserved their seats on the plane.

A tricky balance of finding the points needed while keeping the body intact was required. But, come the end of the Madrid Masters, Henman had done nothing to benefit either. He lost in the third round to Ivan Ljubicic, and felt so wobbly on his feet that he decided to take a blood test to make sure he was suffering from nothing viral. 'I feel similar to the way I did at the French

Open,' he said. 'After four or five games I feel tired. I feel fine from the waist up. I don't feel ill. I just don't have any energy.'

Three days later, while in Basle preparing for the Davidoff Open, he received the result of his blood test. It revealed an unusually low level of magnesium, and it was believed this shortage could be the reason for the tiredness he had been feeling on court. He was advised to undergo a twenty-eight-day course of supplementary medication.

A shortage of magnesium in the blood can manifest itself in many ways, not least a susceptibility to noise, confusion, irritability and nervousness – all of which have a habit of encroaching into a player's psyche during a tournament at this time of year, with so much on the line.

More bad news was to follow, as reports filtered through that Marat Safin had leapfrogged him into 6th spot in the Indesit ATP Race, after winning the Madrid Masters.

Despite these setbacks, Henman battled on. He made it as far as the quarter-finals in Basle, but still his place at Houston was not secure. It all came down to his progress at the Paris Masters, the title he had lifted a year earlier. What he would give for a repeat right now.

He was in one of the two remaining qualifying spots, after Carlos Moya and Guillermo Coria confirmed their places, and was only fourteen points behind Marat Safin. However, he still had Andre Agassi and David Nalbandian breathing down his neck, as they lost finals in Stockholm and Basle, respectively. Henman could secure a place in the £850,000 season finale by winning two matches in Paris, thereby making the quarter-finals.

It was the eve of the Paris Masters, and Henman was busying himself by posing for a photoshoot in front of the Eiffel Tower, when startling news came through that was about to change everything. Agassi had informed French tournament organisers that he was suffering from the recurrence of a hip injury following his defeat in Stockholm. He would be withdrawing from the tournament. Nalbandian had also conceded enough was enough and having struggled recently with foot and leg problems, also pulled out.

Without even hitting a ball Henman had qualified, by finishing 7th in the ATP Champions Race. 'Confirming my place in Houston has been a goal of mine all year so it's very satisfying to qualify,' he said. 'It's the result of a lot of hard work over what has been a great year for me.'

The draw for the group stage of the Masters Cup saw Henman placed in the blue group with Roddick, Safin and Coria. Henman arrived at the outdoor Westside Tennis Club in Houston, the only one of the eight competitors, as the champion of nothing, having failed to win a single title in 2004.

His first opportunity to put that right was against Roddick. Persistent drizzle caused the match to be delayed by ninety minutes, but when it finally got underway the crowd were treated to a fine spectacle.

Both players had chances to take the first set, with Henman averting a crisis in the tenth game to recover from 0-30 down, and then Roddick playing a superb backhand at break point down at 5-5, to preserve his serve. At 6-5 the opening set looked set to be decided by a shoot-out, but Roddick took advantage of his only break point of the entire match to take a one-set lead.

The second set was just as closely contested and needed a tie-break to settle it after Henman wasted two break points. He also led 3-0 and 5-2 in the tie-break but showed a familiar frailty when on the brink of success. Roddick reeled off six of the next seven points to snatch it 8-6, the match ending when Henman sent a forehand long.

Henman had played his part in a high-quality encounter, but found home favourite and world number two Roddick simply too strong on the vital points.

However, he refused to be downbeat in defeat. After all, he still had two more matches to put things right. 'I've no complaints about the way I played. It's certainly my best showing since I reached the US Open last four in September. There was some good-quality tennis from both of us. On reflection, I've won a couple of tight ones against Andy and this was his turn. I was so much more disciplined than I have been recently on each and every point. Losing is never fun but when you play and compete as I did, you have to say "too good" to Andy.'

Henman had to win his next two games, starting with Coria, to stay alive. The Argentinian had lost his first game to Safin in straight sets and appeared to still be suffering from a shoulder injury, which had forced him to retire against Peru's Luis Horna in the first round of the Toronto Masters way back at the end of July. The Masters Cup was his first match back, and he was struggling.

After overcoming a nervous start, Henman dominated the match from every conceivable area of the court with superior serving and extra snap at the net. There were sufficient break points against the Briton for the first set to have become worrying, but he saved three at 5-2 to seal a one-set lead. Once Coria had squandered his serve again to trail 3-2 in the second set, Henman was able to cruise home, a couple of aces in the final game rubbing salt into his opponent's wounds.

With Safin losing to Roddick 7-6, 7-6, Henman's final group match with the Russian would be a winner-takes-all clash for the right to play Roger Federer in the last four.

In front of a sell-out crowd he struggled to make an impact, as the in-form Safin, who had clinched back-to-back ATP

Masters Series titles in Madrid and Paris, won the first set of their eliminator in style. Henman had dropped his serve in the first game, with Safin sealing the break with a cross-court forehand after a series of deuces. He was almost broken again in the third game, but fortunately for him Safin mistimed a forehand from the baseline. Henman, whose forehand consistently failed him, managed to keep serve in the fifth game, but the decisive second break came on his next service, when he double-faulted to gift his opponent a 5-2 lead.

He attempted to make a fight of the second set, powering through his first three service games without dropping a point, and twice forced deuce on Safin's serve, in the eighth and twelfth games, but failed to break. It resulted in a tie-break, and when Safin won the first mini-break at 3-1 he quickly extended to 6-2 for four match points. He cashed in on the first one, when Henman netted a forehand. Safin had won the match and with it a place in the last four at Houston, at the expense of Henman, whose season was now over.

Henman's failure to reach his third major semi-final of 2004, though, should not be allowed to take the gloss off his best year yet. He finished the year at number six in the world, the highest of his eleven-year career, and proved himself capable of living with the company he kept at the Masters Cup. Two semi-final appearances, outside Wimbledon, in the French and US Open, were evidence of that.

If he can maintain his physical fitness he will go into 2005 buoyed by the way he played in 2004, and perhaps have an even better year. Henman certainly thinks so. 'Although I was disappointed not to have qualified for the semi-finals in Houston,' he said, 'I thoroughly enjoyed myself while I was there and I'm even more motivated now to try and qualify again next year.

'I've really enjoyed 2004 and I managed to achieve many of the goals I set out to try and accomplish at the beginning of the year, which is obviously very satisfying. My coach Paul Annacone has had a big part to play in all of it.

'I've been delighted by the way the relationship has developed since we first got together towards the end of last year. Paul has really done a great job clarifying so many situations for me and I feel I've now got a much better understanding of what I need to do on the court in order to make life as difficult as possible for my opponents.

'But there are a few goals that I didn't quite manage to fulfil and I can't wait for next year to begin as I feel I'm a much better tennis player now than I was back in January. There are still aspects of my game that I feel I can improve so if I can stay healthy I don't see any reason why next year can't be even better.

'I've had a good record at Wimbledon over the years but my results at the other Grand Slams have been disappointing. Yet, one of the main reasons why I enjoyed this year so much was because I did so well at both the French and US Opens. It's been a really positive year. My performance at Roland Garros was certainly the outstanding moment of my season. I had never reached further than the third round there. It was a real breakthrough and I had a lot of fun.

'My serve has been a dictating factor throughout the year. When I've played well, I have been very disciplined on each and every point, the way I wanted to play it.

'That's sort of pretty motivating, pretty exciting, because there's absolutely no doubt in my mind that I can play better next year.'

Only time will tell.